BATSFORD STUDIES IN ARCHAEOLOGY
General Editor: Dr Graham Webster MA, PHD, FSA, AMA

The Roman Villa

An Historical Introduction

For
Carole, Alice and Jessica

The Roman Villa

An Historical Introduction

JOHN PERCIVAL

Senior Lecturer in Classics, University College, Cardiff

University of California Press

Berkeley and Los Angeles

First published 1976
ISBN 0 520 03233 0
Library of Congress Catalog Card Number 76-7766

Printed in England

University of California Press
Berkeley and Los Angeles, California

Contents

Preface

The Roman Villa is a subject about which we could be said to know a great deal and understand very little. For the student who has seen Chedworth, say, or Fishbourne, or the Hinton St Mary mosaic in the British Museum and who wants to know more, there is, certainly, an enormous amount of published material to which he can go for information. The standard works on Roman Britain normally contain a chapter on 'The Countryside' or something similar, and provide references to perhaps several dozen villa reports in this country and a handful of comparable ones in France and Germany. These in turn will lead him to others, and before long he is likely to find himself with the problem, not of finding sufficient material, but of coping with the ever increasing amounts of it that seem to be available. Yet, after reading a fair number of such reports, he may well begin to feel that what they have to offer, full and detailed as it is, is nevertheless to some degree unsatisfactory, in that it does not in fact provide him with the right kind of information. The reports will tell him about this or that particular villa, and the more general chapters will compare and classify a wider selection of sites within a particular area or province. But about the villa as an institution, as a social and economic unit and as part of the life and history of the Roman world, they will tell him remarkably little. They will, of course, contain a great deal of the material necessary for acquiring this kind of understanding, and one could hardly begin to acquire it without a fairly close familiarity with the many individual examples, any more than one could understand, say, the art of van Gogh or the music of Beethoven without seeing the pictures or hearing the works. But there is a sense in which, having studied the particular examples, one needs to back away from them and see them in the mass and from a distance. After all, the individual villa, like the individual painting or piece of music, existed within a context, and although its remains reflect that context and so provide us with an introduction to it, there will in addition be large areas which they will not reflect but which will nevertheless be essential for their understanding and interpretation. It is for this reason that in the chapters that follow we shall be trying at each stage to keep this context very much in view, our aim being, not only to study those parts of it on which the villas shed some light, but to establish as much of it as we can from other sources and so interpret the villas themselves more fully. There are, admittedly, certain dangers in this approach: it is all too easy, in moving in this way from the general to the particular, to construct the theories first and look for the evidence later, and we shall obviously need to anchor the discussion by reference to the villas themselves at every appropriate stage. There will, however, be certain matters on which the physical remains of villas can afford us little or no assistance, and for these we must rely on the kinds of evidence which seem to offer a solution; there is no point in condemning a theory because the villa remains do not support it, if in the nature of things they provide no evidence one way or the other. And even on matters where they do, or could, provide such evidence it is often useful to set out a theory in outline, so as to have a more precise notion of the kind of evidence that would be relevant to it, or that we may or may not expect. Provided we regard such theories as temporary hypotheses, to be discarded as soon as they are discredited and adopted as something stronger only when they have been rigorously tested, they are much more likely to help our understanding than to hinder it. Very little of what follows has progressed, as yet, beyond the hypothesis stage, and it is for this reason that the book is described as an Introduction; to describe it also as Historical is not to claim a greater degree of certainty but merely to indicate the approach outlined above.

Acknowledgments

I would like to record my thanks to the many people who by their writings, their conversation or their words of advice and encouragement assisted me in the preparation of this book. While excusing myself from mentioning them all by name I cannot allow the following to remain anonymous: Mr C.E. Stevens, who provided supervision, friendship and (though he would hate the word) inspiration; Dr Graham Webster, who suggested the work and helped with advice throughout; M. Georges Fouet and M. Raymond Agache, both of whom gave generously of their advice and published material; and the Department of Archaeology of University College, Cardiff, whose members dealt patiently with my many queries and made available to me the practical assistance of their photographer, Mrs G. Booth, and their draughtsman, Mr Howard Mason. To all of these people, named and unnamed, I am extremely grateful: I hope they will allow me to reserve my special thanks for the three ladies to whom the book is dedicated.

The Author and Publishers wish to thank the following for permission to reproduce the illustrations appearing in this book:
A.C.L. Bruxelles for fig. 32; R. Agache for figs. 19 and 20; Académiai Kiadó, Budapest for figs 42–3 and 58; G. de Boe and Service National des Fouilles, Belgium for fig. 6; the Bristol and Gloucestershire Archaeological Society and Capt. H.S. Gracie for fig. 31; the British Museum for fig. 36; the British School at Rome for figs 11 and 14–16; Centre National de Recherche Scientifique, Paris for figs 18, 40–1, 44, 54, 56–7 and 59; Clarendon Press, Oxford (M. Rostovsteff, *Social and Economic History of the Roman Empire*) for fig. 7; Espasa-Calpe, Madrid for figs 12–13; H.-P. Eydoux for fig. 55; Walter de Gruyter & Co., Berlin for fig. 24; W.H. Manning for fig. 35; Howard Mason for figs 1, 4, 17, 26, 39, 49 and 53; Museum of Archaeology and Ethnology, Cambridge for fig. 34; National Museum of Antiquities of Scotland for fig. 34; Helen O'Neil and the Royal Archaeological Institute for fig. 46; Prof. E.E.D.M. Oates for figs 14–16; Penguin Books Ltd. for fig. 10; Editions A. & J. Picard, Paris for fig. 21; Dr C.A. Ralegh Radford and the Oxfordshire Architectural and Historical Society for

fig. 30; Rheinisches Landesmuseum, Trier for figs 3 and 37–8; Rheinisches Landesmuseum, Bonn for fig. 5; Warwick J. Rodwell for fig. 52; Schweizerische Gesellschaft für Ur- und Frügeschichte for fig. 25; the Society of Antiquaries of London for fig. 28; the Society for the Promotion of Roman Studies for figs 27, 29, 45 and 52; Thames and Hudson Ltd. (K.D. White, *Roman Farming*) for figs 8–9; J.B. Ward-Perkins for figs 10–11; K.D. White for figs 2, 47 and 48; E.M. Wightman and Granada Publishing Ltd. for figs 22–3 and 50–1; P.J. Woods for fig. 29.

List of Illustrations

I

Definitions

To the question 'What is a villa?' there are at least two kinds of answer. One is a description of the villa as an economic and social phenomenon, an account of its function, an interpretation as it were, and it is such an answer that this book as a whole is intended to give. The other is a definition, a statement of what the word means and an indication of the sorts of things to which we should or should not apply it. Easy as it may appear, this second kind of answer is not in fact easy to provide; we can give examples of what we mean, but as soon as we try to say what it is that makes them villas we run into difficulties. We may say that they are farms, but we can think of establishments other than farms which we would nevertheless wish to call villas, as well as indisputable farms to which the term seems hopelessly inappropriate. We may list the sorts of amenities that villas have, such as hypocausts, painted wall plaster, mosaics and so on, but again there seems to be no list that would include all the sites that we wish to include and exclude those that we do not. Yet, if we are to talk of villas, and of such concepts as the villa system, to any purpose we must have a definition of the term with which to begin.[1]

The literary sources are of only limited use: they give us a range of meaning but nothing which is really precise.[2] A villa is a place in the country, normally (but not always) associated with farming, sometimes with connotations of luxury or relaxation, and in most cases a single house rather than a group of them. A character in a play of Terence asks the way to Charinus' villa, and is told that it is 'the next on the right after this estate'.[3] The consul Aemilius Mamercus, ravaging Sabine country in 470 BC, destroys 'not only the villas but the villages too'.[4] A client of Cicero bought a piece of land when prices were low: 'it had no villa, and was completely uncultivated, but it is worth much more now'.[5] The poet Horace would rather accompany his friend and patron abroad than enjoy broad acres, plough teams, and a villa on the outskirts of a country town;[6] and in a verse epitaph from North Africa a man tells how he set himself up in a villa and lived a life of contentment among his fields and crops.[7] By looking at a whole collection of such passages we can, perhaps, arrive at a definition of sorts, but none of them are themselves definitions and only a few are at all explicit or precise. They tell us what sorts of things are generally called villas, but they do not actually say what villas are, or (more important, perhaps) what they are not. Nevertheless, the range of meaning they give is fairly restricted. It is clear, for example, that a villa is a country phenomenon and not a town one: indeed, the phrase *in villa* is sometimes used almost with the meaning of 'in the country', and the word itself is the regular one for a farmhouse in the Roman writers on farming.[8] There is a suspicion, also, that it is a townsman's word: that is, a villa is not simply a place in the country, but a place in the country from the point of view of someone living in the town. This is not so easy to show by actual quotation, but the contexts in which the word occurs do frequently give this impression, often as part of the vaguely romantic feeling which the country inspires in the town dweller. One wonders if a lifetime countryman would have used the word *villa* for his farm with any more readiness than a farmworker nowadays would show in talking of his 'cottage'.

For something more than impressions we have to turn to the lawyers. The passage of Cicero already quoted uses the term in its strictly legal sense, confirmed for us at a later date in the official codes of law. A *villa* is a building in the country, as opposed to one in the town, which is an *aedes*;[9] a *villa* and its land (*ager*) together form a *fundus*, or estate; land in the town is not *ager*, but *area*.[10] Here at least is a clear and simple statement: nothing about luxuries or amenities or size, and nothing specific about function, though agriculture might seem to be implied as the normal accompaniment.[11] Indeed, in some ways the definition is a little *too* simple: apart from the buildings we normally think of as villas there were many others, primitive dwellings in the native tradition, to which we would hesitate to apply the term but which nevertheless fulfil the legal requirement of being buildings in the country. If we are to include these within the term *villa*, and indeed the single Iron Age farms as well, there seems little point in using the word at all: we might as well say 'farm' or 'rural site' or something similar, and dispense with it altogether.[12] At this point, however, we turn again to the literary sources: it has long been recognized that on the few occasions when Roman writers have to refer to rural settlements of a native type they are reluctant to use the word *villa* to describe them, and seem to prefer more neutral words such as *aedificia* ('buildings'), or less dignified ones like *tuguria* ('huts').[13] This, in view of the Roman fondness for seeing analogies for their own institutions in other societies, and their willingness to give them Roman labels, is of some interest, and what it would seem to suggest is that to be a villa a building must be recognizably Roman, in appearance or function or both.

It is for this reason that modern definitions of the villa have nearly all included a reference in some form or other to Romanization.[14] Thus Collingwood spoke of 'the dwelling of people, somewhat Romanized in manners', while Richmond connected villas with 'the adoption of Roman standards in greater or lesser degree by natives of substance'.[15] Such an approach is entirely reasonable: *villa* is a Latin word and must have applied to something which was part of a Latinspeaker's culture. The difficulty, however, is that being Roman is not a precise and definite thing but rather a matter of degree; the most squalid hovel in Britain or Gaul may be Romanized in the sense that its plan is slightly more regular than those of its Celtic predecessors, or that its inhabitants numbered some items of Roman style or manufacture among their possessions. The choice of a point at which Romanization is sufficient to merit the title of *villa* can hardly be other than arbitrary, and although attempts have been made to define such a point in archaeological terms they have been of value more as rules of thumb for classifying sites than as embodying any real cultural distinction.[16] Indeed, it is hard to see how such a distinction *could* be formulated with any degree of precision: even Rivet's replacement of 'somewhat Romanized in manners' by 'integrated into the social and economic organization of the Roman world'[17] could be said merely to replace an arbitrary definition of Romanization by an equally arbitrary one of 'integration', not to mention the added difficulty of deciding what, if anything, the social and economic organization of the Roman world was.

And yet it is as close, perhaps, as we shall get. Indeed, we may well be mistaken in wanting to get closer. Villas were not things invented at a given point in time, but things that evolved gradually as part of a wider social and economic evolution. There is no reason to suppose that they formed a distinct and easily definable category to the Romans themselves, and to ask that they should do so to us may well be unreasonable. They occurred over a wide area, the contexts in which they arose were very different from place to place, they lasted in some regions for very long periods – all of which should make us wary of being too precise in our attempts to define them. There will always be sites to which one scholar will apply and another refuse the title, but it may be of some comfort to believe that two Romans could well have disagreed in the same way and for similar reasons. In what follows, Rivet's definition will be followed for villas as a class, though it may be that in applying it to particular sites we would not in every case meet with his approval.

2

The Sources of Evidence

As with most historical subjects, the study of the Roman villa involves the drawing together of different kinds of evidence to produce a single coherent picture. The primary material, clearly, is archaeological: the villas themselves and the sites associated with them. But this can be supplemented by literary evidence from contemporary poets, orators, historians and writers of letters, by legal codes and enactments, by inscriptions, papyri and other documents, by representations in painting, mosaic or sculpture, and in some areas by the evidence of place-names. For each kind of evidence there are problems of interpretation and evaluation, and each item, no matter how explicit and unambiguous it may appear to be, must first be checked and tested so that its contribution may be as accurately assessed as possible. To set out the process in detail as each point comes along would obviously be excessive, but it may be helpful at this stage to give a brief account of the material available in each of the categories, together with some indication of its strengths and weaknesses and of the ways in which it is handled.

ARCHAEOLOGY

The most important evidence, if only in the sense that there is so much of it, is that provided by archaeology. Precisely how many villas have been excavated or otherwise examined it is impossible to say, though the total would certainly be in thousands rather than hundreds. The figure for Britain, counting 'Villas', 'Probable Villas' and 'Other Substantial Buildings' as defined in the third edition of the Ordnance Survey Map of Roman Britain, is now well over 600.[1] For Gaul the total is certainly much higher, though in the absence of precise 'official' statistics one can only make a guess. The index to the journal *Gallia* lists 132 villas discovered or re-examined in the period 1943–62: this does not include rural bath houses, which in many cases will have belonged to villas, but even if these and similar sites were added it would only represent a fraction of the total. A survey of sites in Belgium, published in 1940, contains at a rough count some 350 actual or probable villas,[2] and there is no reason to suppose that this is exceptional. Reports are plentiful, as we shall see, from the Rhineland and from the Upper Danube provinces: in Pannonia, for example, a recent study refers to 153 sites, many of them excavated since the war.[3] We can also draw on material from Africa, from Italy and from Spain, though admittedly not in such profusion.[4] Taken together, this is an enormous body of information, sufficient, one might have thought, to provide an answer to most conceivable questions. Included in the lists are villas of every size and character, from every period in Roman imperial history, and from every region likely to be able to support them. Of a particular ground plan, a particular kind of room or a particular amenity we may have not one but dozens of examples to compare and contrast. In some areas, where sites have been dug in large numbers, we may feel able to offer statistical information about the size of estates, the level of production, or population. With such a wealth of concrete evidence available, anything that we can obtain from other sources may well seem vague and imprecise, suitable only by way of general confirmation or as a substitute when the archaeological record is temporarily lacking.

To say that such a view is too simple is not to imply any disrespect for archaeology, but merely to recognize its limitations, some of which are bound up with the nature of archaeological evidence itself and others with the ways in which that evidence was acquired. One of the most obvious points, and one which makes itself felt as soon as one considers excavation reports in any number, is that even over a comparatively short period of time there may be quite fundamental changes, not only in the techniques of excavation but in the emphasis given to particular aspects of the material available. Let us look at this latter point first: reports of villas excavated in the nineteenth century, and in some areas well into the twentieth, tended to concentrate on the residential parts of the buildings, and particularly on mosaics, hypocausts and architectural features such as capitals, friezes and the like. This was linked with, and largely explained by, a tendency to see the villa as a symbol of Roman luxury and comfort, so that a detailed description of each room was often accompanied by an attempt to identify its precise function and a detailed description of the kind of activities that might have taken place in it. The number of times, in this kind of report, in which the reader is taken step by step through the full process of a visit to the baths or through each course of a vast and imaginary banquet is part of the same approach. There was also in these early days an emphasis on objects, not as aids to dating or as shedding light on the villas' economic or social context, but as an indication of the wealth and luxury of the Romans or of the strange and exotic character of their life. There were, of course, plenty of other reasons why those exploring the villas confined themselves to these particular aspects. Barns and stables, and buildings to house estate workers, apart from being less productive of interesting objects, were much less different from their modern counterparts than were the residential wings, and so were of less immediate interest;

they were also frequently of more perishable material and therefore less easy to excavate – even if they attracted attention at all. Whatever the reasons, however, this tendency to concentrate on one particular aspect of the villas did produce a narrow, and in many ways distorted picture, not only of what the villas were like, but, more important, of the part they played in the economic and social life of a given region.

One of the difficulties, of course, and one which goes a long way to explaining this kind of approach, was that of dating. Until comparatively recently, the only dateable objects on a villa site were the coins: the beginning and end of its occupation were determined by reference to the earliest and latest coin discovered, and a rise or fall in its prosperity might well be charted in terms of the frequency or scarcity of coins within a given period. To establish a means of dating by objects other than coins, such as pottery, brooches or domestic objects of various kinds, was a long and complex process which is likely to continue indefinitely and which now requires a whole team of consultant experts on all but the simplest sites. Lacking also on the earlier excavations was the technique of stratification – the establishment of a site's history by studying the layers of earth and other material in the sides of trenches cut across it. More common until fairly recent times was the practice of uncovering lengths of wall, thereby removing such informative layers and at the same time divorcing coins and other objects from their precise chronological context. Without the dating techniques any attempt to discover the detailed evolution of a site was hardly likely to succeed. Villas tended to be treated, even if not explicitly, as if they were static: in some cases there were speculations about 'the owner', as though there were only one in the course of several centuries. Frequently history was, as it were, foisted on them: a villa was said to have been built at a particular date because it was known from literary sources that the area was being opened up at the time, and any signs of burning that appeared were linked to particular known invasions. In other words, the early excavators applied to the evidence they collected such techniques as were available to them; because the ways of collecting evidence and the methods used in assessing it have both been greatly improved since the investigation of villas first began, our main consideration when we read a given report must be the date at which it was written. Only when we know this can we know what knowledge and what skills were available to the author and thus how reliable his report is likely to be on a given point.[5]

Apart from such considerations, however, which arise from the way in which the study of villas, and indeed the science of archaeology, has evolved, there are certain points about archaeological evidence which are to a large extent independent of this evolution and which, though they may have to be modified as more advanced techniques are developed, are likely nevertheless to remain broadly true. Let us again begin with a fairly obvious example: there are some materials which are more or less indestructible and others which disappear almost completely within a comparatively short space of time. It may be that in certain

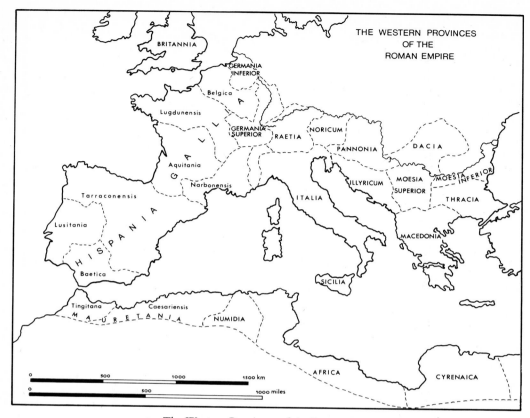

THE WESTERN PROVINCES
OF THE
ROMAN EMPIRE

1 The Western Provinces of the Roman Empire

climatically favoured areas such materials as wood, leather and so on may be exceptionally well preserved, and it is also true that such techniques as pollen analysis or the study of carbonized material can help to redress the balance, but it is unlikely that the heavy reliance on (for example) pottery can ever really be avoided. The problem here is one of distortion, in that certain aspects of villa life are for largely irrelevant reasons given more prominence or less prominence than they would otherwise deserve. There are also more fundamental distortions arising from the fact that the products of archaeology are concrete objects rather than the people who used those objects, though of course it may be possible to make inferences from the one to the other. So it is, for example, that we have so little evidence about the ownership of individual villas, apart from literary references.[6]

There is little either that archaeology can tell us about the social or other relationships of the inhabitants of villas in a particular area or within a single villa estate. Relationships in general are, in archaeological terms, very difficult to establish: we may feel fairly sure that a group of villas in a given area is part of a single property, or that a series of huts and other 'native' sites are the dependencies of a nearby villa, but there is no sure way of proving it. This has other repercussions: it means that systems of land tenure can only rarely be illustrated on the ground, with the result that information about the detailed application of the Roman law in such matters as the ownership and inheritance of land must be gained from other sources. The mention of land reminds us, of course, that the actual villa building is only a part – though admittedly the most important part – of the unit with which we are concerned, namely the villa estate or *fundus*. Quite apart from the outbuildings, to which reference has already been made, there are the dependent dwellings, enclosures and so on – which may well have been some distance away – the system of roads and tracks connecting the various parts of the estate, and above all the fields. There are in Britain and occasionally elsewhere examples of the fields associated directly with the central villa buildings, but there is almost no evidence (apart of course from the so-called 'Celtic' fields) of the systems operating on villa estates as a whole.[7] And even without the fields the excavation of a complete estate would be an enormous undertaking, some idea of which may be gained from the 'total' excavation of the villa at Barnsley Park in Gloucestershire, which began in 1962 and is still proceeding, or from the famous excavation of the villa of Montmaurin and its dependencies in southern France[8] (*Figs.* 40, 41). It is not often, in any case, that we can be sure, either that the limits of an estate have been reasonably clearly recognized, or that within those limits most of the component parts are still discoverable.

As with any other branch of archaeology, the villas which lend themselves most readily to exploration are those which are relatively undisturbed by later building or other destructive activities, and here again there is a danger of distortion; a villa relatively undisturbed in open country and a villa buried almost without a trace beneath a village may well have been virtually identical in (say) the second century AD, but in the sense that the one site had a subsequent history of settlement while the other did not they are, from the wider historical viewpoint, radically different. The fact that our knowledge of villas in archaeological terms has been built up by exploring sites in open country much more than those beneath later settlements can often be safely ignored, but there are some enquiries, such as those concerning the fate of villas in the period during and after the great invasions, where it could well be very relevant, and it would be unwise in any discussion to leave it out of account.[9] Distortion of another kind, though much more easily allowed for, is that resulting from the presence or absence within an area of able and active workers. There are many examples in Britain and France of an area liberally dotted with sites next to another with almost none – and an energetic priest or local official is often the reason.[10] The modern counterpart of this, though on a grander scale, is the work of the aerial photographer: one thinks, for example, of the transformation brought about by aerial surveys in our picture of the river gravels of England or the plains of northern France[11] (*Fig.* 19). Questions of distribution, intensity of settlement and the like are ones which ultimately archaeology alone can really answer; but the answers it gives must always be provisional, and may alter dramatically from one season to the next.

Much of what has been said so far is cautionary, and in some ways even negative, in tone. The great advantages of archaeology, if we may end on a more positive note, are first, that it provides us with a direct link, uncomplicated by any intermediary, with actual villa buildings, second, that it gives us detailed information about particular sites rather than general information about villas in the mass, and third, that it is almost the only area in which the body of material is increasing and likely to increase more or less indefinitely. Gaps in literary evidence are permanent, whereas in archaeology they can generally be filled by looking at a site again or by looking at another site; in the same way theories can be verified, questions asked and answered, doubts and uncertainties resolved. There are, as we have seen, distortions and there are parts of the subject where archaeology is of only limited help, but it is nevertheless upon archaeology that the study of villas is primarily and necessarily based.

REPRESENTATIONS IN ART

As well as uncovering the villas themselves, the archaeologists provide us with most of the items in another body of evidence, namely the representations of villas and their associated activities on such things as mosaics, wall-paintings and other works of art. The study of these as evidence for villas rather than from a mainly artistic viewpoint is not, perhaps, as far advanced as it might be, and discussion has tended so far to concentrate on particular examples rather than on a comprehensive survey of the material as a whole. This is a pity, because the amount of evidence now available in this category is quite considerable; there are, undoubtedly, many problems and uncertainties of interpretation, but used in conjunction with archaeology, and verified where possible by archaeological means, it can be enormously helpful.

Mosaics, apart from being one of the most familiar features of villa sites, are also the best source of information we have about their appearance. They were not, of course, confined to villas, but were common also (indeed, more common) in town houses and public buildings and later in churches and tombs. Among the many and various subjects represented those connected with the country and with country life were naturally very popular, either as a record of the owner's daily pursuits or as a reminder of the many opportunities offered by the countryside for relaxation. Thus hunting scenes were common, as well as more ornamental designs in which animals of various kinds were grouped in a suitably attractive landscape. Common also were representations of the range of farming activities, such as tilling the fields, herding animals and tending vines or fruit trees. A favourite subject in this respect was a sort of farming calendar, in which the seasons, and sometimes the months of the year, were illustrated by the jobs appropriate to them: a famous example of this is the pavement at St-Romain-en-Gal in southern France, which in its complete state had some

2   Mosaic from Tabarka, in Tunisia, showing the residential part of a villa set in an orchard

40 separate panels, all but eight of which depicted some aspect of agricultural life.[12] Examples of all these subjects are to be found throughout the western provinces, but for number and variety as well as for sophistication of technique those of Roman North Africa are in a class of their own.[13] This is an area where some attempt has been made to bring the available evidence together,[14] and the light it throws upon rural life in general and villas in particular is very revealing. Most important for our purposes is that from Africa come almost all the examples in which actual villa buildings are depicted, not only the residential parts (though these are understandably the most frequent) but sometimes the more humble barns and outhouses. A fine example is the early-fourth-century group of mosaics from Tabarka, showing the main house, with its portico and flanking towers, set in a kind of park, and on separate semicircular panels four of its associated work buildings[15] (*Figs.* 2, 47, 48). Very similar, though this time on a single panel, is the so-called Seigneur Julius mosaic from Carthage, depicting once again the villa itself and various farming occupations,[16] and there are equally valuable examples from Zliten, Oudna and elsewhere.[17]

Most of what we have said about mosaics is applicable also to wall-paintings, the main differences being that our best examples of these are on the whole rather earlier than the mosaics and are from Italy rather than from Africa. Apart from this, the kinds of buildings in which they appear and the range of subjects they represent are very similar. The best known examples are those from private houses in Pompeii, dating from the early first century AD, typically the ones from the House of Fronto, which depict a series of luxury villas, some of them by the sea, with colonnades, pavilions and elaborate gardens;[18] and the same kind of subject appears on paintings from Stabiae, from villas along the Appian Way and from Rome itself.[19] More interesting, however, and certainly more representative than these exotic examples is one from another Pompeian house, that of Fortuna Piccola, which shows what is clearly a working farm, with an unpretentious, even rather untidy group of buildings and amongst other things a plough propped up against a wall[20] (*Fig.* 7). A fairly similar painting, dating from a century or so later, was found in Trier; here the villa is a little more imposing, but the inclusion of figures in obviously peasant dress reveals that the establishment is a farmstead rather than something more luxurious[21] (*Fig.* 3). No doubt this kind of thing was fairly common in the north European as well as the Mediterranean villas, but since in the northern provinces very little survives in most sites above the foundations we are not likely to recover many examples in other than fragmentary condition.

With sculpture we are dealing with something at once more durable and

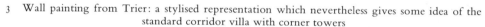

3   Wall painting from Trier: a stylised representation which nevertheless gives some idea of the standard corridor villa with corner towers

much more general in its distribution; on the other hand, it is a medium which lends itself more readily to the portrayal of figures, whether human or animal, rather than to landscape, and it is for rural activities rather than for the villas themselves that its evidence is most useful. Most of the pieces that concern us are monumental, reliefs in the main from funerary monuments of various kinds, depicting the activities during their lifetimes of the people commemorated. In some cases the rural subjects are probably subsidiary to the main ones, so that, for example, a shepherd and some sheep may be depicted on a side panel more or less for ornament, but there are monuments from which a whole series of pieces survive and which are clearly intended more as a factual record. Perhaps the most famous examples of these are the sculptures on the remarkable column-like monuments at Igel and Neumagen near Trier,[22] (*Figs* 37, 38) both of which give a picture of a prosperous family engaged in commerce but with investment also in land. The area from here westwards into Luxembourg and Belgium is particularly rich in sculptures of rural scenes: there are many fine examples from Arlon, among them one of a series of representations of the harvesting machine which is otherwise known only from the work of the late agricultural writer Palladius.[23] Africa again provides other examples,[24] and there are individual pieces from most of the western provinces. In addition to reliefs there are a number of other items to which reference should also be made: students of British villas will be familiar with the little bronze from Piercebridge in County Durham representing a ploughman and his team of oxen, and there are models of ploughs, again in bronze, from Sussex and Cologne[25] (*Figs* 35, 36). These and other representations of tools and implements relating to agriculture have now been assembled and studied together, and much of value has been derived from them.[26]

The primary contribution of all these works of art, and in particular those which show us actual villa buildings, is that they give us some idea of what the villas looked like when they were complete and flourishing, and how the various activities were carried out or the various implements used. Consider, for example, the average villa site: what, essentially, we have are the main foundations and floors, which may be reasonably intact, together with the occasional cellar or other underground structure. Overlying this, in a very fragmentary state, will be such of the superstructure as has escaped destruction by ploughing or removal as building material, and it is on this fairly limited evidence that the archaeologist has to base his reconstruction of what the villa might have been in its original state. The main outlines are often clear enough, but the details and the overall appearance remain a matter of conjecture,[27] so that any help that works of art can give will naturally be gratefully accepted.

There are, of course, a number of problems, and it would be foolish to suppose that representations of villas in art can be used without reservation and without certain allowances being made. As works of art they will have been subject to artistic conventions, some of which will have caused distortions which are obvious (like the paintings in the house of the Vetii in Pompeii, in which the gathering and pressing of grapes is being carried out by a group of winged cupids),[28] while others may well go undetected. The fact that their purpose was to please rather than to inform will have meant that artists were less concerned with authenticity of detail than with the overall effect, even supposing that they were familiar with the detail in the first place. Most of the artists would be town dwellers, many of them foreign to the areas in which they worked; much of their subject matter was secondhand, derived from representations in other regions and in different media. Added to this would be the limitations imposed by technique, and the difficulties involved in working with rapidly drying cement or plaster. The villas depicted in the African mosaics, for example, are generally very two-dimensional in appearance, consisting in most cases simply of a facade with at most the suggestion of rooms and extensions behind.[29] But these are things which can in principle be allowed for, and although the degree of precision is obviously much lower than that possible with excavation the study of villas in art does provide an extra dimension to our understanding which is not possible using purely archaeological evidence. What it does, in fact, is to bring us that much closer to the minds of the villa owners, so that we can understand a little more clearly the part that villas played in people's lives, and something of what they meant to those who lived and worked in them.

WRITTEN SOURCES

To deal in detail with all the literary and documentary sources which have something to contribute to the study of the Roman villa would require more space than is here available.[30] All that we can hope to do is to note the most helpful authors and summarize the main types of evidence they provide, so as to give at least a general idea of what is available and where its value may lie. Much of the written material is directly concerned with villas and villa estates, and it is to this that our primary attention must be given, but there is a great deal also which throws light on farming and rural life in general, as well as on various aspects of the social and economic framework of which the villas were part, and since it is in these areas that the evidence of archaeology is probably least informative we shall need to spread the net a little wider than may at first seem necessary.

Not surprisingly in a world in which agriculture was of such fundamental importance there were, first of all, a number of technical handbooks, written at various periods for the benefit of landowners and offering advice and information on basic as well as more specialised topics. The earliest of those that survive is the work *De Agri Cultura* of M. Porcius Cato.[31] Written in the first half of the second century BC, at a time when agriculture in Italy was being transformed in the aftermath of the second Punic war, with the decline of the small peasant proprietor and the formation of the great estates, it is a confused, haphazard collection of facts, ideas and advice, presented in abrupt and forceful language by a man who deplored the social and moral tenor of his day and saw in the traditional practices of Roman farming the simple virtues whose passing he regretted. Cato was a practical farmer himself and, in spite of its obscurities and lack of organization, his work was drawn upon heavily by later writers; though not directly relevant to the villa as we know it, the development of which came rather later, it is a book which contains much of permanent interest and has the great merit of being written from a wholly utilitarian rather than a literary point of view. On a similar level, though in a rather more literary framework, is the *Res Rusticae* of M. Terentius Varro,[32] written in about 37 BC at the end of the author's long and varied life. Its three books deal respectively with agriculture proper, with animal husbandry (of which Varro had expert personal experience), and with the production for profit of smaller stock such as poultry, game birds and bees – this last reflecting the growing demand for luxury items which was a feature of the period. Its rather rigid arrangement and the author's pedantic interest in antiquarian and philological detail make it a difficult work to read, but like Cato's it is immensely informative and was subsequently very influential.

To move from this to Virgil's *Georgics*,[33] published only a few years later in 29 BC, is to move very obviously away from the informative and factual and into the world of poetry and imagination. Written ostensibly as a didactic poem in the tradition of the early Greek poet Hesiod, it has a similar arrangement in many ways to Varro's, with its four books covering successively the topics of corn growing, vines and olives, cattle and horses, and bees. But it is clearly something very different from a conventional technical handbook, even though later writers tended to use it as such, and it is unlikely that Virgil had any more practical knowledge of farming than one would expect in a man who, though he loved the country and had spent his early years in a farming environment, was primarily interested in matters literary and intellectual. Not all of his information and advice will stand up to scrutiny, and it is probable that much of the technical material on which he draws was taken from other writers, Varro himself being prominent among them.

Roughly contemporary with Virgil (though his exact dates remain unknown) was Marcus Vitruvius, whose ten books *De Architectura*[34] are the only major work on ancient building to survive. Most of it, of course, is outside our scope, but there is in Book VI, which is about houses, a short section dealing with the planning and siting of a villa. As with all the writers so far mentioned, the region envisaged is Italy, and it is among the Italian examples that practical illustrations of Vitruvius' precepts are to be sought. But as an authoritative explanation of villa planning the passage is hard to match, and it serves also as a useful bridge between the handbooks on the one hand and the more literary descriptions of villas (of which more in a moment) on the other.

Of the handbooks, that of L. Junius Moderatus Columella,[35] the next author whose work has come down to us, is in many ways the most important. It was probably written about the middle of the first century AD, and its 12 books cover the whole range of agricultural practice from basic principles through to the production of luxury items and the cultivation of gardens. As one might expect,

Columella draws heavily upon the work of earlier writers, but he relies equally heavily upon his own experience, which was clearly very considerable. There is much in his work that his predecessors do not cover, and much that he takes further than they do, but his main quality is his ability to organize his material and deal with the subject systematically and lucidly, and in a manner which is comprehensive without being tedious.

The same can hardly be said of Columella's rather younger contemporary the elder Pliny, whose encyclopedic work called *Natural History*[36] was essentially a compilation of facts thought worthy of note by the author and drawn together, often somewhat uncritically, from writers of widely differing periods and purpose. Two books in particular are of interest: number XVII, which is about cultivated trees, and number XVIII, about agriculture generally. There is, though, much also in XIV and XV, which are about vines, olives and fruit trees, and at various points elsewhere. Pliny's reading was wide and voracious, and his work is full of peculiar or surprising items for which he is our only authority. Most important, perhaps, his interests were not confined to Italy, and much of his value to us lies in the information he provides on agricultural practices and achievements in Africa, Gaul and elsewhere.

From what we may call the classical period this more or less closes the list as far as technical handbooks are concerned. Otherwise we have a number of works of the later Empire which, though they are by no means lacking in interest, are of somewhat restricted use, either because they deal with particular specialist topics or because they are to a large extent derivative and therefore useful mainly as a means of filling gaps in what we already know. Most interesting in many ways is the work of the fourth-century writer Palladius, who bases himself very closely on Columella but whose 15 books, written mainly in the form of a month-by-month calendar of farming operations, contain much that is not found elsewhere.[37] The so-called *Agrimensores* are a group of writers on surveying, some of them from as early as the first century and others much later, who are mainly of interest in connection with the regular method of land allotment known as centuriation, but who provide information also about the legal aspects of land tenure and a certain amount also about field patterns.[38] More exotic, though rather more central in its relevance, is the compilation known as the *Geoponika*, which comes down to us in its present form from the tenth century but is collected from much earlier writers, many of whom, like Cato, Varro and others, are known to us.[39]

With all of the technical writers there are particular problems of interpretation: with some it is a question of the precise meaning of a passage, with others the problem of establishing the ultimate source of the information, and therefore its reliability, or of cutting through the moral or political overtones of what is said. But there is one more fundamental question that is relevant to all of them, namely the extent to which they can be used as authorities for other periods and other areas than those to which they primarily refer. How far, to put it bluntly, can the writers up to and including Columella, who wrote almost exclusively for the farmers of Italy, be used to interpret and illuminate villa sites in Gaul, Africa or Britain, most of which were not in existence, or at least had not become villas in any real sense of the term, until some time after the works in question had been written? In one sense the answer is fairly clear: if what we are asking is whether, in establishing and running their farm, the villa owners of Gaul or Britain were likely to consult their copies of Varro or Columella at every stage, the answer is clearly no. Quite apart from questions of literacy or language, the idea of working from textbooks was probably as alien to the ancient farmer as until recently it was to his modern counterpart, and the very striking differences in farming practice which still exist from one region to another in spite of the pressures towards uniformity suggest that in antiquity the differences were greater and the value of all but the most general advice proportionately less. It still remains possible, however, that the textbooks, even if they were not directly a guide to the average provincial farmer, might still be a guide to the modern scholar, in the sense that they were to a large extent simply the written record of that body of inherited farming wisdom which the average practising farmer would acquire by other than written means. There still remains the problem of regional variety of practice, but there is some justification for using the handbooks to provide parallels for practices otherwise known to exist or to suggest interpretations for material otherwise unexplained. It would clearly be wrong, however, to take them as a starting point, as was done by some of the early excavators, and to explain a given site in terms of them rather than the other way round.

In any case, important as the handbooks are, their value is limited for us in the sense that they are concerned mainly with the practice of farming itself and only rarely or partly with the villa as an institution. In this sense there are a number of writers who, though not concerned with writing handbooks, are none the less of considerable value. The *Satyricon* of Petronius,[40] the central character of which is the freedman Trimalchio, contains a great deal of material about landed estates (the basis of Trimalchio's wealth), and although the work is fictional and humorous in intent there is much to be gained from it in a general way about the situation in Italy in the middle of the first century AD. The letters of the younger Pliny,[41] who achieved public distinction in the reign of Trajan, make frequent reference to his own estates and the problems involved in running them. Indeed, it is hard to find any work of literature which does not at some point provide information of one kind or another that is of interest, from Cicero or Horace right through to Ausonius or Salvian. How useful such information is depends on the context in which it appears, on the nature of the work of which it forms a part and on the purpose of the author in writing it. Thus, for example, apart from exercising obvious caution with a work like the *Satyricon*, we must allow for exaggeration of gloom in a sermon of Salvian or for false modesty when Ausonius refers to an estate of some 700 acres as his 'little bit of property'.[42] On the other hand, there are items of information in sources of this kind which, because they are mere incidental details as far as the main purpose of a work is concerned, are at least as reliable, if not even more so, than if they had appeared in an authoritative treatise.

Within the literary material there is one recurring item which became something of a literary convention, and which will concern us again later in another context. This is the practice of describing one's villa, whether in prose or verse, in a certain amount of detail for the benefit, ostensibly, of a friend but also as a kind of literary exercise. The first signs of it appear in Horace's odes,[43] but the earliest extended example, and also the most famous, is that of Pliny's Laurentine villa which occurs in the 17th letter of his second book.[44] Obviously modelled on this is the equally detailed account provided some two and a half centuries later by Sidonius Apollinaris of his own estate at Avitacum in the region of Clermont-Ferrand,[45] and there are other examples from the late Empire in the poetry of Ausonius, Fortunatus and a number of others.[46] Such descriptions are the literary equivalent of the villas depicted on mosaics and wall-paintings which we have already considered, and their value to us is broadly the same: they give us an insight into the villa as a living institution, together with some indication of the attitudes of villa owners and of those aspects which seemed to them to be of importance.

More straightforward in many ways, though naturally less particular in its relevance, is the evidence provided by the great legal compilations of Theodosius and Justinian in the fifth and sixth centuries AD. Both emperors produced a *Codex*, or collection of laws, many of which date back a number of generations before the compilation, and Justinian also provided a sort of introductory handbook known to us as the *Institutes*.[47] But the most important collection for our purposes is that known as the *Digest*,[48] which brought together opinions of distinguished jurists on detailed points of law, being given originally in connection with particular cases but acquiring a more general authority with the course of time. The great period for jurists of distinction was that of the Antonine and Severan dynasties, that is to say roughly the second and early third centuries AD, and a great deal of the material in the *Digest* is from this period. The main interest of the law, in this as in any other period, was in the relations between people, both groups and individuals, most notably in connection with property, and the bulk of what the *Digest* has to offer us concerns the mutual rights and responsibilities of the estate owners and their *coloni*, farmers holding their lands on a fixed but renewable lease. In other words, it sheds light on the social framework of the villas rather than on the villas or their estates as such, reaching once again some of the areas which in archaeological terms are largely intangible.

The same is true, broadly speaking, of what little documentary evidence exists. With the exception of such things as funeral monuments, the purpose of which was to provide not only a permanent but a public record, most of the documents concerning the affairs of private citizens were in the Roman period as in all subsequent ages inscribed on fairly impermanent materials. Deeds of sale, wills, census returns, inventories of equipment, accounts and all the other records likely to concern us in connection with villas existed in the form of papyri, wooden tablets or the like, and only in freak conditions would they be likely to survive at all, let alone be recognized for what they were and adequately preserved and restored. Egypt, of course, was a well-known exception to the general rule, and the profusion of papyrus records enables us to understand a great deal by analogy about the less favoured areas where the villas mostly occur; but Egypt was an exception in many more ways than that of its climatic conditions, and so many of its institutions are peculiar to it that without specific supporting evidence any extrapolation from it to other provinces is likely to be misleading. Apart from an odd scrap of material here and there, this restricts us, as far as these other provinces are concerned, to a number of inscriptions in which the running of individual estates is tied up in some way or other to wider public issues. Such are the inscriptions of the early second century relating to the so-called *alimenta* system in Italy,[49] or the well-known series from North Africa dealing with imperial estates,[50] and immensely valuable as these are it would be wrong to suggest that they shed light on anything more than a small corner of the subject.

Clearly then the written evidence for villas and villa life, whether it be in the form of literary works or documentary records, is uneven both in reliability and distribution. There are, of course, the obvious historiographical techniques that one can apply in order to evaluate written material, but it can never be as specific and as concrete as the evidence of archaeology. On the other hand, there are aspects of the subject on which it rather than archaeology is most likely to enlighten us, and its very generality can often be of value as a counterbalance to what one often feels is the excessively narrow picture provided by individual sites.

PLACE-NAMES

In any study of human settlement the evidence of place-names is likely to be fairly central: such names have a tenacity which is frequently greater than that of the things which originally gave rise to them, and the extraction of their meaning by the philologist is both analogous to, and as valuable as, the more physical extractions of the archaeologist, for whom they serve both as a way of interpreting the evidence he has and as an indication of where additional evidence may be found.

As evidence for villas, their value in most areas is that they record the discovery of sites at various periods by people who often had little notion of what they were and certainly no thought or means of recording them in any other way. If in a particular field the plough was frequently obstructed by building stones it might become regular to refer to this in conversation: the field became the 'stony field, *le champ des pierres*, the *steinmäurles äckern*', and so on.[51] In France and Belgium the name 'Mazières' or 'Maizières' is very common: derived from the late Latin *maceriae*, meaning 'walls', it usually indicates the discovery of wall foundations under farm land, and although these may not necessarily be Roman they frequently are.[52] Similarly, the appearance of Roman bricks or tiles can give rise to the names 'Ville Rouge' or 'Maison Rouge',[53] and burnt material, whether from hearths or a destruction, produces 'Terres Noires'.[54] Frequently, indeed usually, the exact nature of the site was misunderstood: the extent of villa remains, which often seemed greater than they in fact were because of the scatter of debris over a wide area, led to the assumption that they were ancient towns,[55] so that names involving *Ville* were common in France and ones involving *Burg* in the Germanic areas.[56] The same kind of thinking probably produced 'Altstadt' in Baden,[57] and (with more justification) 'Borough Field', the site of the Great Chesterford villa in Essex.[58] Occasionally, one finds names which appear to be corruptions of actual Latin words, such as *Sioutat* for *civitas* or *Questel* for *castellum*,[59] and it may be that these are part of the same kind of process at a much earlier age, when Latin was still spoken, or at least remembered. More frequent, and often comparatively modern, are the names which indicate popular attribution; many German villas are on sites associated by name with pagan peoples ('Heidenschloss', 'Heidenhäuser'[60] etc.), and in France it is common to attribute ruins to the Saracens (*le champ Sarrazin, les Sarrazinières*[61] and so on). On its own, of course, this kind of evidence is not particularly valuable, in that it is really only part of the popular traditions of a given area which are as likely to be misleading as to inform; but it can often point the way to more concrete discoveries, and as a supplement to more scientific enquiries it is of considerable value.

Far more important, and worthy of separate treatment on its own, is the survival in some regions, not of popular beliefs about villa ruins, but of the actual names of villa estates, preserved, often in very large numbers, in the names of modern farms and villages. France and Belgium are particularly rich in names of this kind, but they are found in Romance areas generally and to some extent also in Germany. The names in question are those with the suffix *-acus* or *-acum*, which is the Celtic version of the regular Latin *-anus*, the use of which was confined largely to Italy, Spain, Africa and the more Romanized parts of southern Gaul. The regular practice in Italy was to attach the suffix to the gentile name of an estate owner (i.e. 'Julianus', 'Antonianus', etc.),[62] and although this seems to have been considerably extended in the Tres Galliae to include the names of various geographical features the overall value of the names remains the same.[63]

More often than not such names are easily recognizable, in that their development within a particular area tends to be fairly regular. In the Midi and in Britanny, for example, their modern equivalents will normally end in -ac, in Limousin and Auvergne in -at or -as, and in most of Languedoc in -y, -é or -ay.[64] Individual examples often escape us, and some names with the right ending derive from other roots, but so long as one is concerned with settlement patterns rather than individual sites they are not likely seriously to mislead us. The likely margin of error can be demonstrated by a particularly well-documented area just south of Paris, where from the 1 : 50,000 map one can quickly discover some 30 names in -y, which is the local *-acum* form.[65] (*Fig.* 4) Of these, no less than 21 can be found with the *-acum* termination in documents earlier than the twelfth century, and a

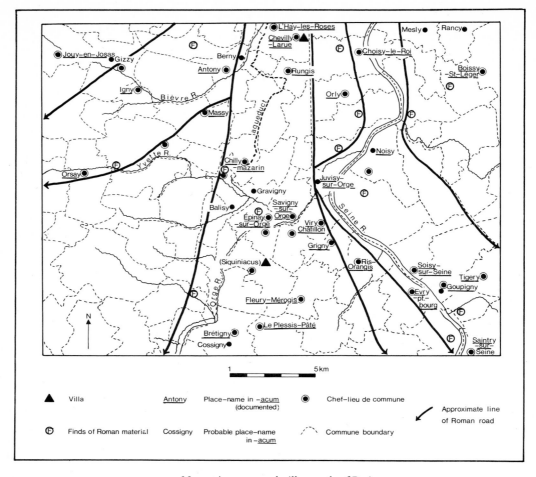

4   Names in -*acum* and villas south of Paris

further six are documented as -*acum* names in other areas where they occur; one
is doubtful, and only two are shown by the documents to derive from other
roots. As it happens, the documents also bring to light some six modern names
which come from -*acum* forms but have developed differently, but since three
of these now end in -ay and three in -is we might well have suspected them
in any case. Clearly, an individual example must be carefully documented before
any reliance is placed on it, but taken in the mass the names have a surprising
degree of accuracy, provided of course that they are used with caution. The
numbers involved, after all, are often very large indeed. The examples just
quoted are from a single sheet of the map of France, that is, an area of some
25 by 20 km, much of it covered by urban development, and areas elsewhere in
France are just as productive. A study of the Gironde *département* published in
1936 contains no less than 281 examples, all of them documented, and there
is no reason to suppose that this is exceptional.[66]

We are, of course, assuming that names in *-acum* do in most cases indicate the existence of a villa, and this may seem a little hasty in view of the large number of examples where there is little or no support from archaeology. Simply because estates were named in this way we should not suppose that nothing else was: it is hard to believe, for example, that Roman York, which had one of the very few *-acum* names known to us in Britain, is of very much help, or indeed Gesoriacum, which is one of the names for Boulogne. Nevertheless, the evidence is that broadly speaking the equation of *-acum* names and villas is a legitimate one. Of those appearing in documentary and literary sources the vast majority are applied either to villas or to *fundi*, which is strictly speaking the same thing in that according to Roman law a *fundus* consists of buildings as well as land.[67] And although there are very many *-acum* names which have not yet been authenticated by the discovery of actual villa remains, there are certainly very many which have – enough at any rate to justify the view that the association is not accidental. Added to this is the fact that the distribution of *-acum* names is very much what we would expect the total villa distribution to be if it could be recovered. It was pointed out some time ago[68] that in Aveyron such names are constantly appearing on traditional villa locations, such as the meanders of rivers and southward-facing slopes, and this is certainly true elsewhere. Wherever one looks, in fact, the patterns are seen to be similar: *-acum* names quite often occur at regular intervals, a phenomenon which, with villas, has been taken as an indication of regular-sized estates; and it is not uncommon to find *-acum* names, like villas, sited just a little way off the Roman roads rather than on the actual line. As with the names themselves, the individual cases still need individual proof, but taken as a class their meaning seems to be clear.

3

Origins and Historical Development

In 31 BC the battle of Actium brought to an end the long period of civil war in which the Roman Republic had foundered. Within little more than a decade its victor, by then known as Augustus, had not only established himself as the unassailable ruler of Rome but had inaugurated throughout the Empire a policy of peace which was to remain in force, in practice as well as in theory, until the disasters of the third century AD. Within this period of peace, which in the western provinces was only locally and temporarily broken, the villas began, developed and prospered, the product of settled conditions and economic stability and an indication of the extent and intensity of Roman cultural influence. We are dealing, of course, with a gradual process rather than a sudden transformation. For some recently conquered areas, such as the north-eastern part of Gaul, the process of consolidation under a largely military authority was bound to last for some time yet, and the process itself could lead to further military activity, such as that in Britain or eastwards beyond the Rhine. There were, on the other hand, provinces which had enjoyed comparative peace and its accompanying benefits for some time already: Africa, Spain and Gallia Narbonensis. But the one essential point was that now for the first time in generations the attention of the central government of Rome could turn to the activities of peace as its primary concern, so that from the provinces' point of view the source, not only of their security, but of their cultural and economic advance, was no longer encumbered with costly and negative demands.[1]

The effects of all this, at least in general terms, are fairly clear. At the public level the establishment of peace was an opportunity for developing the new provinces and consolidating the old, for providing or improving road net-works, for setting up administrative systems based on new or existing urban centres, and in some cases for the establishment of frontiers. By such means, together with the development of something like a colonial civil service and the gradual incorporation of individual provinces into the Roman census, the collec-tion of taxes could be made more efficient and an opportunity given for the provinces to contribute more effectively to the economic life of the Empire as a whole. For agriculture, with which we are primarily (though not exclusively) concerned, such activities could hardly be other than beneficial, even if in the short term they represented something of a challenge. The towns, with their growing business communities and increasingly cosmopolitan populations, provided markets on a scale unknown before and therefore an incentive to efficient management and the production of an agricultural surplus. In the military provinces the army had the same effect, with the more permanent camps attracting the familiar native settlements and again providing a market for goods and services of various kinds.[2] The more basic needs of the army, of course, were met by requisitioning rather than by normal trading processes, and the provision of corn, hides and so on must have been a considerable burden to native farmers, even without the corruption and gratuitous inconveniences of which Tacitus gives us examples.[3] But even this, provided it was fairly organized, was a welcome stimulus: the increased efficiency needed to meet the demands would serve as its own recommendation and a generally healthy economic situation would do the rest.[4] Such a situation, moreover, as well as presenting opportunities to the provincials themselves, was an attractive prospect also to people from Italy and other parts of the empire, so that alongside the official and public development programme there was an equally energetic and no less beneficial private one. Some of this was carried out at a distance, with business men (Seneca is a famous example) providing capital for building and other projects to communities or prominent individuals.[5] But much more was done by people on the spot, by merchants and craftsmen travelling from place to place and eventually by settlers, sometimes former soldiers, eager to reap the benefits of a new and developing world. Here again the effect on a predominantly agricultural economy was positive and generally beneficial. The availability of a whole new range of manufactured goods was a powerful encouragement to farmers to produce a surplus – the only means by which they could acquire them – and these goods, seen in the context of the settlers' comparatively sophisticated life style, could lead to a degree of Romanization beyond their immediate use.

How this came about, and how the villa emerged as one of the more obvious examples of it, is what we are here mainly concerned with, but before looking at this particular aspect of Romanization it may be helpful to have some understanding of Romanization as an overall process.[6] What one has to avoid is the concept of a militant missionary government imposing its culture on a world regarded as barbarian. This is not to say that the Romans were not proud of their civilization or that they did not wish to share it with their subject peoples. On the contrary, they were very quick to stamp out in the provinces any behaviour which was thought to be out of keeping with accepted Roman standards – their attitude to the more exotic local religions is a case in point – and from Caesar and Augustus onwards it was regular policy to reward Romanization with an increasing scale of privileges culminating in Roman citizenship itself. So Claudius, advocating the admission of Gauls to the Senate in a famous speech of AD 48, points first to their loyalty, then to their wealth and then to their Roman ways.[7] But as a general rule it was for the provincials themselves to take the initiative; once evident, this initiative was encouraged, assisted and rewarded, and if not immediately forthcoming it could be stimulated, but without it there was a general reluctance to force the issue. Individual governors might take things further: Tacitus says that in Britain Agricola chided the sluggish as well as praising the willing.[8] But perhaps a better guide to what happened in particular cases is provided by Pliny's letters to Trajan, in which there is encouragement for Romanizing projects and chiding only for overenthusiasm leading to financial difficulty or for dishonest speculation and profiteering.[9] Indeed, if these letters are anything to go by, there was no lack of readiness on the part of the provincials; towns vied with each other in putting up the status symbols of theatres, baths and the like, and this was no doubt matched by a similar rivalry among individuals. Desire for Roman amenities not infrequently outstripped the ability to cope with them: buildings were erected after inadequate surveys and by inexperienced architects, and the lack of capital, putting the provincials at the mercy of the big Italian financiers, was a constant source of trouble.[10] The consternation caused in Britain when Seneca called in his loans under Nero is well known, and there are plenty of examples elsewhere; debt was one of the factors behind the revolt of Florus and Sacrovir in AD 21, and the attacks on merchants which tend to accompany local revolts are probably connected with the same basic problem.[11] Problems indeed there were, but the greater part of the Romanization process was the work of the provincials themselves; as such, it was unsystematic, uneven and at times a little comical, but being willed rather than imposed it was genuine and above all durable.

Agricola's encouragement to the Britons was to build temples, *fora* and town houses – that is, to adopt an urban way of life to which they were but little accustomed but which was essential for the efficient administration of the province. The adoption of Roman ways in the countryside could be left to individual initiative and general economic forces. At its lowest level this might mean simply the acceptance of new types of tools or equipment within the traditional life style; in this sense even the most primitive hutment could be 'Roman' in that it had succumbed to what Haverfield called 'the heavy inevitable atmosphere of the Roman material civilisation'.[12] Villas are something more: once we feel able to apply the term to a given site we are giving recognition, no longer to the unthinking adoption of available objects, but to the acceptance, even to a small degree, of a new and different way of life – to the beginning of that integration into the social and economic organization of the Roman world which is Rivet's definition of the term itself.[13]

There are not many sites on which this process can be illustrated with any degree of detail: the earliest phases of villas, particularly those built largely of wood or other perishable materials, were likely to be submerged in later reconstructions, if not actually dismantled and removed. But parts of the process can be seen in numerous examples, and the villa of Mayen, in the Rhineland near

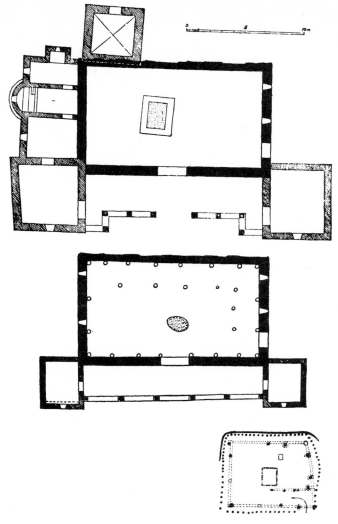

5   Mayen, Germany, Phases I–II (bottom), III–IV (centre) and V (top)

Coblenz, is one of the best.[14] (*Fig.* 5) The earliest phase here is a small hut of wattle and daub, rectangular and without any sophistication except for what seems to be a sort of vestibule, intended perhaps to allow people in and out without letting the weather in as well. The first real sign of influence from outside is in the third phase, early in the first century AD, in which the primitive hut is replaced by a more strictly rectangular building, still largely timber-built but with stone footings. In most respects this is no real advance on the hut – there is still only one room for all the occupants, animal and human together, and even at this stage the structure is supported on rows of wooden posts running inside the stone foundations – but what is important is that even at this level the influence of a superior culture is making itself felt; the establishment remains the same socially and economically, but is translated into the new language. Once this has been achieved it can develop in a way that was not possible within the earlier pattern, a point which is clearly seen in phase IV, when the single large room is given a simple colonnade along one of its longer sides and a pair of corner rooms, one at either end. The term 'villa' now becomes appropriate, not simply because the building is now one of hundreds built on the same basic plan throughout the western provinces, but because it represents a gesture towards, if not the whole-hearted adoption of, a new kind of life and even a new set of values. Socially it is different from the hut of phase II and the single-roomed building of phase III in that segregation is now possible between humans and animals or between different ranks of humans – and not only possible but presumably also desirable. Economically, it is different because, with the construction of a colonnade, however simple, the owner has moved beyond what is strictly utilitarian to something designed for physical, even visual, pleasure, the taste for which will ultimately involve him in the production of a surplus in order to satisfy it.

Similar, though less complete examples may be cited from other parts of the Roman world. In Britain, where Iron Age dwellings were almost exclusively round or oval in shape, the appearance of even a hut with a rectangular ground plan may reasonably be taken as indicating a degree of Roman influence: the first-century huts under the Park Street villa are a case in point, as is the rectangular pattern of post-holes, dated to *c.* AD 70, beneath that of Ditchley[15] (*Figs* 30, 46). The earliest villas in Britain, of which Park Street is one, are built on a simple rectangular plan, usually with a row of small rooms rather than one large one as is more usual on the Continent. Lockleys began in this way, with a range of five small rooms (*Fig.* 28), and there were very similar buildings in the early phases of Brixworth (Northants) (*Fig.* 29) and Hambledon (Bucks).[16] Corridors in Britain seem to appear from the second century onwards: Park Street and Lockleys are again the most obvious examples, though Lockleys (and apparently Brixworth also) had rudimentary timber verandahs at an earlier stage.[17] This is in line with what evidence we have from Gaul also: there the conquest was roughly a century earlier, and corridors appear, as at Haccourt (Liège) (*Fig.* 6) and Cadeilhan-St-Clar (Gers) in the course of the first century rather than the second.[18]

What we are trying to illustrate, of course, is the gradual adoption of a Romanized life style in the early part of a province's development. There will, clearly, be sites which omit some or all of the stages described, and others which go through the stages but at a much later date (a good example is the development of the villa at Frocester Court, Gloucestershire, in the late third and early fourth century)[19] (*Fig.* 31). Moreover, in talking of Romanization, we are assuming that in the majority of cases the owners and builders of the individual villas were not themselves Romans but natives of the province in question. There were, however, exceptions, which can be seen, not so much as illustrations of the Romanizing process but rather as part of the force behind it. Most of

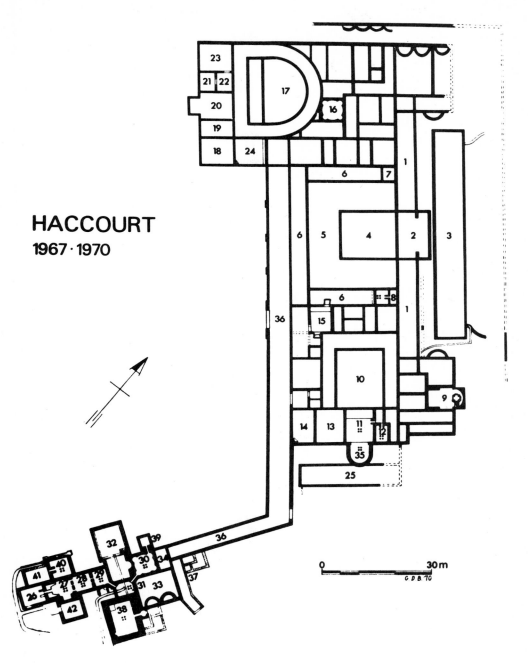

HACCOURT
1967·1970

6   Haccourt, Liège, Belgium

the western provinces can provide one or more sites, built close to the beginning
of the Roman period, whose size or amenities or both would seem to indicate an
owner from Italy bringing his life style with him in the familiar 'colonial'
manner, or perhaps a provincial magnate rich enough to import his Romanization
in one fell swoop rather than allow it to evolve in the fullness of time.[20] The
great villas of Chiragan and Montmaurin in south-west Gaul, which were begun
around the middle of the first century, were built on a grand scale from the
beginning and in a style directly comparable with that of houses in the Hellenistic
tradition at Pompeii and elsewhere.[21] Similar sites appear at an early date along
the frontiers and in association with major military and administrative centres:
such, for example, are the villas of northern Switzerland associated with the early
development of Vindonissa, that of Seeb, near Zürich, being one of the best
known[22] (*Fig.* 25). In Britain the villa at Fishbourne clearly falls into the same
category, and there are grounds for believing the same to be true of the villa at
Eccles in Kent.[23] Whether the owners in each case were rich natives or immigrant
Romans can hardly be established with any certainty; but that sites of this kind
have a special role in the normal Romanizing process is fairly clear.

Whatever the factors influencing individual provinces, the steady emergence
of villas throughout the western Empire was part of a larger growth in prosperity, begun in the early principate and culminating in the reigns of Nerva,
Trajan, Hadrian and the Antonines, when, in the words of Gibbon, 'the Empire
of Rome comprehended the fairest part of the earth, and the most civilised
portion of mankind'.[24] During this period, from AD 98 to 180, the stabilization
of the central government, the securing of the frontiers and the establishment of
effective provincial administration provided the basic framework within which
the full benefits of the Roman Peace could be enjoyed. What this meant at one
end of the social scale we have already seen in the early palatial villas, and although
such sites must be regarded as exceptional there is no doubt that the opportunities
for accumulating wealth at this period were very considerable – in the provinces
perhaps even more than in Italy itself.[25] Nor is it likely that the owners of villas
were immune from the tendency towards conspicuous expenditure that we
have seen at this date in the towns: it may be that we cannot point to half-
completed houses or anything like the collapsing buildings in Pliny's *Letters*,
but the great porticoes and splendid facades of villas like Haccourt in Belgium
or Montcaret (Dordogne)[26] (*Figs* 6, 56) are part of the same picture. It would be
wrong, however, to suggest that luxury was the primary consideration at this
or at any other period in the history of the Roman villa. There were, it is true,
establishments built solely for pleasure, particularly near the major towns and
close to the fashionable resorts, but elsewhere even the most lavishly appointed
villas were farms to a greater or lesser extent, even if the intention was merely
to produce enough for the day-to-day needs of the resident staff. And once we
move away from these richer sites, which numerically, after all, were in a minority, a truer picture begins to emerge. What is typical of the period is not the
palatial establishment like Chiragan, or even the obviously wealthy one like

Haccourt, but sites like Guiry (Seine-et-Oise) (*Fig.* 18) or Noyers-sur-Serein (Yonne), or the scores of modest farmsteads in Württemberg or the northern lowlands of France.[27] Sites such as these could not be described as poor: most of them are solidly built, many have heated rooms and some have mosaics or other signs of wealth. But they are not large, their amenities are designed for comfort rather than ostentation, and the most frequent thing that strikes the eye is a tidiness of layout and a general air of efficiency. In other words, their prosperity is a responsible prosperity, steadily acquired and firmly based, and with every prospect (or so it might have seemed) of further and greater increase.

That things turned out differently, that in the course of the third century the villas as an institution came near to extinction (and in some areas did in fact disappear for good), is well known and attested by clear and abundant evidence. Part of the story – the successive invasions by Germanic and other peoples, and the resulting abandonment and destruction of villa sites – is easily told; the underlying problem, essentially economic and sufficient to have caused a major recession even without the pressures from outside the empire, is less precise and marked by less tangible evidence. But from both points of view the third-century troubles are worthy of careful attention, not only for their own intrinsic interest but because in the late fourth and early fifth centuries a similar situation arose once more. Precisely what happened then is one of the great questions in European history, and any light that the earlier crisis can shed will be of value.[28]

As early as AD 166 the movement of Marcomanni into the Danubian provinces had given an indication of what was to come, but it was during the first part of the third century that the extent and seriousness of the danger became evident. Instead of the individual tribes, often at war with one another, with which the earlier emperors had had to deal, the frontiers were now threatened by great confederations of tribes – the Franks beyond the Rhine, the Alemanni beyond the upper Rhine and Danube, the Goths beyond the lower Danube and the Black Sea provinces. Until the early 250s their incursions were largely sporadic and were dealt with as occasion arose, but the inability of the Roman army to deal effectively with the danger became increasingly clear: in AD 234 the Alemanni were persuaded by a gift of money to leave the *Agri Decumates*, between the upper Rhine and Danube, and in 252 the Goths withdrew from the Illyrian provinces in return for an annual payment of gold. The ineffectiveness of such desperate measures was almost immediately revealed: in the reigns of Valerian and Gallienus (AD 253–68) not only the frontier regions but the greater part of the western provinces were overrun. The Franks broke through the Rhine defences to the north and south of Cologne, came west through northern Gaul to Paris and then moved south. Around Langres they were met by a wave of Alemanni who had crossed the bend of the Rhine near Belfort, and from here the two peoples moved southward and westward into Spain and eventually to northern Africa. About the same time, another group of Alemanni crossed the Danube and moved through the Raetian Alps into northern Italy, while further east the Goths renewed their attacks on the provinces of the Black Sea area.

The Goths were eventually defeated, by Claudius (who earned the title Gothicus) and by Aurelian, but only at the cost of the province of Dacia; the Franks and Alemanni, after a temporary lull, invaded again in the 270s, and by the time the western provinces were fully recovered in the last decade of the century their condition was radically, and in some respects irredeemably, different from what it had been less than a century earlier.

Two developments, among many, are worth noting. Under Probus (AD 276–82) began the policy of recruiting the Germanic peoples into the Roman army and of settling them within the imperial frontiers. The effects of this upon the army and upon the fortunes of Rome in the later invasion period are well known; for the villas their influence is less easy to predict, though the effects of their distinctive social structure, their law and their way of life in general could hardly be negligible. Much would depend on their ability to adjust to their new circumstances and on the extent to which they were willing and able to mix with and be influenced by the provincial population. The precise character of their settlements is not at all clear: one assumes that once an area had been assigned to them they were left to settle it in their own way, and the frequent occurrence in Gaul of Germanic tribal place-names (e.g. Allaines-Alani, Gueux-Gothi, Marmagne-Marcomanni, etc.)[29] suggests, perhaps, that the settlers tended to keep to themselves and away from the local people. In one respect, however, there was some fraternization, and this is the second of the developments that merit our attention. The third-century troubles, both external and internal, made life extremely difficult for the poorer peasant populations, and it is hardly surprising that as a result of the pressures upon them many found it preferable to leave their lands and take to a life of brigandage, often, it seems, in company with groups of Germanic tribesmen.[30] The evidence for this is scattered and imprecise, but there can be little doubt that the phenomenon was both extensive and long lasting. The first appearance of what seems to have been the popular name for such brigands, *Bagaudae*, is in the 280s at the time of their temporary suppression by Maximian, but they were probably behind the revolt of the army deserter Maternus a century earlier and the extent of the problem is illustrated by the provisions for the return of deserters in treaties with the Germanic peoples from the late second century onwards.[31] In general perhaps, we may see them as an illustration of the overall economic depression rather than as a principal cause of it, but the links between their movement and the invaders may well have had an effect on such things as the vulgarization of Roman law and so, for example, on the later tenurial development of the villa estates.

Mention of the *Bagaudae*, of course, leads on to the wider and more fundamental problem of the third century – economic recession and near collapse. To deal with this separately from the invasion problem is necessarily to oversimplify; even if they were not connected, the external and the internal crises each intensified the other and, more important, dictated the form of each other's solution. There can, however, be little doubt that, even without the added complication of pressures on the frontiers, there would still have been a major crisis, the symptoms of which are numerous and plain enough.[32] There was, on the one hand, a falling-off of production, not only of manufactured goods, but in agriculture too. Lands went uncultivated, farms were abandoned or maintained for subsistence only; the resulting fall in revenues led to stricter demands from the central government, and these, falling on a shrinking acreage, merely made the problem worse. Small farmers turned to brigandage or went for refuge to the nearest towns, where things were little better; great land-owners saw their incomes falling, their standards of living at risk, and their labour disappearing; the local councillors, landowners themselves in the main, came increasingly under pressure to maintain the flow of public income, and an office that had once been the subject of competition and a source of pride became rapidly a burden to be avoided.[33] Alongside all this, and linked with it at every point, was the worsening problem of the currency. To meet the cost of the long series of wars from the reign of Marcus Aurelius onwards, successive emperors reduced the silver content of the *denarius* from 85 to less than 5 per cent.[34] Prices inevitably rose, as people hoarded older issues and demanded more of the new to meet the devaluation, and in the inflationary situation government and individuals alike relied increasingly on payment in kind. The speed with which the crisis developed, combined with the rigidity of the Roman fiscal system, made radical measures impossible to put in hand, and a succession of crude and temporary expedients gave rise to as many problems as they solved. Only with the coming of relatively stable government at the end of the third century could the long-term solutions be sought, and by this time the context, and the Empire itself, had changed for good.

To point to a single underlying cause for all the troubles is not so easy. For some historians the debasing of the coinage was the result of a shortage of precious metals, which they see as a motive for Trajan's Dacian wars;[35] but as has been pointed out,[36] the exact reverse is just as likely to be true, with the shortage of gold and silver being caused by the known tendency of bad money to drive out good. More convincing is the suggestion that the cost of the armies needed to deal with attacks on the frontiers could be met only by the sale of public property, the confiscation of private estates, or the debasement of the coinage, the last in many ways being the easiest.[37] Quite apart from its cost in terms of money, the prolonged campaigning will, as in earlier periods, have affected agriculture and production generally; and the insecurity of the times and uncertainty about the future will have acted as a brake on the improvement of property and on investment. Similar in their effect, though less easy to evaluate without more detailed information, are the widespread plagues of which the sources make mention from the second century onwards;[38] these and the wars together could certainly have started a decline which then got out of control. Nor should it be forgotten that the prosperity of the early Empire was in many ways unstable: as early as the reign of Trajan the dangers are clearly visible, and one can hardly say that the economy of the provinces as we see it illustrated in the correspondence of Pliny was likely to stand up to prolonged and serious pressure.[39] For this reason alone it is probably unrealistic to look for a single primary cause for all that happened in the course of the third century; granted that a single factor may have set the crisis in motion, other factors will have contributed to its development, and it is with the total effect that we are here mainly concerned.

Turning to the material evidence for all this, and in particular to that concerning the villas, we find a picture which in outline is clear enough but in detail still leaves much to be desired. That the third century was a period of destruction and decay is plain from almost every villa site in the western provinces that has been excavated with any degree of care.[40] The gap in the pottery evidence or in the coin list, and on continental sites the layer of burnt material, are features so regular in villa reports that if they fail to appear one assumes they were not discovered rather than that they did not in fact occur. It is hard to find a site anywhere of which one can say with confidence that it survived the third century unscathed,[41] and even if one could find a score or more the evidence on the other side would be overwhelming. In individual cases there is often room for doubt: layers of burnt material are not always easy to date with accuracy, and there is a definite temptation to assign such evidence to known invasion periods; many of the destructions will have been accidental rather than the work of invaders, and the chances of telling the difference are fairly remote; in some cases, perhaps, what seemed at first sight to be signs of destruction could well turn out to be the results of normal domestic processes. More important than such individual doubts, which tend to complicate the picture rather than falsify it, is the problem of knowing whether abandonment or destruction is the appropriate term for a particular villa site. One is, after all, in the majority of cases, dealing with sites which were later cleared and rebuilt, so that the chances of obtaining clear and unambiguous evidence are not high. Farms left empty would presumably suffer the same fate in an invasion as those remaining in use, and would in any case run the risk of accidental burning from casual occupation by squatters or passers-by. One would like to know more, for example, of what happened at Guiry-Gadancourt (Seine-et-Oise), where there is evidence both of destruction in about the 270s and of abandonment earlier in the century.[42] If there was a lengthy period when the farmstead was derelict, the later destruction is of less significance, and the basic pattern much the same as that of Lyons-la-Forêt (Eure),[43] where the site was abandoned and the roof fell in, but as far as one can tell no destruction occurred. Clearly, the picture is complicated, and as more detailed evidence becomes available the variation from one site to another is likely to become more marked. But whatever distinctions we make the sheer scale of the destruction can hardly be overstated.

There will, again, have been regional variations, with some areas suffering greater or more permanent damage than others. One would expect, for example, that sites away from the main routes, particularly if they were modest in size, might escape the invasions themselves, though if their markets were removed, and they were left in some sort of economic vacuum, the privilege of not actually being destroyed can hardly have brought much benefit.[44] In any case, sites of this kind may well have been in areas which were opened up to development in times of exceptional prosperity, and would thus have been feeling the effects of the various economic and social ills some time before the invasions. Even so it would be surprising if there were not many areas which, like southern Britain, suffered primarily from economic recession and only secondarily from actual invasion, and where, instead of destruction or abandonment, the pattern was one of what Rivet has called 'a general lack of maintenance'.[45] It is also well to remember, both here and in connection with the later invasions, that the decay or destruction of villa buildings, indicative as it may be of economic and social upheaval, is by no means the same thing as the decay or destruction of agriculture. Owners, or their agents, might leave the villas themselves and live elsewhere, perhaps in the towns, perhaps for a time with their workers, but the workers themselves, who did not enjoy such mobility, could do little else but carry on as best they could. People in general survived, food continued to be needed, and farming, unless prevented by actual physical force, went on as it had always done.

The ultimate recovery, therefore, is of the villas rather than of agriculture itself, or, to put it differently, is a return to something more than subsistence farming of a fragmented and precarious kind. The first signs that this was beginning to happen appear in the closing years of the third century, and this is what we would expect. The accession of Diocletian in AD 284, though not in itself a solution to all the existing problems, was the beginning of a long and determined effort to set the Empire on its feet and to take the radical measures which, even without the invasions, had long been overdue. Diocletian remained in power, alone or as a member of a Tetrarchy, until his abdication in AD 305, and after a brief interval was succeeded by Constantine, who ruled until his death in 337.[46] Thus for over half a century in these two reigns alone the Empire enjoyed a competent and relatively stable government. The invasions, already past their worst, were gradually brought under control, the frontiers once more secured; areas like Britain and Gaul which had sought to solve their problems by adopting emperors of their own were brought back into the fold. Peace and security assured, the work of recovery could begin; in a major reform of the currency gold and silver coins of a new and acceptable standard were issued; the census system, the major source of public revenue, was overhauled and generally made more effective; attempts were made, remarkable even if not wholly successful, to regulate prices; and administration generally, for long at the mercy of generals, usurpers and invaders, was reorganized and placed once more on a sound footing.

But great as these achievements were, and impressive as the recovery certainly was, the chances of a complete return to the situation before the invasions began were non-existent. Most obviously, the continuing danger of invasion required, and was now acknowledged to require, a large and permanent army; much of this was composed of the invading peoples themselves, who were given lands along the frontiers, and its cost was necessarily borne by the people at large. In every aspect of public policy the dominant consideration was from now on that of military security: the emperor was now a soldier, his court a general's camp, his whole administration increasingly military. Society at large was regimented: to make the collection of taxes more efficient more and more restrictions were placed on those who paid them, so that in the end people became tied to their craft or profession and even to a particular area. Preferable as this may have been to the anarchy and chaos of the invasion period, it was a far cry from that earlier age when security was still compatible with freedom and when injustice, if not immediately dealt with, was at least not encapsulated in an increasingly static society. In some respects, admittedly, this is an unfair assessment of what the reforms achieved: society itself was changing, and there is a sense in which, far from moulding that society, the reforms were simply an acknowledgement of the change. Forces long before the third century had begun the process which from one point of view was the decline of slavery and from another the rise of serfdom; the adoption of what Finley has called 'a broader spectrum of statuses'[47] was a return to a much older and more primitive social pattern, the effects of which will have been similar, though less formal, to those of the various enactments. The fact remains, however, that what emerged from the period of reform was not the world of a century before but one with a character of its own, in many ways less attractive, in some ways perhaps more real. Prosperity there certainly was: in some areas, as we shall see, it was spectacular. But taking the overall picture, and thinking primarily of the western provinces, with which we are here mainly concerned, it would be more accurate to see the fourth century as a period, not of conspicuous wealth, but rather of economic stability on a lower and generally more sober level. For this period, more perhaps than for any other, the villas provide an excellent illustration.

For some areas, of course, the third-century invasions marked the end of the villa system, and there was to be no fourth-century recovery at any level. The regions north of the Danube and east of the Rhine, most notably Dacia and the so-called *Agri Decumates*, were no longer part of the Empire: their villas, in any case, will not have had time to develop to anything like the standard of those in the longer established areas, and in this sense their (apparently) total disappearance is hardly surprising. More striking, perhaps, is what happened in northern Belgium, where the villas north of a fortified line from Bavai to Köln seem largely to have been given up after the invasions as a matter of policy.[48] A similar picture, though not always as stark as this, is found along much of the northern frontier: some areas recovered while others did not, and although the factors affecting an individual site may not be clear the pattern overall is plain enough. Areas close to those parts of the frontier through which the main invasions had come will have suffered most devastation and for this reason will have been least likely to be resettled afterwards. These and other vacant areas would lend themselves most conveniently to occupation of an official or semi-official kind by groups of Germanic peoples, and although one should be wary of jumping to conclusions the chances of this bringing about a revival of villas on any significant scale were not high.

Away from the frontier regions, and leaving aside the exceptions for the moment, two main features may be discerned: a general lowering of standards, and a certain contraction of the areas occupied. The first of these appears in numerous reports, and although in many cases one is dealing with an overall impression rather than a fully documented assessment the cumulative effect is quite considerable. To quote just a few examples: the rebuilding at Palaminy (Hte-Garonne) and Plouhinec (Morbihan) was on a less lavish scale than that before the invasions;[49] at Camblanes (Gironde) the new walls were slighter than before and built of earlier débris;[50] at St-Just-Pépiron (Charente-Maritime) the later building was less careful;[51] at Banon (Basses-Alpes) and Noyers-sur-Serein (Yonne) re-occupation was only partial;[52] at Villerest (Saône-et-Loire) the fourth-century finds were poor compared with those of earlier phases,[53] and so on. The picture is one of individual sites engaged in a cautious revival rather than that of a whole system bouncing back to prosperity. The second feature, that of a contraction of occupied areas, is very well illustrated by Dr Wightman's work on the territory of the Treveri.[54] Here the central lands around Trier itself saw rebuilding and re-occupation as the normal pattern, whereas the less attractive outlying areas, such as the Hunsrück south of the Moselle, were clearly less fortunate. What we have here is a retreat into the easier and older settlement areas, a reversal of the process of expansion which had been prompted by the prosperity of earlier periods. The pattern is not so clear elsewhere, no doubt because few other areas have been so thoroughly studied, but there are traces of it in parts of the northern lowlands of France, and as the evidence becomes more plentiful it is likely to appear more generally.

It would be unwise, however, to generalize too readily. There were, as we shall see, exceptional areas, and even where the evidence seems at first sight to fit the pattern suggested we would do well to give a second look before jumping to conclusions. A case in point is the famous villa of Chiragan (Hte-Garonne), which, after reaching a peak of luxury and prosperity under the Antonines, would seem in its final Constantinian phase to have gone into something of a decline.[55] The excavator pointed to the much less lavish residential quarter at this date, with its smaller rooms and poorer amenities, and noted a tendency to use what had formerly been living rooms for agricultural and other purposes. So Grenier, summarizing Joulin's report, concurs in the verdict of decadence during the fourth century and points to the Antonine and Severan period as that of greatest prosperity.[56] Even if we confine ourselves to the site of Chiragan itself this could well be a somewhat over simple view: the spread of work buildings into a residential wing, which is what seems to have happened at Chiragan, is a decline in one sense but arguably an improvement in another. Given the date of the main report, we can hardly speak with certainty, but it would seem at least likely that the change of emphasis that took place in the fourth century may have been connected with the establishment of a completely new villa a kilometre or so away at the village of Martres-Tolosane: that is, a new and more manageable residence was now constructed, and the old and uneconomic one converted to other uses.[57] The questions, of course, remain: was there an increase in farming and other activities generally, or was there simply a policy of centralizing storage, workshops and so on at the estate centre; was there, in the uncertain economy of the late third century and after, a tendency for estates to move towards self-sufficiency? Whatever the answers, they are unlikely to be found within a single site; but the decline or growth of luxury amenities may not be as useful a guide as it has sometimes seemed to the economic fortunes of a given estate or area.

Whatever their implications, the kinds of restraints and tendencies that are common in this period on the Continent are seen on a number of sites in Britain as well. The rash of corn-drying ovens, often, as at Brading (Isle of Wight) or Atworth (Wilts), inserted ruthlessly into former residential areas,[58] is clear enough evidence that the need for production was more important than the desire for comfort; the similar encroachment of industrial activities, such as the iron-working establishment in the latest phase of the villa at Sutton Courtenay (Berks), is evidence in the same direction.[59] But to suggest that this was the normal situation in Britain, as it undoubtedly was over much of the Continent, would be to give a very wrong impression. The truth is that Britain is quite exceptional, that on this side of the Channel we are not in fact dealing with a general decline in standards or even a shrinking of areas, in spite of the fact that the overall economic climate might seem to be roughly the same. It was not simply that the majority of British villas continued into the fourth century, nor yet that a number of examples (such as Witcombe or Frocester Court in Gloucestershire)[60] (*Fig.* 31) were built for the first time in the late-third-century recovery, but that in this period the standards of luxury and amenities which on the Continent had been characteristic of the Antonine and Severan age were at last achieved in Britain. Far from lowering their sights and concentrating on a modest and careful advance, the owners of the British villas were able to make a leap forward which elsewhere had been the product of long years of peace and stability. Why this was so is not by any means clear: the evidence for a migration to Britain of Gaulish landowners seeking refuge from troubles nearer the frontier is now fairly considerable,[61] but although such a movement would give an added boost to any revival it will have been more in the nature of a symptom than a cause. What seems inescapable is that in the fourth century Britain had an economy which was relatively healthy and relatively firmly based, and one can only suppose, with Rivet,[62] that the roots of this are to be sought in the third-century troubles themselves.

There seems little doubt that in spite of considerable suffering Britain was spared a direct involvement in the invasions and civil wars on anything like the continental scale, so that simply in comparison with Gaul and elsewhere her recovery was likely to be more rapid.[63] There is also the point that by being cut off for long periods from continental markets and products she was compelled for her own survival to become more self-sufficient; this, for example, may be one explanation, if not by any means the only one, for the growth of the British pottery industry in the later imperial period.[64] Whatever the reasons (and much more work is needed before we can know with any certainty what they were), there can be no doubt that the economic climate of fourth-century Britain was favourable for farming, and that the villa owners were well prepared to take advantage of it. The results are villas like those already mentioned, which were begun in the latter part of the third century and continued developing throughout the fourth, or ones like North Leigh (Oxon.) or Bignor (Sussex) and several dozen more, which in the fourth century grew to their greatest size and highest point of prosperity.[65] It may be, indeed, that the encroachment of agricultural and other activities upon former living quarters, which we have hitherto tended (though with some reservations) to regard as a sign of economic stringency, was part of the same development, with certain sites being incorporated into larger units and converted to specialist functions. If this is so, the pattern is even more striking.

Britain, it must be said, was not the only area in which this late flowering of villas occurred, even though it was the largest area so to benefit. Something very similar happened in parts of Pannonia, where again it was in the fourth century that the great estates came really into their own,[66] and even in Gaul there were some areas in which something more than a mere recovery was achieved. One such was the immediate neighbourhood of Trier, where there is evidence, not only of a good deal of rebuilding and extension at existing sites, but of major villas appearing now for the first time.[67] Two of these new establishments have been plausibly identified as being imperial houses, and it seems likely, as Grenier suggested, that the area as a whole was able to benefit from the rise of Trier itself as an imperial capital.[68] In this connection the famous reference in Ausonius to the villas along the Moselle may not be quite so idealized as it has sometimes been thought to be, and if this is so there may well have been other areas, associated also with Ausonius, which experienced a similar revival.[69]

Whatever the fortunes of particular areas, however, the temporary nature of the recovery is plain enough. The great reforms of Diocletian and Constantine, effective as they were in creating stability, could not restore the old impetus, and there is a sense in which, even before the danger from new invasions became acute, emperors had turned their backs upon the western half of the Empire in favour of the more congenial East. So it was that when the pressures built up once again there was no longer the ability, and in some senses not even the will, to cope with them, and from the end of the fourth century, as they had done in the third, the villas began to go under. What exactly happened, and to what extent, if at all, the recovery of the late third century was repeated in the fifth, are questions which we shall seek to answer later. That the villa as we have so far come to understand it ceased to exist as a result of these later invasions is in one sense obvious enough: an institution which we have defined as being integrated into the social and economic organization of the Roman world was not likely to survive the collapse of that organization and still remain the same. But whether, though obvious, such an assumption is perhaps a little simple, is something that will need further study.

4

Regional Types and Distributions

One of the more obvious difficulties in talking or writing about villas is the enormous variety of examples which fall under the one single heading. At its lowest level the villa may be little more than a hovel with only a certain regularity of plan to distinguish it from its Iron Age predecessors, while at the other end of the scale it may be an establishment so vast and palatial that its ruins are mistaken for a town.[1] Within this range the variety of individual plans and styles is endless, and the broad distinctions between 'corridor', 'courtyard' or 'basilican' type are simply a preliminary, and by no means exhaustive, way of sorting the material out into manageable units. Plans, in any case, are only one criterion for classification, and other criteria, such as size, will produce quite different results. Nor is it possible to see the villa in purely static terms; each one had its history, and as the techniques of the excavator become more advanced so the more complex these histories are seen to be. Villas grew and shrank, were destroyed and rebuilt, changed or modified their functions, and although in a very broad sense they often did so together, the local variations and exceptions were such as to make the wider patterns a good deal less instructive than they seem to be. The scale, both of time and space, is enormous. Drawing as it did upon an Italian tradition going back to the Republic, the villa followed hard upon the pacification of a new province. Already in the first century of the Empire it was becoming a regular feature in Africa, Spain and Provence, and was extending rapidly through Gaul and into Germany and the Danube provinces. In Britain, as part of the pattern of Romanization enjoined upon the province by such governors as Agricola, it had by the turn of the century begun to make its mark upon the south east and further afield. And since, on even the most cautious view, it persisted in Britain to the late fourth century and in Gaul perhaps to the fifth, the period with which we are dealing is one of at least five hundred years – or roughly what separates our own day from the fall of Constantinople and the end of the Roman Empire in the East. The areas involved are if anything even more daunting: the villa extended from the Black Sea to Portugal and from Yorkshire to the Sahara, flourishing in regions as different from one another in character as they were distant in miles. It is an interesting question whether there is anything *other* than villas which links, say, the Bagradas Valley with Lake Balaton or the Côte d'Azur with Glamorgan, or whether anything more than the most empty of generalizations would cover the villas in all of them.

Generalize, however, we must, if only to say where, broadly speaking, the villas were and what they tended to be like. Having in this way placed them, as it were, on the map, we can then go on to a more detailed analysis of their economic and social function. The temptation to begin with Britain and move southwards is naturally strong, but there is much to be said for seeing the picture as far as possible from the Roman point of view and for taking the various regions where villas occur in the order in which they became incorporated into the Empire. Appropriately, therefore, we begin with Italy itself.

THE ITALIAN PENINSULA

The great curving range of the Apennines, though more hospitable than other mountain masses in the Mediterranean, confines the good arable land of Italy to the river valleys and to the eastern and western coastal strips. There might, at first glance, seem little to choose between the Adriatic seaboard and that of the Tyrrhenian Sea, but as is clear from the distribution of major towns the western side, in antiquity as in our own day, was always more favoured and more densely settled. The reasons are not hard to find: the volcanic area most obviously visible at Etna in Sicily and Vesuvius above the Bay of Naples extends in fact along the whole western seaboard to Etruria, producing a richness in the soil which made the farmlands of Etruria itself and more especially Campania further south proverbial for their fertility; while the major rivers Arno, Tiber and Volturno, all flowing into the western sea, extend the cultivable areas and contrast very noticeably with the smaller streams and lower rainfall of areas like Calabria, down in Italy's heel. The great exception to all this, of course, is the river Po, which flows from the western Alps across to the top of the Adriatic and waters one of the most extensive plains in the whole Mediterranean basin. Development here was difficult, in that the abundant water produced by rain and melting snow in the Alps made widespread flooding normal and maintained a thick covering of forest over much of the area; but once the technical and administrative skills became available it could hardly fail to achieve prosperity on a grand scale.[2]

Not surprisingly, the distribution of villas in Italy is largely in keeping with this general picture. They cluster thickly all along the western coastal strip and in the lower Po Valley, and are markedly absent from the Adriatic coast south of Rimini. What this suggests is that in the great majority of cases the determining factor was the availability of good farm land, and that villas built and sited solely or even primarily as luxury retreats were in a minority. It is true that in such areas as the Bay of Naples this must have been a strong contributory factor, and there is also plenty of evidence that particular areas went in and out of fashion

7   Wall painting from the House of Fortuna Piccola, Pompeii, showing a country house: in the
foreground, a plough is propped against a wall

as the years went by.³ But the archaeological evidence so far available makes it
quite clear that even in the fashionable areas the most luxurious villas tended
more often than not to include a section devoted to farming, and even if this was
intended simply to support the resident staff rather than to produce a surplus
we are justified in supposing that the villa was only very exceptionally other than
a business enterprise. And if this is true of Italy there is every likelihood that, at
least in the early Empire, it is true of the western provinces.

With the great wealth of Roman material in the towns, work on the countryside in general and on the villas in particular has understandably been somewhat
neglected, with the result that, for example, a field study of villas around Pompeii,
done in the early 1930s, is still a basic source of material⁴ (*Figs 8, 9*). There have,

however, been a number of more recent surveys, together with some individual excavations, and it may be useful to summarize the evidence so far assembled. The most detailed work to date has been in the part of southern Etruria immediately to the north of Rome, where members of the British School have carried out field surveys of the lands surrounding Veii and of the adjoining area of Capena.[5] Even from such a comparatively small region a number of general points emerge. One is that the development of farming in the Roman period was very firmly based on earlier cultures, in this case mainly that of the Etruscans. This is an advantage which the Romans enjoyed, not only in this part of Italy, but also further south, where the underlying tradition was less Etruscan and more Greek – though it must be said that the Greek contribution was likely to be general prosperity rather than any particular agricultural expertise. The point at which the pattern changes is that at which increasing Roman activity in northern Italy and beyond necessitated the construction of the major north–south roads, which not only provided new focuses for settlement, but opened up whole areas to new markets and wider contacts than before.[6] Another result of the surveys is that it is now possible, albeit still in a small way, to illustrate a number of trends which had hitherto been known largely from literary evidence: one example, that of the changes in fashionability of particular areas, has already been mentioned, and another, which in the long run is far more important, is that of the growth of large estates (the so–called *latifundia*) at the expense of the smaller ones.[7] With the older surveys this extra dimension of time is less available, and their main interest is in questions of distribution, such as the relationship of villas to towns and road networks; that on the Campanian villas, however, has thrown light on an important social trend, namely the increasing investment in land by freedmen in the first centuries BC and AD, which is the kind of study that is rarely possible elsewhere.[8] Here again the Po Valley has to be taken separately. To the difficulties of drainage and forestation already mentioned were added the dangers of inroads from Alpine tribes, which were only removed by the final subjugation of the Alpine region under Augustus. Once security was assured and the major development work was in hand, the area was ready to reap the benefits of being on the main land route to the Danube provinces and beyond, and the importance of centres like Ravenna in the late imperial and early medieval period was no doubt reflected in the prosperity of the region as a whole. There are no surveys here comparable to those further south, but the excavation of individual sites, such as that at Russi, near Ravenna, is beginning to bring the region's history into focus.[9]

To attempt a description of a 'typical' Italian villa would be extremely difficult, if not wholly impossible, but clearly some general impression is needed, if only for purposes of comparison with those of other regions. Perhaps the best approach is to classify them first of all in terms of function, and then, by looking at particular examples, to establish a group of representative sites rather than one to stand for all.[10] First, then, there is what is known as the *villa suburbana*, distinguishable from a town house only by being on the outskirts of a town

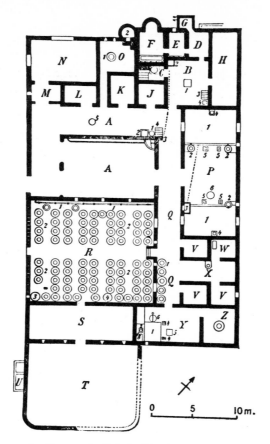

8   Boscoreale, S. Italy (Carrington, No. 13)

rather than at its centre. It is primarily, if not entirely, residential, and belongs in all meaningful senses to the town rather than the country. Such, at one end of the scale, is Hadrian's villa at Tivoli, and less spectacular examples can be found near most of the major towns. It is of course possible to build such a villa at some distance from a town and to use it solely as a luxury retreat; but as we have seen there was a marked tendency to provide such villas with a basic farming establishment, so linking them, to some degree at least, with rural life and economy. The usual practice at these sites, which fall into our second main category, was probably for the owner to use them from time to time as a place to stay, and to leave them for the rest of the time in the hands of a small resident staff, for whom the farming activities were both a means of employment and a way of contributing to the costs of maintenance. An arrangement of this kind is common in all the main areas of Italy: of the 39 Campanian villas in the survey already mentioned some nine examples are thought to be of this type, and it is to similar sites that the term 'villa' rather than 'farm' has been applied in the field studies of the *ager Veientanus.*[11]

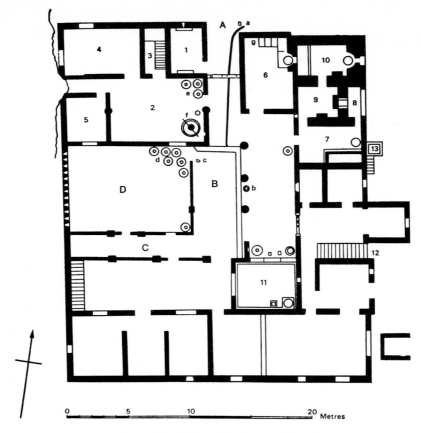

9   Boscoreale, S. Italy (Carrington, No. 29)

One of the best illustrations of such a villa, and of the contrast between it and
the more workaday kind, is provided by the recent excavations at Francolise,
near Caserta: here, in the villa of San Rocco, is a primarily residential establishment with farm buildings attached, while roughly a kilometre away, at Posto,
is an essentially working villa with a small residential wing[12] (*Figs* 10, 11). This
latter type will, in the nature of things, be more common than either of the two
already mentioned, and it is fair to say that the majority of the excavated examples
fall into this category. In some cases, of course, we are still dealing with absentee
landlords, in the sense that the residential wing may have been occupied, not by
a small landowner, but by the manager of a larger one; to say in a given case
whether or not this is so is an almost impossible task, but it is difficult to believe
that in normal circumstances it was true of more than a minority of cases. A
further type of establishment, which is sometimes added to the list, is what
Rostovtzeff called 'an agricultural factory run by slaves', in which the residential
section is so minimal as to be indistinguishable from the work buildings.[13] Two
of the villas near Pompeii have been thought to fit this description, and as we

shall see there are similar sites in Africa,[14] but it is arguable that this is a false category. Unless such establishments were fairly closely linked with a villa of the more residential type they can hardly have operated without some kind of steward or overseer, who may well have lived in a separate building nearby instead of in the 'factory' itself; in either case the 'factory' is not a villa at all on its own, but should be seen rather as part of a larger unit, which will resemble one of the earlier types in all the important respects.

Clearly these categories of villas are by no means as distinguishable from one another as we have suggested: one category will merge into another, a single category may include a wide range of sites in terms of size or amenities, and the classification will tend to change as the prosperity of a given region rises or falls. They are nevertheless a reasonably useful method of labelling sites, provided we are not too rigid in applying the labels, and provided we recognize that other sets of labels are equally valid. A similar rough classification is possible in the matter of architectural plans, though here the distinctions are rather less precise than those of function. As a general rule, the closer a villa is to the life of an urban centre the more its design and general layout will resemble that of a normal town house, with its rooms grouped on either side of an *atrium* and around an inner colon-

10   San Rocco, Francolise, S. Italy

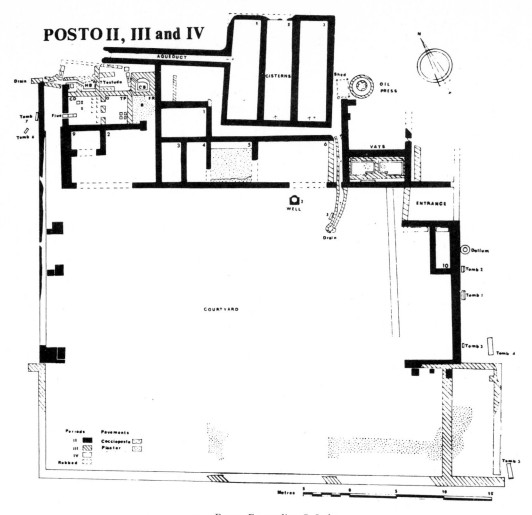

11   Posto, Francolise, S. Italy

naded court or peristyle. This is evident, not only in the 'surburban' villas, which one would hardly expect to be otherwise, but also in those sited away from the towns which are primarily residential. The Campanian villas include several of this kind, and the San Rocco villa already referred to is a perfect example, the main attention being given here to the designing of the living quarters with the various working rooms to all appearances being simply added on where convenient. When we come to the sites which were primarily working establishments, however, the urban influence is much less evident, and the layout is determined much more by the requirements of farming practice than by the dictates of architectural fashion. On sites of this kind, of course, the amount of detailed conscious planning is much more variable, though it is clear from

Vitruvius (to take the most obvious example)[15] that the basic principles of such planning were known and available. It is perhaps worth saying in this connection that as one concentrates on what we have called the working farms so the resemblances between Italian and provincial villas become more marked – which argues, if not for conscious planning, at least for a common recognition of, and willingness to cater for, the basic farming needs.

SPAIN

'It is fruitful', said Justin, 'in every kind of crop – so much so, that it provides an abundance of all things, not only for its own inhabitants but for Italy and the city of Rome as well.'[16] To a certain extent he was exaggerating, for only about a third of the Iberian peninsula is now strictly arable, and the proportion is not likely to have been greater in antiquity. On the other hand, the areas that were

12   La Cocosa, near Badajoz, Spain

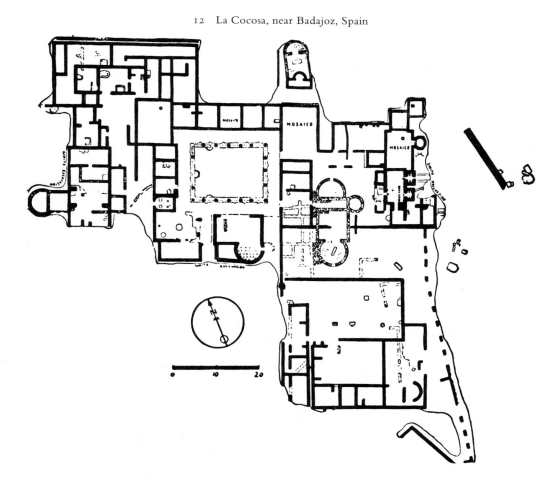

fertile were very much so, and there is plenty of evidence of their ability to export corn from the beginning of the second century BC onwards.[17] The areas in question were the old province of Hispania Citerior, which was essentially the eastern coastal strip from Catalonia in the north through Valencia to Murcia in the south, and the southern part of Hispania Ulterior, later to become the province of Baetica and corresponding roughly to the modern Andalusia. These areas were not only among the first to be incorporated into the Roman sphere of influence, but were settled by a large-scale programme of emigration and colonization from Italy, with generous land allotments enabling the newcomers to assume the role of overlords of the native population and so to hasten the process of Romanization and the growth of a villa system.[18] Already in the time of Augustus the rich farms and thriving urban centres were a feature of this part of the Empire, and less than a century was to elapse before the local gentry produced their most illustrious members, the emperors Trajan and Hadrian. Work on villas and other rural sites is not so advanced in Spain as in some of the other provinces, but as one would expect the pattern and style of villas is in keeping with the historical picture so far described.[19]

The distribution throughout the peninsula is explicable first and foremost in

13   Cuevas de Soria, near Numancia, Spain

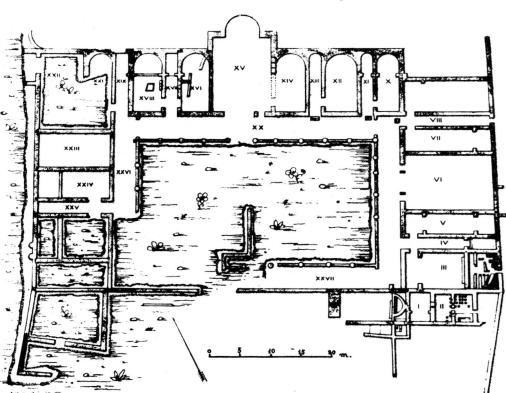

terms of arable land: with few exceptions, villas occur in areas below the 1,500ft contour, and are to be found either along the coastal plains or in the valleys of the major rivers, most striking in this respect being those along the Ebro in the north east, the Baetis (now the Guadalquivir) in the south, and the Tagus over in the west. The most obvious exceptions are those around Valladolid and Ciudad Real, in Old and New Castile respectively, both of which groups are close to major rivers but may perhaps have been associated with the exploitation of mineral resources rather than with farming. The latter, certainly, is in the heart of the rich silver-producing area of the Sierra Morena, and it may be that in other areas too, such as the hills overlooking the Ebro Valley, the presence of metals was at least a rival attraction to the fertile valley soil. In Spain, of course, we are entirely within the Mediterranean area so far as climate and patterns of agriculture are concerned, and it is no surprise to find the plans of villas still strongly influenced by those of Italy, with rooms grouped round an inner colonnaded court. The so-called villa of Fortunatus at Fraga, near Lérida, is a good example, as is that of la Cocosa near Badajoz[20] (*Fig.* 12); similar also is the enormous villa of Liédena (Navarra), which is strongly reminiscent of the Chiragan villa on the other side of the Pyrenees.[21] Types more familiar to north-European eyes are by no means absent, however, and there are standard corridor villas at Cuevas de Soria (*Fig.* 13) and Ramalete, near Tudela, to name just two examples.[22] The older excavations tended to concentrate on the more spectacular sites, and one should perhaps be careful of making too much of the undoubted luxury of the examples so far cited. Luxurious indeed they are, and this is in keeping with the prosperity documented in other sources, but we would probably be well advised to take as typical, not these examples, but such sites as Villanueva y Geltru, near Barcelona, where to all appearances a much more workaday site is indicated.[23]

AFRICA

The first Roman province in the north of the African continent was an area of some 5,000 square miles around Carthage, annexed by the Romans after the destruction of the city in 146 BC. Military activity during the next century extended this to the south and east, so that what came to be known as Africa Proconsularis included most of modern Tunisia and the north-west corner of Libya. To the west, the kingdom of Numidia, which had for long been closely linked to Carthage, was finally incorporated into the province in 25 BC, and the creation of the two additional provices of Mauretania by Claudius in AD 42 completed the extension of Roman authority through the northern half of Algeria to the Atlantic seaboard of Morocco.[24]

Under the rule of Carthage the central part of this area had been intensively and efficiently developed. The river Medjerda, which flows into the sea by the ancient Utica just north of Carthage itself, is fed by a series of tributaries, of which the Bagradas is the most important, and the resulting river basin was and is the most fertile corn-growing region in the whole of northern Africa. Wealthy Carthaginians had their estates in the eastern part of it, and it was these, no doubt, which helped to build the reputation of Carthage as a centre of agricultural knowledge and expertise. Roman writers on farming make frequent mention of a lengthy textbook on the subject by the Carthaginian Mago, and although little is known of his date or the contents of his book there is enough evidence to show that the book did exist and was influential.[25] Thus, whatever the situation may have been elsewhere, here at least there was a solid body of experience on which the Roman development of the region could be based. Nor was this experience entirely limited to the immediate area of Carthage itself: the belt of fertile land extends westwards as far as Sitifis (Sétif in Algeria), and most of it had benefited in some measure over the years from the more advanced techniques of its eastern neighbours. Quotations from Mago in Roman writers refer more often to trees and stock rearing than to corn growing, and it has been suggested that Carthaginian landowners may have concentrated on these aspects of farming and left the production of cereals to their native subjects;[26] alternatively, we might suggest that the pattern was in reality a mixed one, and that Mago's writings, or the quotations from them, were in some way selective.

This, certainly, is the most likely pattern in the Roman Republican period, when much of the province was parcelled out to settlers from Italy in a series of colonization programmes.[27] Not all of these holdings were small, and there is some evidence that large estates quickly built up again; but for the first generation or so it is probably fair to assume that family farms were the rule and that the colonists' primary concern was to establish themselves on a broad basis rather than launching immediately into specialized farming for profit. After this initial period, however, when the successful settlers had made their mark and the unsuccessful ones had given up, the tendency towards larger holdings and more specialized operations seems to have increased. The famous remark of the elder Pliny, that six men owned half of Africa until Nero brought them to ruin,[28] was no doubt an exaggeration, but it is not an isolated example. The rapidly expanding markets, not only in the new towns of Africa itself, but in Rome and other Italian centres, will have given an added attraction to an area already known for its fertility, and all the signs are that Africa was a part, and perhaps the most conspicuous part, of the complex economic and social upheaval which is associated with the growth of *latifundia*. Pliny's remark is merely an illustration of something far more general: '*latifundia* were the ruin of Italy, and before long of the provinces too.'

Morally, perhaps. Economically, certainly not, at least in Africa. The growth of large estates was accompanied, as we have seen, by an extension of the area under Roman control, so that much of the Aures Mountains and regions as far south as the Schotts on the edge of the desert itself became at least potential farming land. Little of this extra land was suitable for cereals, but with extensive irrigation systems and the careful application of dry-farming techniques much of it was ideal for the growing of olives. And so a pattern quickly established itself: the corn-growing lands already in being were used more exclusively for corn production, and the newer lands were developed for olives. The distinctive remains of the olive presses, which tend to survive even when the rest of the farm buildings are reduced to a pile of rubble, have enabled the main olive-growing areas to be plotted with some degree of accuracy.[29] Apart from a strip along the southern edge of the main cereal belt, the greatest concentration of them was in the area known as Byzacium, that is to say the coastal region of Tunisia from Cape Bon in the north down to Sfax at the western edge of the Gulf of Gabès, but there were other areas in the more favoured parts of the interior, and pockets of them more or less everywhere.

Outside the original province development was not so spectacular, but none the less real for that. For much of the north African coast – apart, that is, from the area immediately around Carthage – incorporation into the Roman Empire was the first opportunity for large-scale programmes of development in comparatively peaceful conditions that had ever arisen, and investors, both from Italy and from Africa itself, were quick to seize their chance. Broadly speaking, the pattern throughout the region was similar to that in Africa Proconsularis: belts of land suitable for cereals, such as the Sidi-bel-Abbès plain in Algeria or the western plateaux of Morocco, were more intensively cultivated, and large areas, often of newly developed land, were brought into use for olive production.[30] For Algeria, the *Atlas Archéologique de l'Algérie* gives detailed information on these developments; for Morocco, and for Tripolitania further east, we are dependent on surveys of more restricted areas, such as those of the Tarhuna plateau and its immediate neighbourhood in the eastern Gebel.[31] Local variations will naturally have been numerous; variable rainfall, uneven distribution of water supplies, sudden changes in soil quality from one area to another, will all have contributed to breaking up the pattern and to making much of it precarious. But the overall picture – the extension of the cultivated areas by improved farming techniques, the marked increase in the growing of olives, and (at least in the central region) the growth of the large estate – is fairly clear, and it is in this context that the individual villa sites are to be seen.

Significantly, perhaps, the type of villa which springs most readily to mind in Roman Africa is the small olive farm – the kind of site, that is, which not everyone would necessarily regard as a villa at all. It is not simply that these farms are very numerous, though the thousands of examples naturally make them difficult to ignore; there is also the feeling that their starkly utilitarian character is most appropriate to a country which, though rich in potential, nevertheless needs constant work and attention to make it give of its best. Outside the immediate neighbourhood of the towns, and perhaps the more favoured parts of the Bagradas valley and similar areas, there can have been little opportunity for sitting back and waiting for the profits to come in, and the olive farms make this abundantly clear. Those surveyed by Oates in the eastern Gebel of Tripolitania, for example, are with very few exceptions entirely devoted to the business of

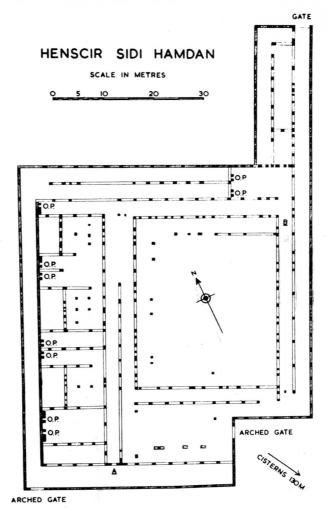

14   Olive farm at Henscir Sidi Hamdan, Tripolitania

farming. Some of them are almost unplanned, giving the impression of having grown up spontaneously to meet the particular agricultural needs[32] (*Figs* 15, 16). Others, like the large site at Henscir Sidi Hamdan, are clearly very carefully designed[33] (*Fig.* 14), but all are very obviously working farms, without luxuries and with only the most rudimentary residential provision. Consisting as they did of a series of rooms grouped round, and looking into, a rectangular central yard, they must have presented a fairly uncompromising, if not actually military, appearance to the outside observer. In the cereal-growing areas, situated mostly in the older parts of the provinces and within reach of major flourishing towns, a greater range of amenities was appropriate, though even here the emphasis on utility rather than luxury remained. It is surely no accident that representations of villas on African mosaics are generally of a building fronted by a corridor or

colonnade, and flanked by a pair of rectangular tower-like rooms at its corners –
that is to say, the 'Portikus-villa mit Ekrisaliten' of the German writers. Such is
the establishment depicted on the so-called 'Seigneur Julius' mosaic from
Carthage, which was very much a working farm, as the careful portrayal of its
outbuildings and various agricultural activities makes clear, and the admittedly
rather more lavish example on a series of mosaics from Tabarka[34] (*Figs* 2, 47, 48).

On the same sort of level, though not in fact of the corridor type, are the
farms in the region of Tangier and Volubilis in western Morocco, of which
those at Jorf el Hamra and Bab Tisra can be cited as representative examples.[35]
There were, of course, establishments built mainly or primarily with luxury in
mind, as one would expect in a province where towns were so markedly
flourishing. There are examples of suburban or near-suburban villas from most
of the main towns, and also many examples of maritime villas – villas, that is,
which may well be near good farming land and contain an element of farming
in their establishment, but which are obviously sited with the comfort of their
residents as the main consideration. There is a good example from the coast just
east of Sabratha, a splendid one at Tagiura in Tripolitania, and others from

15   Olive farm (Oates, No. 10), Tripolitania

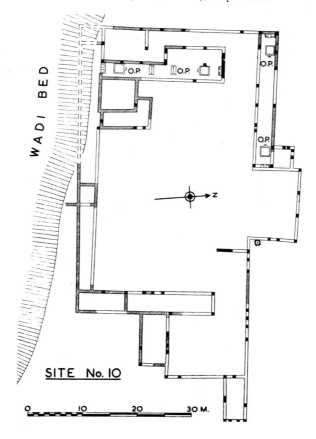

SITE No. 10

0   10   20   30 M.

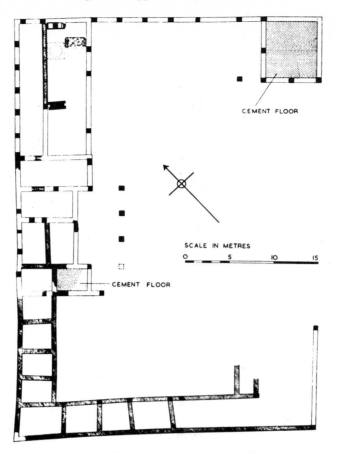

CEMENT FLOOR

SCALE IN METRES

0   5   10   15

CEMENT FLOOR

16   Olive farm (Oates, No. 14), Tripolitania

Tipasa, Hippo Regia and elsewhere.[36] Even so, the overall impression, though certainly one of prosperity, is of a prosperity closely linked to work and a high degree of efficiency.

The date of these various establishments is not always easy to determine, especially those which are more remote and more utilitarian; coarse pottery, often from local kilns, is notoriously difficult to date in any area, and in Africa less work has been done in this field than elsewhere. Many of Oates's sites in Tripolitania had fragments of *sigillata* on them, which enabled him to say that they were in existence by the second century AD,[37] but clearly this kind of evidence is only of limited use. On the richer sites, the presence of imported goods makes dating more possible, and mosaics also, though by no means easy to date accurately, offer at least some guide. On general historical grounds we would expect sites in the central corn-growing lands to appear as early as the first century BC, with the olive farms in the newer lands coming perhaps a few generations later, and on the whole the evidence we have confirms this.

GAUL

The Mediterranean coast of France, from the Côte d'Azur to the foothills of the Pyrenees, was settled by colonists from Greece from the late seventh century BC.[38] Centred at this time on the mouth of the Rhône and in particular on the town of Massalia (Marseilles), the Greek communities owed their prosperity not only to their share of seaborne trade in the western Mediterranean but also to the overland tin route from Britain of which they controlled the southern end. From about 500 BC this particular source of wealth was to pass out of their hands, but by this date their culture and economy were sufficiently well established, not only to survive, but to continue to prosper, so that when in the second century BC the Romans began to be drawn to this part of the world they found themselves in contact with an advanced and stable society almost as Greek as Greece itself. Here already established were flourishing cities, ordered patterns of government and administration, thriving agricultural and business communities – all the institutions which elsewhere it was the task of the Romans to create – and it was hardly surprising that the area came rapidly and fairly easily to provincial status.

Leaving aside the activities of individual traders, Rome's interest in Gaul was a direct result of her second war with Carthage at the end of the third century BC. Hannibal's march from Spain through southern Gaul and over the Alps into Italy, recalling as it must have done an earlier invasion of Gaul in the 380s, made clear the need for a frontier province beyond the Alps; and the acquisition of Spain as a result of Hannibal's defeat made this doubly necessary as a means of securing an overland route to the west. Trouble from Gaulish tribes in the 120s provided a pretext, and within a few years the whole area had been annexed and the province of Gallia Narbonensis established, with new Roman towns at Aquae Sextiae (Aix-en-Provence) and Narbo (Narbonne) and the beginnings of a road through the province and into Spain. It soon became clear, however, that this was only a first stage: the great invasions of the Cimbri and Teutones in the closing years of the second century revealed the need for a secure frontier to the north, and it was this need which led in due course to the campaigns of Julius Caesar in the 50s, as a result of which the whole of Gaul from the Mediterranean up to the English Channel became part of the Roman Empire and Rome advanced for the first time out of the Mediterranean basin and into northern Europe. Begun by Caesar himself and carried on with great energy by Augustus, the task of developing this vast new area was again accomplished with surprising speed, and apart from a few short interludes the Gaulish provinces were to remain as peaceful and as loyal as any part of the Roman world for the next four hundred years.[39]

In studying the villas of Roman Gaul we have at our disposal a body of material which, though vast, is very uneven in quality. As in Britain, the evidence has been assembled over many generations by a wide range of people from professors of archaeology to the local amateurs. Of the many hundreds of known villa

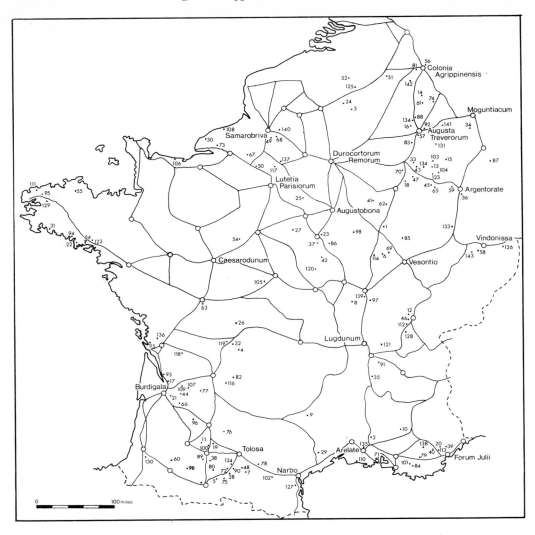

17   Map of Gaul and adjacent areas showing location of villas mentioned in the text

sites some were explored in the last century, some examined in a single season or by a small confirmatory dig at the time of their discovery, the majority simply recorded as existing with a note of surface finds. Only a very few have had the benefit of a recent and thorough excavation extending over several years. The tendency of the older workers to concentrate on the larger sites and on the residential wings of villas rather than on the working buildings has helped to distort the general picture, and the distribution of known sites is affected by the presence or absence in a given area of a local archaeological tradition or even of a single devoted field worker. Nevertheless, the sheer amount of material is impressive: the Gaulish provinces are the villa provinces *par excellence*, and much of the evidence in succeeding chapters will inevitably be drawn from them. What is

KEY TO FIG. 17

1 Andilly-en-Bassigny
2 les Angles
3 Anthée
4 Antone
5 Arnesp, Valentine
6 Attricourt
7 Auterive
8 Aynard, Cortevaix
9 Banassac-la-Canourgue
10 Banon
11 Beaucaire
12 Bernex
13 Berthelming
14 Blankenheim
15 Böckweiler
16 Bollendorf
17 Bourg-sur-Gironde
18 Bouxières-aux-Dames
19 Cadeilhan-St.-Clar
20 Callas
21 Camblanes
22 Carnac
23 la Chapelle-Vaupelteigne
24 Chastres-lès-Walcourt
25 Châteaubleau
26 Chateauponsac
27 Chateaurenard
28 Chiragan
29 Clermont-l'Hérault
30 Colleville
31 Concarneau
32 Condat-sur-Vienne
33 Courcelles-Urville
34 Dautenheim
35 Erôme
36 Eschau
37 Escolives
38 Espaon
39 Fayence
40 Flayosc
41 Fontaines-sur-Marne
42 Fontenay-près-Vézelay
43 Frécourt
44 Frontenac
45 Gondrexange
46 Grange
47 Grémecey
48 Grépiac

49 Grivesnes
50 Guiry
51 Haccourt
52 Hosté
53 Izaux
54 Josnes
55 Kergollet, Landebaëron
56 Köln-Müngersdorf
57 Konz
58 Kulm
59 Kuttolsheim
60 Lalonquette
61 Leutersdorf
62 Liffol-le-Grand
63 Liqugé
64 Lodo
65 Lorquin
66 Loupiac
67 Lyons-la-Forêt
68 Malapart
69 Mantoche
70 Marly-aux-Bois
71 Martigues
72 Martres-Tolosane
73 Maulevrier
74 Mayen
75 Mazères-sur-Salat
76 Moissac
77 Montcaret
78 Montferrand
79 Montfort-sur-Argens
80 Montmaurin
81 Morken
82 la Mouthe, Sérandon
83 Nennig
84 Néoules
85 Noroy-lès-Jussey
86 Noyers-sur-Serein
87 Ödheim
88 Odrang, Fliessem
89 Ornézan
90 Palaminy
91 Penol
92 Pfalzel
93 Plassac
94 Plouhinec
95 Plouneventer
96 Pompogne

97 Préty
98 Prusly-sur-Ource
99 Pujo
100 Puységur
101 la Roquebrusanne
102 Rouffiac
103 Rouhling
104 Saaraltdort
105 St.-Ambroix-St.-Hilaire
106 St.-Aubin-sur-Mer
107 Ste.-Colombe
108 Ste.-Marguerite-sur-Mer
109 St.-Émilion
110 les Stes.-Maries-de-la-Mer
111 St.-Frégant
112 St. Gervais
113 St.-Hermentaire,
    Draguignan
114 St.-Julien
115 St.-Just-Pépiron
116 St.-Léon-sous-Vézère
117 St.-Maximin
118 St.-Preuil
119 St.-Priest-sous-Aixe
120 St.-Revérien
121 St.-Romain-de-Jalionas
122 St.-Symphorien
123 St.-Ulrich-Dolving
124 Sana
125 Sauvenière
126 Seeb
127 Sigean
128 Sion
129 Sizun
130 Sorde-l'Abbaye
131 Sotzweiler
132 Stahl
133 Steinbrunn-le-Bas
134 Téting
135 Trinquetaille, Arles
136 la Vergnée, Romegoux
137 Verneuil
138 Villecroze
139 Villerest
140 Warfusée
141 Weitersbach
142 Wollersheim
143 Zofingen

here attempted is a brief summary of the overall pattern of villas, with a view to bringing the Gaulish evidence in relation to that of the western provinces generally[40] (*Fig.* 17).

Not surprisingly, villas developed early in the original province of Narbonensis. Most of the sites have yielded material of the first century AD, and the appearance at several sites of Iron Age evidence also – like the cemetery at Sigean south of Narbonne, which was apparently in use from the early Iron Age through to the early Middle Ages[41] – suggests that the first steps towards a villa economy were taken right at the start of the province's history. Markets were readily available in the older and newer towns, and with the beginnings of a road network and an assurance of reasonable security this area was rapidly developed. Settlement then, as now, was mainly on the belt of land between the lagoons and salt marshes of the coast and the *garrigue* and hill country which marked the beginning of the central massif. The geology here is complex, but much of the usable land, like that of lower Provence between the Rhone Valley and the western end of the Côte d'Azur, is a series of limestone ridges, cut into by rivers whose valley floors and surrounding hillsides are now used for small scale but very intensive mixed farming. In the Roman period the farm units seem to have been rather larger, though the comparative scarcity of mosaics and other luxuries suggests that the villas were primarily working establishments. That at Martigues, some 30km west of Marseilles, is probably fairly typical.[42] Further west, in Languedoc, the pattern is much the same, with villas dotted thickly along the Aube Valley as far as Carcassonne, though here if anything the standard of luxury seems rather higher, probably as a result of the more extensive areas of corn-growing land and the involvement of villas in the production of wine. The large courtyard villa at St-Bézard, near Clermont-l'Hérault, is one of several obviously prosperous farmsteads in the area.[43] Villas are absent, as one would expect, from the Crau and Camargue areas at the mouth of the Rhone (though there is a rather spectacular exception at les Stes-Maries-de-la-Mer, which was possibly connected with the salting and marketing of fish),[44] from the Maures and Esterel massifs between Cannes and Toulon, and also from Roussillon, where the extreme summer drought and the need for extensive schemes of irrigation made settlement less attractive than in the easier lands nearby.

To move from Narbonensis into the basin of Aquitaine is to move for the first time outside the strictly Mediterranean area, for although much of the region has an agreeable climate the influence of the Atlantic, resulting most noticeably in wetter summers than those further south and east, makes it appropriate to regard this as the first part of northern Europe rather than the last of the Mediterranean. The region is mostly lowland, with gently undulating hills and valleys, though some of the rivers, such as the Tarn in its upper reaches, have cut deep and often spectacular channels. The rivers, in fact, are the most obvious feature: in the north the Dordogne and its tributaries flow westward from the central massif through Périgord to the Gironde Estuary; from the south the Garonne flows down from the foothills of the Pyrenees and then, joined by the Tarn, the Aveyron, the Lot and numerous others, turns northwest to link up with the Dordogne just north of Bordeaux; and the Adour, rising not so very far from the source of the Garonne, takes a similar though shorter route, enclosing a little *pays* of its own and emptying into the Atlantic near Bayonne. Outside Bordeaux, the region is not densely populated but is nevertheless quite intensively exploited agriculturally: the river valleys, where practicable, are given over to market gardening and the plain land to cereals, mostly wheat and maize, while around Bordeaux and a number of other areas there are extensive vineyards, and to the south of the region, near the foothills of the Pyrenees, an emphasis on sheep rearing, mostly on the basis of transhumance. Holdings nowadays are mostly small, and *métayage*, or share leasing, is relatively common. To judge from known villa sites the primary settlement in the Roman period was very much along the main river valleys, and only in Périgord and neighbouring Quercy does there seem to have been any extensive development of the ground in between the valleys, well watered as it normally is. In Périgord there is evidence of very active iron working,[45] and the attraction in Quercy may well have been the isolated pockets of fertile land known as *cloups*; elsewhere the alluvial valley floors and gravel terraces were sufficient to meet the demand. Along the valleys settlement varied considerably in density, depending on the presence or absence of good farming soil and also, no doubt, on the variable risk of flooding. Thus in the upper Garonne basin, for example, villas are more common around Montauban than they are further south around Toulouse; or again, in the Agenais, there are several sites along the Garonne and Lot before they join streams, but very few after. The presence of an urban centre clearly had its effect also, but the availability of water transport made close proximity less necessary, and the concentration of sites around major towns with which one is familiar elsewhere in Gaul is here very much less marked.

Settlement in the region seems to have begun early, with the basic pattern probably established by the end of the first century AD; dating evidence for the early phases of villa sites is very sparse here, but most areas contain at least a handful of sites where first-century material is present in significant amounts. Clearly for the majority of sites the main period of prosperity was the fourth century, a point to which we shall return. Prosperity, in fact, is the general impression one gets when looking at the villas in the region as a whole; mosaics, for example, are very common, with some sites, such as St-Émilion (Gironde) or Pompogne (Lot-et-Garonne),[46] having a whole series. On the other hand, with one or two exceptions, this is not a region of grand palatial villas, but rather of medium to large establishments in which the keynote is comfort rather than ostentation. Typical, perhaps, (though in such a large area it is difficult to regard any one site as properly representative) is the villa of Cadeilhan-St-Clar (Gers), a winged corridor villa with a main range at least 60m in length and probably nearer a hundred; midway along it is an impressive apsidal room with a mosaic of perhaps the late third century, but the rest of the rooms were floored in cement.[47] In a different class altogether, and exceptional by any standards, are

the enormous villas of the upper Garonne and Save valleys in the southern part
of the Haute-Garonne *département*: Chiragan, the most famous villa in France,
Montmaurin (*Fig.* 41), which is now by far the best documented, and (less
spectacular because as yet less thoroughly explored) Arnesp.[48] There are also some
impressive sites in the pays d'Adour; that of Lalonquette (Pyrénées-Atlantiques)
being particularly striking.[49] A point worth mentioning here is that Aquitaine
in general, and areas like the Bordelais in particular, are more than normally
rich in place-names in -*acum*, the Roman estate names to which we referred
earlier and to which we shall return. Generally speaking, their distribution
coincides more or less with that of known villas, though there are occasional
surprises, such as the heavy concentration of them on the western side of the
Gironde estuary – the area of the Médoc vineyards. Linked with these names is
what one might loosely call continuity evidence: villas under churches or abbeys,
villas with early medieval cemeteries and so on, which are here so common
as to be almost the rule. With the wider implications of such evidence we shall
be concerned in later chapters: for the moment we may merely note its existence,
and observe, perhaps, that this is an area which merits more detailed study.[50]

North of the Gironde Estuary the number of villas gradually declines, and in
western France it is not until we get to Britanny that we find anything like the
concentration of sites that we saw in Provence or the Aquitaine basin. One has to
beware of jumping to conclusions: there are some areas in which a fairly high
concentration of names in -*acum* may suggest that a lack of a local archaeological
tradition is part at least of the explanation – one such area is the southern part
of the Charentais, where these names are as frequent as in the Bordelais further
south, and there is a similar concentration around Brive-la-Gaillarde in Corrèze.
Nevertheless, the basic pattern is fairly clear, and the explanation not hard to find.
This whole tract of land from Bordeaux northwards to the mouth of the Loire
is a kind of corridor between the Atlantic in the west and the northern hills of
the Massif Central in the east, and between the sand dunes and salt marshes on
the one hand and the upland scrub and permanent pasture on the other there is
only a fairly narrow belt of land which is not at all easy or attractive for settlement. Apart from the obvious difference in climate the pattern is fairly similar
to that in Provence, though it would be unwise to press this too far. Taking the
main settlement area first, one can say that villas are fairly common in Bas-
Limousin, and also along the middle Charente Valley and the Roman road from
Saintes to Limoges; there are also concentrations in the Vendée, along the
Sèvre-Niortaise near Niort, in the lower basin of the Thouet around Airvault,
and further east on the network of roads around Poitiers.

Outside these concentrations both villa sites and -*acum* names are fairly scarce,
and it is clear that the primary factor which influenced settlement was the
presence of good communications by road or water, and in most cases proximity
to an important urban centre. Where such conditions were met the villas were
by no means small or struggling. It is true that mosaics are comparatively
infrequent – the large one at Condat-sur-Vienne (Hte-Vienne) is something of

an exception,[51] and there are signs that in some areas, such as Bas-Limousin, there may have been a general recession after the third-century troubles. But there are also some very large villas, both in Bas-Limousin itself and more notice-ably in Charentais: the excavated area at Antone (Hte-Vienne) is about 110 by 90m and clearly only a fraction of the whole;[52] the site known from air photographs at St-Preuil (Charente) is a courtyard villa about 100–150m square,[53] and the villa of La Vergnée (Romegoux, Charente-Maritime) is not only of comparable size but has a great farmyard almost 300m long with a range of stables and other buildings grouped around it.[54] As in any area, one has to allow for the fact that it is the big villas which attract attention, but we are probably justified in saying that here at any rate the evidence suggests fairly large estates within fairly restricted regions. All of the sites so far mentioned are in the central settlement strip, and as already suggested villas are much less frequent (and less distinguished) in the less favoured areas to east and west. There is, however, one important exception to this: the coastal strip between the Gironde Estuary and the mouth of the Charente contains a number of villas, one of which, that of St-Just-Pépiron, is large enough to merit attention on its own.[55] It is built on a fairly lavish scale, the main block so far dug being some 65m in length, and seems to have had a continuous history from the first to the fourth century, with evidence of a late Iron Age occupation for good measure. What is most striking, however, is that it lies on a narrow strip of land which must in antiquity have formed little more than a causeway surrounded on all sides by mud flats and salty marsh-land; the resemblance to the site at Stes-Maries-de-la-Mer on the southern edge of the Camargue[56] is very marked, and it seems probable that its income came from something like fish or the manufacture of salt rather than from conventional farming.

Once at the mouth of the Loire we are at the southern edge of Armorica, that is to say Britanny, the Cotentin peninsula and the Vilaine and upper Sarthe basins. In antiquity much of this area was covered in oak and beech woods, but once these were cut down the poor, gravelly, rather acid soil made it impossible to replace them. The pattern now is one of *bocage*, that is, small enclosed fields, growing rye or buckwheat, interspersed with areas of often bleak moorland offering pasture to sheep or cattle. It is no surprise, then, to find that over the greater part of Armorica villas are extremely rare – rarer, indeed, than in any area of France outside the Massif Central. But there is one area where more fertile soils and more favourable climate made settlement much more attractive – the coastal parts of the Breton peninsula – and here the villas are once more both frequent and flourishing. Known in the Breton language as Armor (that is, the sea-country, as opposed to Arcoët, the woodland country, further inland), this coastal strip accounts nowadays for about three-quarters of the population of Britanny. It is given over mainly to arable farming, especially to market garden-ing, though there is also a thriving fishing industry. Villas occur all around the coast, with particular concentrations between Brest and St-Brieuc in northern Finistère, the whole of the Quimper peninsula to the south, the area round

Vannes and Carnac in Morbihan, and that around Landebaëron in the *département* of Côtes-du-Nord. There are some very large sites among them – the main facade at Lodo (Morbihan), for example, is about 100m in length[57] – but more typical would seem to be the medium-sized villas at Carnac (Morbihan) and Concarneau and Plouneventer (Finistère), all of which have a main building roughly within the range 50–60 by 20–30m in size.[58] Most of the plans so far published are of the corridor type, and there are no obvious local peculiarities of style. None of the sites could be called luxurious: mosaics, even painted wall plaster, are rare, and we are clearly dealing with working establishments. Early dating material is hardly sufficient for any firm conclusions about the first settlement period; several sites have first-century material, but those which have been more thoroughly explored, such as Concarneau or Sizun[59] (Finistère), seem to have begun quite late in the century. Plouneventer is apparently earlier, but again the site at St-Frégant (Finistère)[60] is perhaps a century later. At the other end of the Roman period evidence for occupation in the fourth century is fairly plentiful. The main factor in settlement must have been the availability of good farm land, though there is also evidence of iron working in association with some of the sites. Villas are very frequently located on the coast itself, and although in most cases this was probably for reasons of scenery and general agreeability some of them may well have been associated, at least partly, with fishing; no real evidence either way has yet come to light.

From eastern Armorica right across to the borders of Flanders, the Ardennes and Lorraine, from Picardy in the north down to the edge of the Massif Central, are the great lowlands of northern France. Covering something in excess of 6,000 square miles, they are subdivided, usually by rivers, into literally dozens of *pays* of varying size and importance. Within so large an area there is obviously room for considerable differences in soil and natural features generally, and so in the pattern of settlement, and inevitably there is a danger of oversimplification in talking about it, but an attempt must nevertheless be made. A good area with which to begin, and one which shows very clearly the quite startling variations from one *pays* to another is the basin of the middle Loire, of which the main components are Touraine, the Sologne and Berry. Here Touraine itself is clearly the main area of settlement; the rich alluvial land in the valleys and terraces of the Loire and Cher, now either lush meadows or market gardens, vineyards and orchards, supported a heavy concentration of villas, for which the close proximity of Tours with its associated road network was an added advantage. In spite of the large number of sites there is very little up-to-date information on this area, so that a detailed assessment is not at the moment possible; but the large number of mosaics suggests a general prosperity, even though the evidence that we have seems to indicate small to medium villas rather than large ones. Lying as it does on major routes of communication, the area not surprisingly suffered considerably in the troubles of the third century, but the indications of destruction at this period are fairly evenly matched by those of repair and reoccupation afterwards, and individual coin lists, such as those for the villas around Josnes,[61] away to the north east, would seem to imply occupation until the end of the fourth century and perhaps even later. Outside Touraine the picture is very different: Sologne, with its heavy impermeable clays and marshy, waterlogged ground, was not cleared of its forest cover until the Middle Ages, and even now is only very thinly populated. Berry is more attractive, with a reddish loamy soil which if heavily manured is suitable for cereal growing; but clearly the labour required, and the better lands nearby, were enough to deter any large-scale development, and there is little evidence, either of archaeology or of place-names, for any significant Roman settlement.

These sharp contrasts between adjacent areas are a feature of the lowland region as a whole, and they appear even in the areas around Paris, which with its complex road network and its geographical position as the natural centre of the lowlands might have seemed likely to attract a more regular pattern of settlement. The main villa areas here are Vexin to the north west, to a lesser extent the Oise and Marne valleys, and the southern part of Brie; elsewhere, villas are scarce or non-existent, and there is a whole tract of land to the west and south west, covering Beauce and the old forest of Yvelines, with only the odd villa site here and there.[62] Clearly the most favoured areas here were the low, limon-covered plateaux with a good supply of water: Vexin and southern Brie were ideally suited, northern Brie less so because an impermeable layer of residual clay makes it waterlogged, and Beauce problematical because the low water table required the sinking of very deep wells. The river valleys, on the whole, were less favoured than the plateaux; many of them will have been marshy and liable to flooding in the Roman period, and it is really only more recent reclamation that has made them profitable. One exception to this rule is the Oise valley, where the villa sites we have, such as Verneuil and St-Maximin,[63] are along the valley itself; this is in other ways an interesting area, because the plateaux here, which are still fairly heavily forested, were worked largely by settlements of native type.[64] It is worth noting that much of the Paris region formed part of the estates of the early Frankish kings, and it is at least a possibility that in the Roman period some of it was imperially owned and organized rather along the lines suggested for Cranborne Chase. Equally interesting, though for other reasons, is the lower Marne Valley, which abounds in names in -*acum* but has so far not produced a comparable number of villa sites. Turning to the villas that we do have, the general picture seems to be one of initial settlement fairly late in the first century, widespread destruction or abandonment in the third and then repair and recovery (though often at a somewhat lower level) in the fourth. There are no really lavish sites, and mosaics are uncommon, but some of the villas are nevertheless very large: St-Maximin already mentioned is one example, and there is probably another at Châteaubleau (Seine-et-Marne).[65] The majority, however, are medium or small working establishments, and we would probably not be far wrong in regarding the recently excavated site at Guiry (Seine-et-Oise)[66] (*Fig.* 18) as representative; this is a corridor villa of average size, with a range of farm buildings around a yard, the whole complex neat and evidently prosperous but

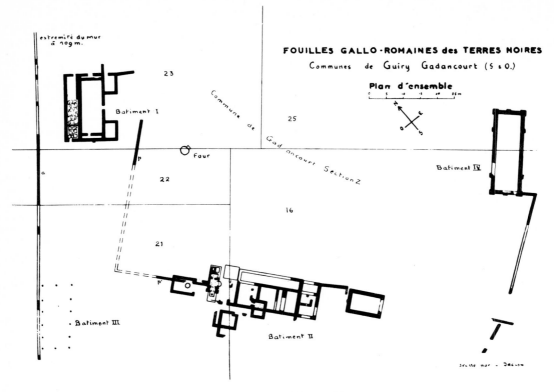

extrémité du mur à 109 m.

FOUILLES GALLO·ROMAINES des TERRES NOIRES

Communes   de   Guiry   Gadancourt (S & O.)

Plan d´ensemble

23

Commune de Gadancourt Section Z

25

Bâtiment I

Four

22

16

21

Bâtiment IV

p

Bâtiment III

Bâtiment II

18   Guiry, Seine-et-Oise

without pretensions.

Until fairly recently the same or similar comments could have been made about the whole stretch of chalkland from Bas-Normandie in the west, through Caux, Picardy and Artois to the borders of Flanders in the east. Basing oneself on the *répertoires* of Cochet and Deglatigny,[67] one could have built up a picture of modest or medium-sized villas, concentrated mainly along the Channel coast and in the basins of the major rivers – the Orne, the Seine and the Somme. As typical sites one might have offered a couple from Cochet's *répertoire* of Seine-Maritime: the little corridor villa at Maulevrier,[68] or the more luxurious peristyle villa at Ste-Marguerite-sur-Mer.[69] In recent years, however, the study of villas in northern France has been given a whole new dimension by the work of aerial survey carried out in Picardy by M. Roger Agache, the implications of which have still to be worked out[70] (*Fig.* 19). What requires adjustment is not so much the distribution pattern – the factors affecting settlement remain, as before, the basin of the Somme and the Roman road network around Amiens – but our notion of the density and character of settlement. As revealed by air photography villas are far more frequent than was suggested by earlier field archaeology, and there is a far wider range of sites than had hitherto been realized. Most striking among Agache's photographs are the large number of

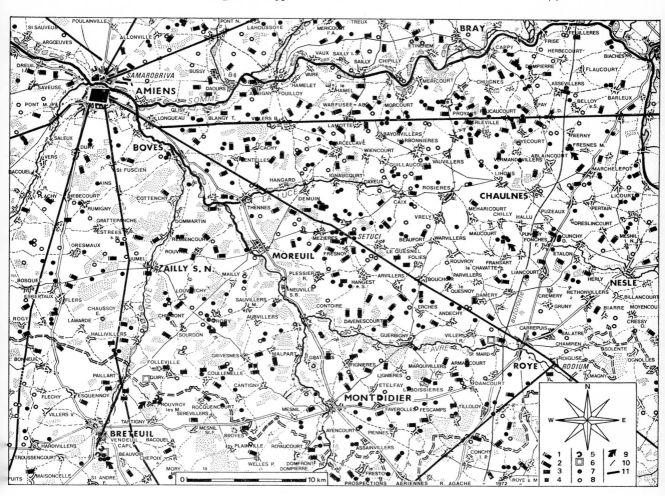

19 Villas and modern settlement in the Somme basin. (Symbols 1 and 2 on the Key indicate villas,
3 a probable villa)

enormous courtyard villas – sites like Malapart, Grivesnes, or Warfusée[71] (*Fig.* 20),
with their great enclosures more than 100m across and up to 400m in length – and
until one of these has been dug, and similar surveys conducted in other parts of
the northern lowlands, any general summary must be tentative.

Moving to the eastern part of the lowland region, one encounters once again
the complexity and contrasts typical of the lowlands as a whole, and all one can
do at this stage is offer examples. Thus along the broad alluvial valleys of
Champagne and Laonnais, and on the sandy clays of the Pays d'Othe, villas are
fairly numerous, while in the heavier clay regions of Gâtinais or Argonne they
are much less common. Variations of soil quality, and particularly of drainage,
clearly dictated the pattern to a large extent. In the Pays d'Othe the chalk is
overlaid extensively by deposits of good arable soil, and the pattern of settlement

in the Roman period is consequently less dominated by the great rivers than in Champagne proper, where such deposits are more rare. In the Gâtinais, or in the narrow strip known as Champagne *humide*, the problem is one of too much clay, resulting in bad drainage and presumably in antiquity fairly thick forest cover. The most favoured areas, as far as villas are concerned, were the Barrois, a low undulating limestone plateau running from Bar-le-Duc down to Auxerre, and the similar plateaux around Dijon and Langres, where villas are as thick on the ground as anywhere in this part of France. To generalize about so large a region would clearly be unwise, though one can say that in most areas where villa sites are at all common there are definite signs of prosperity in the form of mosaics, painted wall plaster and so on, and no lack of large, and sometimes very large, individual sites. At the upper extreme is the villa of St-Julien (Côte-d'Or),[72] an impressive L-shaped corridor house with a great walled enclosure; in the medium range are a number of clearly very prosperous sites, such as Andilly-en-Bassigny (Hte-Marne) or Noyers-sur-Serein (Yonne),[73] while at the lower end of the scale are the small working villas of which Fontenay-près-Vézelay (Yonne) or Fontaines-sur-Marne (Hte-Marne)[74] are typical examples. As one would expect in this part of Gaul the evidence for third-century destruction is widespread, and there are signs in some areas of retraction after this date, but most parts saw a certain amount of fourth-century rebuilding and revival, though often at a somewhat lower level than earlier.

20 Warfusée-Abancourt (Nord) (*Photo*: R. Agache)

Once at Dijon, we are at the top end of the Saône–Rhône valley, which serves as a natural route between these northern lowlands and the Mediterranean and which at an early stage in the development of Gaul received a major north–south road. Not surprisingly, the towns along this route were quick to attract settlement, and most of them supported a fairly vigorous villa population. The stretch between Mâcon and Chalon through Tournus, and especially the Mâconnais itself, is a particularly striking example. Here the villas cluster along the hillsides west of the Saône, most of them, to judge from finds, being already in existence early in the first century AD, and most of them large and well appointed establishments. Clearly, the presence of ready markets and relatively easy communication with markets further afield were the main contributory factors in this prosperity; whether, as one is tempted to suggest, its basis was the cultivation of vines is a question which must await more detailed excavation. Certainly the prosperity lasted well into the fourth century, and there is here (as around Bordeaux) a good deal of what we there called 'continuity evidence', suggesting that the economy of the area, whatever its character, was well founded. The same degree of prosperity is found further up the Saône valley, to Vesoul and beyond, and also along the Doubs through Besançon to Montbéliard and around such centres as Salins. Further east the route from Narbonensis up to Vindonissa through Geneva and Lausanne is similarly lined with large and prosperous sites of which Grange and Zofingen[75] are typical examples. All through this region mosaics are the rule, and some villas, such as Attricourt or Mantoche (Hte-Saône),[76] have a whole series; most of the excavation here was done in the last century, and detailed dating evidence is therefore lacking, but such plans as have been published are of very large corridor villas, many of them with courtyards or enclosures attached. Such obvious signs of wealth, in a region not everywhere blessed with strikingly fertile soil, are a clear illustration of the effect on rural prosperity of reliable and readily accessible markets, and of that integration into the social and economic organization of the Roman world which has been suggested as the essential characteristic of villas in general.[77]

For Lorraine the analysis made by Grenier[78] has not been much affected by subsequent discovery. As he pointed out, villas are very common in what was the territory of the Mediomatrices (that is to say, roughly the modern *département* of Moselle) but comparatively rare elsewhere. Part of the explanation must no doubt be geological, in that the soils outside the villa area, though easier to work than the Keuper and other clays of Moselle, are rather more meagre and variable in quality; but the differences in this respect are by no means striking, and one is bound to look for other explanations. As Grenier observes, the areas not favoured with villas were settled fairly extensively by sites of native character, suggesting that there might have been some policy of not extending the villa culture into them; one possible reason for such a policy might have been the presence here of public or imperial lands (again with Cranborne Chase as the British parallel), and there is some evidence to support this. As we shall see, the same sort of problem appears in Alsace, and it would be interesting if the same solution were possible there. Turning to the villas themselves one can say that, more than in any area of Gaul so far considered, they fall into two distinct categories: on the one hand there are the small working villas, either of a simple corridor type like Frécourt or Courcelles-Urville, or of a square plan typical of the region like Lorquin or Marly-aux-Bois;[79] and on the other hand the vast palatial establishments of which St-Ulrich-Dolving is the most spectacular but which are found also at Rouhling, Téting[80] and elsewhere. These two kinds of villa are not segregated into separate areas, but occur side by side with one another, and it is tempting to suppose that some at least of the smaller ones were actually dependencies of the large ones. Grenier suggested[81] that the presence of the larger ones was explicable in terms of the rise of Trier as an imperial capital from the late third century onwards, and this too is attractive. If so, the pattern may well have been one of small settlements in the early stages, with an increase in wealth leading later to the building up of large estates and the construction of villas to match. Whether one can guess also at the earlier settlements is another matter, though the regular spacing of villas around Gondrexange[82] (to cite the most famous example) would seem to suggest some kind of official distribution of land, perhaps of a military nature.

Whatever the answer to this particular question may be, it is clear that in eastern and north-eastern Gaul the history of villa settlement is likely to have been much more complex than elsewhere. To the varied and varying effects of military factors throughout the Roman period must be added the increasing importance of penetration, both forcible and peaceful, by the Germanic peoples, the long-term consequences of which are evident to this day in the linguistic divisions of this whole region. Nowhere are such complexities more evident than in Belgium, where the villas, now admirably catalogued, have been the subject of fairly intensive study,[83] and though we are here concerned primarily with questions of distribution and overall character it will be difficult to avoid discussion of at least the major underlying influences. One area can, for the moment, be left on one side: the Belgian province of Luxembourg lies to a large extent within the Ardennes, and the many villas which it contains, notably along the Roman road from Bastogne to Arlon and the upper reaches of the Semois, can most conveniently be dealt with alongside those of Trier to the east. Apart from these, the vast majority of Belgian villas are in the central low plateau, most of them being located within a somewhat bulging triangle of which the corners are Mons near the French border, Maastricht on the German one, and Marche-en-Famenne to the south. West of this triangle lies Flanders, whose sandy soils, now heavily manured and intensively cultivated, were clearly less attractive to villa settlement than the loams of the central provinces; and to the north, the heathlands of Noord-Brabant and Limburg, now developed industrially but never much of a prospect agriculturally. Within the triangle villas are distributed fairly evenly, except for concentrations around centres like Mons or Tirlement and along the great road from Bavai to Tongres, which is part of the route from the North Sea to the Rhine. In terms of villa type, size and so on the picture here is very similar to that of Lorraine, in that we have on the one hand the

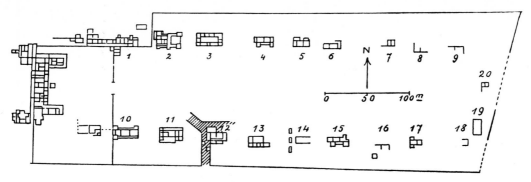

21   Anthée, Namur, Belgium

fairly modest villas (usually of a simple corridor type) like those of Sauvenière or Chastres-lès-Walcourt (Namur),[84] and on the other the very large sites (again usually corridor villas but on a much more lavish scale) such as Hosté (Brabant), Anthée (Namur) or that recently excavated at Haccourt (Liège)[85] (*Figs* 6, 21). The main difference, however, is that the prosperity here comes fairly early (the phase II villa at Haccourt, extending 103 by 44m overall, is tentatively dated to the first half of the second century), and that there was a very clear recession after the third-century invasions. Whether this makes a reconsideration of the Lorraine villas desirable is an open question; here, certainly, there is little evidence of prosperity as a result of the rise of Trier, and the suggestion that the second-century prosperity was the result of corn production for the Rhine armies has much to commend it. In this connection the discovery at Buzenol, in Hainault, of one of the reliefs depicting a Roman harvesting machine[86] (*Fig.* 32), is clearly significant.

Finally in Gaul, and as a suitable introduction to the frontier regions themselves, one turns to the district of Trier, the leading town of Gallia Belgica which became, from about AD 90, the administrative centre for the two Germanies and ultimately a seat of imperial government. For present purposes, one can include the south-eastern corner of Belgium, the duchy of Luxembourg, and much of the Rhineland Pfalz, that is, a rather greater area than that covered by the *civitas Treverorum* itself. A recent study of the region has brought the available material conveniently together,[87] and one can hardly do better at this stage than summarize those of its conclusions which relate to rural settlement generally and villas in particular. Occupation was thickest, and most tenacious, in the central fertile area of which Trier itself is the centre and Bitburg and Luxembourg the northern and western extremities. Here the soils were easily worked, and here the most prosperous villas, in terms of size and amenities, are generally found; but such was the prosperity of the region as a whole that other less hospitable areas were developed also, and there are villas in northern Luxembourg and in the Hunsrück in what has long since reverted to forest.[88] Settlement began early, and by the end of the first century the basic pattern of villas seems

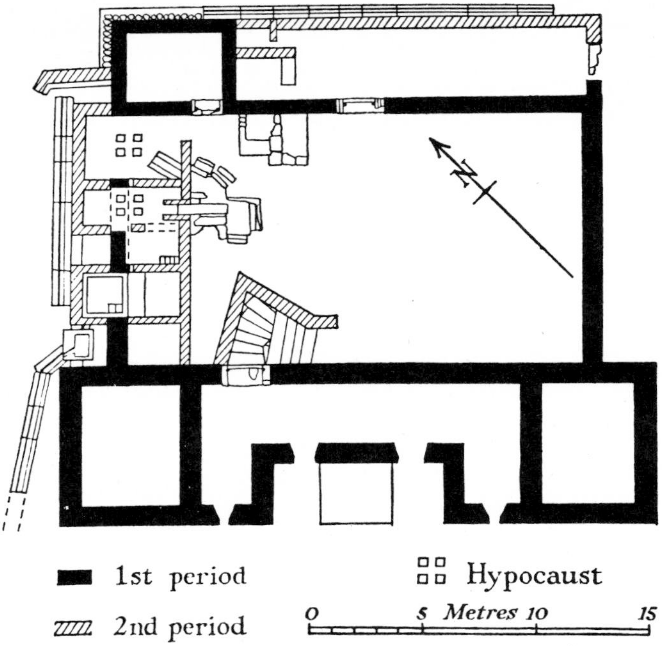
1st period
Hypocaust
2nd period
0
5 Metres 10
15

22 Bollendorf, Germany

to have been well established, dominated, not unnaturally, by the extensive road networks around Trier and Arlon. A period of expansion and great prosperity lasted throughout the second and into the early third century, after which the area felt the full force of the upheavals of the 250s onwards. The recovery that followed, however, was striking, though one has to say that outside the central area the destruction wrought by the invasions was more permanent. Within the central area there was extensive rebuilding, often (as at Bollendorf (*Fig.* 22) or Sotzweiler[89]) on a grander scale than before, and there are some sites, such as Konz or Pfalzel[90] (*Figs* 50, 51), which were actually begun in the fourth century. Ausonius' well-known reference[91] to villas flourishing in his own day along the banks of the Moselle could well be overstated, but it could hardly have been made if there were actually something of a recession. As in Lorraine, and indeed to a greater extent than there, the proportion of large luxurious villas is high – a clear indication of the prosperity of the region as a whole and of the richness of Trier and the other urban sites as market centres. There are no sites quite so lavish as St-Ulrich or Téting,[92] but Nennig to the south of Trier and Odrang[93] (*Fig.* 23) to the north are both on a grand scale and are by no means alone. Apart from these, and the others already referred to, one ought perhaps to mention Blankenheim and Leutersdorf[94] as examples of the large corridor houses so typical of the area, Stahl or Weitersbach[95] as examples of the more modest type, and Mayen[96] (*Fig.* 5) as one of the best and most informative individual reports still available. This, in any case, is an area to which we shall frequently need to return.

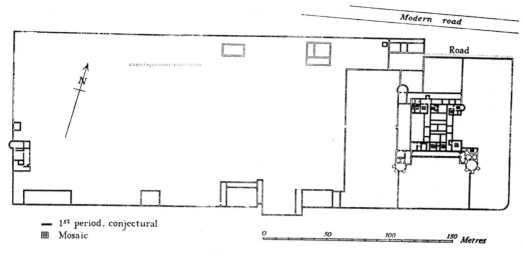

— 1st period, conjectural
⊞ Mosaic

0   50   100   150 *Metres*

23   Odrang, Fliessem, Germany

RHINELAND AND UPPER DANUBE PROVINCES

The advice of Augustus to his successor, that the Empire should be kept within its existing boundaries,[97] could be taken to imply that the northern frontier should consist essentially of the Rhine and Danube rivers, and this, after the campaigns of Germanicus in the first three years of the reign of Tiberius, seems generally to have been assumed. The decision of Vespasian to advance beyond the Rhine and to occupy what is now roughly Baden-Württemberg was not an abandonment of this policy so much as an improving modification, the need for which had been made abundantly clear by the troubles of AD 68–9. Ideal as they were for much of their length, the Rhine and Danube had one serious weakness as a frontier, namely the large re-entrant angle between their upper courses, which, if it were left unoccupied, would not only make rapid communication between the Rhine and Danube armies more difficult, but would offer a route for prospective invaders through the Black Forest to the very approaches of Italy. And so it was that under the emperors from Vespasian to Hadrian this angle was gradually straightened out and a fortified frontier established which left the Rhine some way north of Coblenz, circled the Taunus Mountains, continued south-south-east to Lorch, and then ran parallel to, and some 50km north of the Danube, which it ultimately joined beyond Ingolstadt. For rather more than a century this frontier remained secure, and the lands behind it were gradually settled and developed; it was, however, a largely man-made frontier, without any major natural feature to support it, and in the troubles of the third century, when troops were so frequently called away to assist some claimant or other to the throne, there was little prospect of keeping it intact against the pressures from outside. Not surprisingly, therefore, it failed to survive the third-century invasions, and after order had been restored by Diocletian and his colleagues the Rhine and Danube became once more the principal line of defence. Again, there was a brief period of relative security, and within the restored frontier life began again. But it was hardly a return to normal: lands which under the Antonines had been well inside the Empire were now once more part of the frontier zone, and the memory of the recent disasters would take more than a couple of strong emperors to erase. Moreover, with the growing barbarization of the army and the increasing settlement of Germanic peoples within the Empire, the frontier itself was becoming difficult, not only to maintain, but to define, and to this extent the fourth-century revival which is evident in other parts of the west was here, if not absent, a restrained and even gloomy phenomenon.

Dominated as they were by such events and processes, the villas of these frontier regions could never enjoy the solid prosperity which in more favoured areas was the result of secure and stable conditions over relatively long periods of time. For much of the imperial period any site in the provinces of Upper and Lower Germany, and also (though perhaps to a lesser extent) Raetia or Noricum, might be subject to disturbance by military or barbarian settlement, destruction by invasion or sudden raids, or economic ruin by the advancement of the frontier and the consequent loss of markets. Prosperity there was, but it was precarious, something to be grabbed while it was available, converted if possible into transportable wealth rather than being spent on lavish amenities which might suddenly have to be abandoned. With few exceptions, the villas throughout these frontier provinces are primarily working establishments, their plan and design dictated by the needs of security and working efficiency rather than of ostentation or even comfort, and the characteristic site, from Köln-Müngersdorf in the Rhineland to Merklingen in Württemberg or Burgweinting near Regensburg in Bavaria,[98] is a small or medium-sized residence, surrounded by its farm buildings, and enclosed by a wall or palisade. Mosaics are rare, wall paintings not very common, bath blocks utilitarian in size and plan. Nevertheless, as Grenier pointed out,[99] it would be wrong to look solely at size and degrees of luxury and to see these regions as only marginally Romanized. Though small and lacking many of the obvious trimmings, these German villas are often very numerous – Paret's estimate for Württemberg in 1932 was over 800[100] – and in terms of intensity of settlement this is Romanization on an impressive scale. The greater the attention to efficiency and profitability the greater the resilience in the face of disaster, and there is a sense in which the sites in these troubled regions were less affected by major upheavals than were the more lavish sites elsewhere by changes in economic climate.

Within this overall picture the various regions have their characteristic patterns, and it may be useful to run briefly through them. In the north, the area around Trier and the Moselle Valley has already been dealt with, but outside this the lands along the Rhine, from Köln to Mannheim and beyond, were settled by small but numerous villas on the lines already suggested. The villa at Wollersheim,

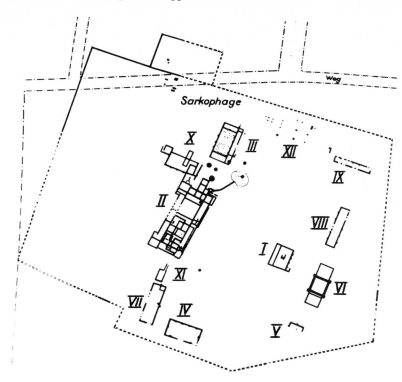

24 Köln–Müngersdorf, Germany

one of a cluster of sites round Berg-vor-Nideggen, near Düren,[101] is probably fairly typical: it consists of a small corridor house with a granary and other farm buildings nearby, and could be paralleled by sites all down the Rhine and upper Danube. Many of them are associated with the legionary fortresses,[102] and there are some areas, such as Dautenheim, where the regular spacing of villas would seem to suggest a military or other organized settlement.[103] Further south, from Mannheim down to Strasbourg, villas are rather less common, and the absence of sites in much of the fertile loess areas of Alsace has led to the suggestion that these areas were part of large, possibly imperial estates and worked in the native manner.[104] In spite of the difficulties this would seem at the moment to be the most likely explanation: it is hard, certainly, to believe that they were unoccupied. South of Strasbourg the familiar pattern returns, though the presence of mosaics in some of the villas around Mulhouse and along the upper Ill would seem to indicate a somewhat higher level of luxury; for the rest of the area the site at Steinbrunn-le-Bas (Ht-Rhin)[105] is probably representative. Moving across the river and into the great belt of land that begins with the Black Forest and extends through Baden-Württemberg to Bavaria (or in Roman terms the so-called *Agri Decumates* and the province of Raetia), the pattern becomes more regular. The sites at Merklingen or Burgweinting already referred to are chosen at random from dozens of sites, all remarkably similar in size, layout and general standard of comfort. From the range of buildings and the overall impression they give of self-sufficient units it seems likely that they were based on mixed farming, though clearly there must have been differences of emphasis from one region to another. Dating evidence is scarce, but it would be surprising if there was anything more than temporary reoccupation after the third-century invasions; the most common feature is an abandonment some-time during the century, making dating even more tentative than it would normally be. In this advance area, which was not made fully secure until well into the second century, one can hardly expect the carefree luxury that we find elsewhere.

25   Seeb, near Zürich, Switzerland

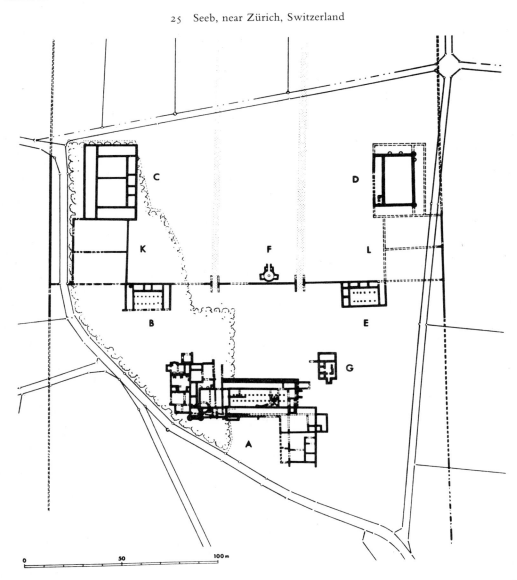

Further south, however, and back behind the Rhine, the situation was very different: just as the prosperity of Trier extended down the Moselle to Coblenz, so along the upper reaches of the Rhine, especially around Augst and Windisch, sites are noticeably more lavish and more lasting than those to the north of the river. The villa at Seeb, near Zürich[106] (*Fig. 25*), is no doubt an extreme example, with its enormous residence and seven-hectare enclosure; but there are several sites in the same general area, such as Zofingen or Kulm in Aargau,[107] where corridor houses up to 100m in length are clearly more than working farmsteads. Here, of course, the proximity of major centres, with well-established communications down through the Jura to the south, was all important; in addition, with Windisch a legionary fortress as early as Tiberius, sites in this area had more than a head start on those to the north, as well as a greater chance of recovery once the worst of the invasions had passed. The pattern here in northern Switzerland is repeated, in fact, in the neighbouring province of Noricum;[108] here again there were villas from the first century onwards in the northern part of Austria from Salzbourg across to St Pölten, and these were followed, with an interruption during the Marcomannic wars of the 170s, by others in the southern part of the province around such centres as Teurnia, Virunum and Solva. Again, there are large and luxurious establishments, such as those at Löffelbach, near the border with Pannonia, and Thalerhof, in the Mur Valley south of Graz,[109] though the smaller and more simple sites like Wimsbach, south of Wels,[110] which recall the working farms of southern Germany, were probably more numerous than the record at present suggests. Many of the Norican villas continued to the end of the fourth century, some of them perhaps even longer; in this, and in their general development, they have less in common with the German examples than with those of the provinces further along the Danube, and it is to these that we now turn.

BALKAN AND LOWER DANUBE PROVINCES

In the establishment of the northern frontier the primary consideration as we have seen was to improve communications between east and west and at the same time to secure the approaches to Italy through the Julian Alps. In this connection the Balkan and Danube provinces were of prime importance: from the Alps across to the Black Sea were tribes potentially or actually hostile, and beyond the Danube were peoples whose identities and relationships were only dimly known and whose power to inspire terror was correspondingly greater. And so it was that the campaigns in this area, and the eventual establishment of a frontier along the Danube, were prompted by motives of consolidation and security rather than by a desire to gain possession of lands attractive in themselves; and though the initial military phase was quickly followed by a programme of economic development, military considerations were nevertheless to remain primary throughout the Roman period, and the provinces here established were frontier provinces with all that this implied.[111]

As in other parts of the Empire boundaries tended to move and names to change, but the provinces that concern us are basically as follows. Dalmatia was a triangle of land, bounded by a line running from south of Trieste, across almost to Belgrade and then south to Albania, that is to say rather less than modern Yugoslavia. Apart from some isolated campaigns in the late Republic, the main work in subduing the area was carried out by the future Augustus from 35 to 33 BC. To the north, and bounded by the river Save, the Alps and the middle reaches of the Danube, was the province of Pannonia, conquered first in the years from 13 to 9 BC and then reconquered from AD 6 to 9 after a major rebellion. Further along the Danube to the east were the two provinces of Moesia, leading eventually to Thrace and the coast of the Black Sea. North of the Danube, in the south-eastern part of the Carpathians now known as Transylvania, was the area soon to become the province of Dacia, annexed by Trajan in AD 106 and finally abandoned by Aurelian in the 270s. Though linked historically and part of the same strategic pattern, each of these areas had its own particular features and can for our purposes be considered separately.

The great mass of the Dinaric Alps, with its lack of water and, except in the occasional isolated depression or *polje*, its lack of usable land, made most of Dalmatia unattractive to the settler and inappropriate for large-scale capital development.[112] Most of the population, and most of the Romanization and consequent prosperity, was in the coastal strip and the immediate offshore islands, where there was fertile (sometimes very fertile) land, abundant supplies of fish, and a good Mediterranean climate. Settlers from Italy moved in from an early date, colonies and *municipia* were established all along the coast, and although not so spectacular as North Africa or Narbonensis a prosperous urban culture was soon in being. Associated with this were the beginnings of a villa economy;[113] at present our information comes largely from one area, that around Narona in the lower Naretva Valley, but we are probably right to assume that the same pattern existed, though perhaps less intensively, in connection with other centres. What we have near Narona is a series of villas, built apparently in the first century AD to fairly high standards of comfort and design.[114] Though not large or complex in plan, they were well provided with hypocausts, mosaics, painted wall plaster and occasionally marble veneers. Generally speaking, they are on good farming land and give every appearance of farm centres, inhabited by their owners on a permanent basis. All the relevant evidence suggests that the original owners at least were Italian immigrants: the early date of the villas would suggest that they were the product of a culture brought ready-made from outside rather than of one acquired locally, and the dependence of the early owners on Italian imports, not only of the regular manufactured goods but of actual building materials such as roof tiles, points strongly in the same direction. As has been aptly observed,[115] the remark of Pliny about Narbonensis, that it was more like Italy than a province, would apply with equal force here.

Outside the coastal strip the opportunities for a villa pattern were, as we have seen, less obvious, but there are one or two areas in which quite a flourishing pattern was nevertheless established. Villas are known, for example, on the upper reaches of the Naretva around the town of Konjic, in the north of the province around Bihać on the river Una, and at isolated points in between.[116] Generally speaking, the standard of construction and of the amenities in these villas is lower than those near the coast. Mosaics are rare, building materials are prepared or acquired locally, and there is little in the way of imported goods. Farming tends to be mixed, and there is not surprisingly an impression of subsistence farming and self-sufficiency rather than of specialization and the production of a surplus. What these villas represent, in fact, is the adoption by the local people of Romanized methods and life styles, and the date at which they were built (most of them seem to be of the third or fourth century) is an indication of the slowness with which this adoption took place. Away from these special areas life must have gone on much as it had before the conquest; indeed, in most of the Balkan and Danube provinces the same was true, and the gap between the Roman or Romanized minority and the rest of the population seems to have been more marked here than almost anywhere else.[117]

Pannonia, geographically, is very different. The Danube and its tributaries, chief among them being the Save and Drave which flow eastwards from the foothills of the Alps, ensure a good supply of water, and most of the province is either plain or low hills. In antiquity a large percentage of its territory was covered in forest, as indeed is the case now, but there were areas of workable farmland and also some areas, such as the slopes around the northern side of Lake Balaton and the Neusiedler See south of Vienna, where climate and scenery made settlement specially attractive.[118]. Work on Pannonian villas has been particularly extensive and efficient, and it is possible to use the distribution map of known sites with a fair degree of confidence.[119] The earliest villas appeared in the Save and Drave valleys, in particular the triangle contained between Poetovio on the Drave and Emona and Siscia on the Save but also further along the Save as far as Sirmium. This area was the primary target in the Roman conquest and the base from which the rest of the region was brought under control. Many of these villas have material suggesting an occupation in the first century AD, and it is likely that by about AD 100 the basic pattern of settlement was already beginning to emerge. What exactly they were like at this date is impossible to say, but in their later stages they were well-to-do farms, prosperous but not lavish, and it is likely that this was their character throughout. The villa at Šmarje-Grobelce, a simple dwelling house with outbuildings grouped in an enclosure wall, for which one could provide numerous parallels from southern Germany, is probably a typical example.[120] Once the Danube frontier was established, of course, there would very naturally be a tendency for settlement to be attracted to the fortress towns of Aquincum (Budapest), Brigetio, Carnuntum and Vindobona, and it is clear from the distribution of villa sites that this did indeed happen. These villas again are primarily working establishments, though many were well provided with heated rooms, mosaic floors and other amenities. Among the larger examples is that at Csúcshegy, in Budapest itself, where the main dwelling house is still only about 35 by 20m;[121] more typical, perhaps, are sites like Testvérhêgyi nearby, which seem to have doubled as inns or staging posts on the major roads for at least part of their occupation.[122] Away from the immediate neighbourhood of the towns the date of development here is rather later: many of the villas seem to have begun about AD 200 or shortly after, and to have reached their peak a century or so later still.

The crucial factor in all of this is, of course, the situation with regard to Dacia: during the period when it was part of the Empire, Pannonia could profit both from the security it afforded and also indirectly from its mineral wealth, whereas during the troubled period leading to its conquest and in the period after its abandonment things were likely to be much more uncertain. It was in this middle period of security and prosperity that certain areas of the interior seem to have been developed and properties of considerable size and luxury assembled and maintained. The settlement around the Neusiedler See in the north might on its own be thought of as simply an extension of the frontier area, but the similar, more concentrated settlement of Lake Balaton shows that it is in fact a new departure, and a very striking one at that. It is here that the really large villas are found, villas with imposing residential blocks and whole ranges of out-buildings, reminding one of such sites as Köln-Müngersdorf or in some cases of Anthée in Belgium. Among the more spectacular examples one may cite that of Nemesvámos-Balácapuszta,[123] with its large peristyle villa and a series of subsidiary buildings arranged in an inner and outer courtyard, and the impressive establishment at Keszthely-Fenékpuszta[124] (*Fig.* 42), where an equally large residential block and a dense assembly of outbuildings were later transformed into a veritable fortress by the addition of a turreted enclosure wall. The evidence from the latter site is that although it may have begun at the end of the first century its main phase may well be as late as the fourth, and it would not be surprising if this were generally true of the villas in these particular areas. The question of fortification is one which we encounter also in Africa, and we shall need to discuss it in due course; suffice it to say for the moment that this particular example, though a remarkable one, is not without parallel elsewhere in the province. With villas as large as these one naturally thinks of imperial ownership, and although the evidence is largely circumstantial there is much to be said for the view of local scholars that imperial estates throughout this part of the Empire were both numerous and extensive. Fenékpuszta itself is an obvious candidate, as is the equally impressive site at Parndorf, south of Carnuntum (*Fig.* 43), though without documentary evidence (which we have, for example, for the palace of Mediana in Upper Moesia) we need to be cautious in individual cases.[125]

The remaining Danube provinces can be quickly dealt with. In Dacia, although the main motive of the conquest was the exploitation of the area's mineral resources, and in particular its gold, there were landed estates with villas at their centres. Oddly enough, the attractiveness of Dacia to settlers and its tenacity in holding on to Roman ways after its abandonment were both, if anything, greater than in the other provinces of the region, a situation reflected in the status of Romanian as one of the most Roman of Romance languages.[126] Evidence of particular sites, however, is very sparse, and at present there is little of any significance that one can say. What evidence we have suggests fairly small working farms, with largely wood-built outbuildings, enclosed by walls or palisades and looking very much like those of, say, Baden-Württemberg,[127] though there were more luxurious ones near urban centres as in most provinces.[128] Further east, in Upper and Lower Moesia and in Thrace, the general pattern, as far as one can tell from the evidence at present available, is roughly that of Pannonia, with villas appearing first in the lands behind the frontier and around such centres as Serdica (Sofia) or Adrianople (Ederne). Here again there are major sites, such as Armira and Chatalka in Thrace[129] or Bela Palanka and Kolarovgrad in Upper and Lower Moesia respectively,[130] which are presumably, like their Pannonian counterparts, of fourth-century date. Without more plentiful and detailed information, however, any general conclusions here would be unwise.

BRITAIN (*Fig. 26*)

'Those who inhabit Cantium,' says Caesar, writing a century before the permanent occupation of Britain by Roman forces, 'are by far the most civilized, and differ little from the Gauls in their way of life[131].' The particular point he mentions is that, unlike the peoples further inland, they were cereal farmers, but it is likely that they resembled their Gaulish cousins in more than this. How far the Belgic areas had in fact advanced in such matters as private property or the growth of a landed aristocracy is open to question, but here in the south-east corner of Britain, so open, as Caesar himself recognized, to influences from across the Channel, the adoption of Roman customs in general, and of the villa in particular, was likely to be fairly rapid. In this sense it is no surprise to see villas like Eccles or Lullingstone appearing within a generation or so of the Claudian invasion,[132] or to find that many of the earliest establishments, such as Eccles again or Cobham Park, were on sites already occupied by Belgic farmsteads.[133] It was no doubt at this stage that the broad pattern of settlement that we find in later centuries was first established, the main villa area being the broad stretch of country from eastern Surrey through Rochester, Maidstone and Canterbury to Dover, along the northern and southern edges of the Downs.

   The most striking concentration of sites within this area was that around the subsidiary centre of Durobrivae at Rochester, and in particular along the Darent and Medway valleys; the comparative lack of sites in the neighbourhood of Canterbury (Durovernum), the cantonal capital, is in this sense rather surprising, though as we shall see there are other areas in which the same phenomenon occurs. The absence of villas in the Weald, and to some extent from the heavier

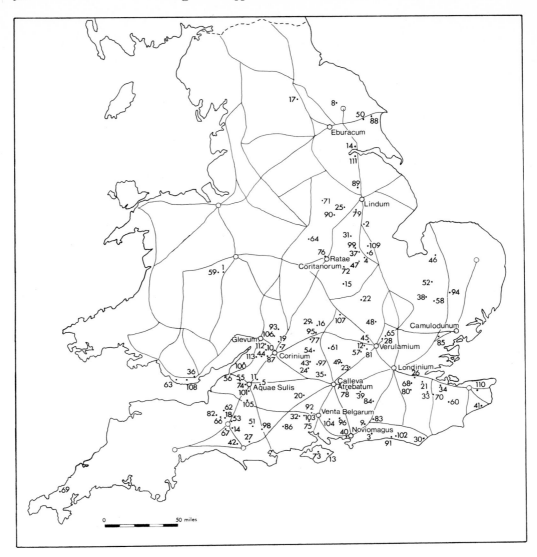

26   Map of Britain showing location of villas mentioned in the text

clays elsewhere, would suggest that types of soil were a major determining factor, the preference generally being for the valley alluvials and the lighter and medium loams. This is not to say that the heavier wooded lands were entirely neglected: as Applebaum has observed, a number of villas, such as Little Chart or Otford, are sited on the edge of the Gaults and other clays, suggesting at least an interest in the woodland, and perhaps an attempt at clearance and cultivation.[134] The general coincidence of villas with what is now good arable land would imply that the cultivation of cereals remained the major concern, as it had been in Caesar's day, though it seems likely that use will have been made of the exten-

KEY TO FIG. 26

1 Acton Scott	39 Farnham	77 North Leigh
2 Ancaster	40 Fishbourne	78 North Warnborough
3 Angmering	41 Folkestone	79 Norton Disney
4 Apethorpe	42 Frampton	80 Otford
5 Atworth	43 Frilford	81 Park Street
6 Barholme	44 Frocester Court	82 Pitney
7 Barnsley Park	45 Gadebridge Park	83 Pulborough
8 Beadlam	46 Gayton Thorpe	84 Rapsley, Ewhurst
9 Bignor	47 Great Weldon	85 Rivenhall
10 Bisley	48 Great Wymondley	86 Rockbourne
11 Box	49 Hambledon	87 Rodmarton
12 Boxmoor	50 Harpham	88 Rudston
13 Brading	51 Hinton St. Mary	89 Scampton
14 Brantingham	52 Hockwold	90 Southwell
15 Brixworth	53 Ilchester	91 Southwick
16 Callow Hill	54 Islip	92 Sparsholt
17 Castle Dykes	55 Keynsham	93 Spoonley Wood
18 Catsgore	56 Kingsweston	94 Stanton Chair
19 Chedworth	57 Latimer	95 Stonesfield
20 Clanville	58 Lidgate	96 Stroud
21 Cobham Park	59 Linley	97 Sutton Courtenay
22 Cosgrove	60 Little Chart	98 Tarrant Hinton
23 Cox Green	61 Little Milton	99 Thistleton Dyer
24 Cranhill	62 Littleton	100 Tockington Park
25 Cromwell	63 Llantwit Major	101 Wellow
26 Darenth	64 Lockington	102 West Blatchington
27 Dewlish	65 Lockleys	103 West Dean
28 Dicket Mead, Welwyn	66 Low Ham	104 West Meon
29 Ditchley	67 Lufton	105 Whatley
30 Eastbourne	68 Lullingstone	106 Whittington Court
31 East Denton	69 Magor Farm, Illogan	107 Whittlebury
32 East Grimstead	70 Maidstone	108 Whitton
33 East Malling	71 Mansfield Woodhouse	109 Wilsthorpe Mill
34 Eccles	72 Medbourne	110 Wingham
35 Eling	73 Newport	111 Winterton
36 Ely	74 Newton St. Loe	112 Witcombe
37 Empingham	75 Newtown	113 Woodchester
38 Exning	76 Norfolk Street	114 Yeovil

sive pasture available on the salt marshes of the Thames estuary, and it is hard to
believe that the great orchards which are so much a feature of the modern landscape were entirely lacking in Roman times. Mention should also be made of
the possible fulling mill at the Darenth villa,[135] which would imply a certain
emphasis on sheep farming, and of the numerous pottery kilns in the Upchurch
marshes north of Rochester, which are close enough to some of the villas to
suggest that they might have been connected.[136] As yet, however, no villas have
been associated with the major iron-working areas inland from Hastings, and in
general the worlds of industry and agriculture would seem in this area to be
clearly separate.

Of the individual sites here very few have been thoroughly excavated, and
only two (those at Eccles and Lullingstone) have been examined in any detail in
recent years. The overall picture, however, is one of prosperity: Eccles itself and
Darenth are major sites by any standard, and several other villas had one or more
mosaic pavements, including those at Maidstone, East Malling, Wingham, Little
Chart and Otford.[137] Here, as elsewhere, the troubles of the third century seem
to have had their effect, the most striking instance being at Lullingstone, which
seems to have been actually abandoned for some 50 years after AD 200; the
continuing expansion of Eccles at this period is to this extent all the more surprising,
though it may be that there were special circumstances. The size and luxury of
the establishment, and in particular its early appearance, are such that in general
terms a comparison with Fishbourne in Sussex is not inappropriate; and if, as
seems possible, it was some kind of official residence, its fortunes may well have
differed from those of more ordinary sites. Mr Stevens, indeed, has suggested
that other sites were rather special too: Folkestone, as being possibly connected
with the British fleet, Darenth, as perhaps being under the control of an imperial
procurator, and even Lullingstone itself, as the *procurator*'s possible residence.[138]
This, clearly, is something on which further evidence would be welcome,
though it might fairly be argued that the small size of the Lullingstone villa
would seem to make it a less likely candidate for official status than some of the
others.

The kind of situation envisaged by Stevens for Kent is rather more easily
detectable in Sussex, in the territory of the Regni,[139] where there would seem to
be a clear distinction between the villas which appear in a rich and fully developed
form in the first century, and those which evolved more slowly and more
normally from timber buildings to modest stone buildings by the early third
century, with a possible further expansion to something more lavish in the fourth.
As examples of the first category, regarded by Professor Cunliffe as 'a reflection . . .
of an imposed politico-economic system',[140] we may quote the extraordinary
site at Fishbourne, together with those at Angmering and Southwick, and
possibly also Pulborough and Eastbourne;[141] and of the second, the villas at
West Blatchington, Rapsley and Bignor – the last of which became a major
site in the fourth century but was still comparatively modest in the third.[142]
For Kent, if such a distinction existed, there is little definite that we can offer by

way of explanation, but here in Sussex the picture is rather more clear, if still somewhat conjectural in detail. If, as seems likely, the Regni (or Regnenses) derived their name from the *regnum* or kingdom bestowed on King Cogidubnus for his services to Rome after the invasion of AD 43, and if, as also seems likely, the villa at Fishbourne was originally his, it is natural to suppose that the large villas of the first century, and the great estates of which they were no doubt the centres, were the property of philo-Roman chieftains from among Cogidubnus' people. This, as Professor Cunliffe has observed,[143] is certainly more plausible than the alternative possibility, that the villas were built by immigrants from across the Channel; one would hardly expect Cogidubnus to be rewarded with a kingdom of his own and then have much of its land transferred into the hands of outsiders.

The distribution of villas generally is similar to that in Kent, with preference being shown for the better soils on the edge of the Downs, but also for those in the coastal plain. Among the more favoured sites are ones along the rivers flowing south from the Downs to the sea, many of them at points on the slope where the chalk and the valley soils meet; this would suggest, not only a concern for adequate supplies of water (this being the spring line), but possibly also a preference for a mixed type of farming, with stock raising and arable combined. A good example of this kind of thing is the villa at Bignor, which was well placed to exploit not only the fertile greensand scarplands, but also the grazing on the nearby Downs and perhaps also the woodland of the Wealden clays.[144] As in Kent, the link with industrial activities seems to be slight, except for a concentration of villas to the north of the area, at the western end of the North Downs; pottery kilns are numerous, and two at least of the villas, those at Farnham and Rapsley Farm, Ewhurst (Surrey), were clearly associated with them.[145] Apart from the spectacular development of the late first century on a few individual sites, there seems to have been a gradual growth of prosperity throughout the region from the second century through to the third, after which the pattern is somewhat unclear. A number of sites, such as Angmering and West Blatchington, appear to have ceased to function, while others, such as Bignor, went on to greater prosperity; the region as a whole would be vulnerable to the seaborne raids of the later Empire, though whether the apparent reduction in the number of occupied sites is the result of these or of an accumulation of lands by fewer and larger owners remains to be seen.

The kingdom assigned to Cogidubnus had earlier formed part of the Atrebates, which at one time extended over much of southern Britain; in the reorganization which followed the conquest this was broken up, the territory of the Regni being taken away in the southeast and a new territory, that of the Belgae, in the southwest, the result being that under Roman rule the lands of the Atrebates consisted of what is now Berkshire and parts of the surrounding counties.[146] Not surprisingly, perhaps, in such circumstances, there were no rich early villas like those of Sussex and Kent; the typical site for this area is a simple corridor villa, emerging perhaps in the course of the second century and developing

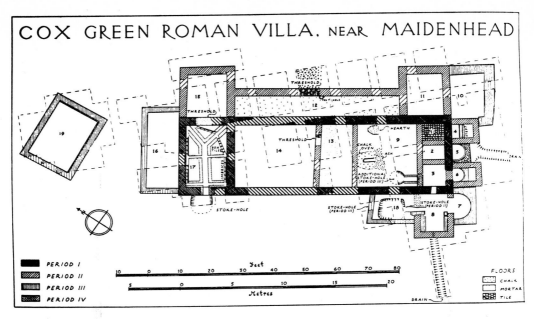

27   Cox Green, Berkshire

steadily thereafter. Such, for example, is the villa at Cox Green, near Maiden-head[147] (*Fig. 27*), which began as a single range of rooms like those at Park Street and Lockleys, acquired a bath suite and corridor in its second phase, and continued through at least two more phases into the mid fourth century. The site at Frilford[148] is comparable to this, and there were similar ones (to judge from what evidence we have) at Eling, to the northeast of Newbury, and Cranhill, in the parish of Letcombe Regis.[149] The Eling villa had a mosaic pavement, which for this area would seem to be fairly exceptional. The overall distribution of sites is of some interest, in that they tend to favour the subsidiary centre at Mildenhall rather than the cantonal capital of Calleva at Silchester; the pattern is not so striking as its counterpart in Kent, but is no doubt explicable in similar terms – that is, that the lands in the immediate neighbourhood of the capital were assigned directly to it, and administered from within the town itself.

More fortunate than the Atrebates, in spite of their record of resistance, were the Catuvellauni, who before and after the conquest were the dominant people in the eastern part of Britain; even under Roman rule their territory extended from the Thames Estuary to Northamptonshire, and was to include, in addition to its capital at Verulamium, a dozen or more centres of importance.[150] Surprisingly, perhaps, it was not one of the major villa areas: villas are less common, certainly, that in areas further west, there are very few of the lavish sites that one associates with such centres as Bath or Cirencester, and with two exceptions there are no obvious concentrations of villas in any particular areas. One very recent site which alters the picture somewhat is that at Rivenhall, where an extensive stone-built villa appears, like some we have seen in Kent and Sussex, immediately after the conquest[151] (*Fig.* 52); one thinks of a local chieftain rewarded for his services, or perhaps of a Roman official, but either way the site is likely to have been exceptional, and was in any case strictly Trinovantian rather than Catuvellaunian. The areas of greatest interest, which have in consequence received most attention, are those around Verulamium itself in the south and the town of Durobrivae at Water Newton in the north. The sites around Verulamium, which extend in a broad band south-westwards towards Reading along the Chilterns, include those of Park Street and Lockleys, which have figured so frequently and so prominently in British villa studies, together with ones like Gadebridge Park and Boxmoor, near Hemel Hempstead, and Latimer in the Chess Valley, on all of which there has been extensive recent work.[152]

The overall pattern of development is typical of that in much of Britain, with the first houses appearing in the latter part of the first century and developing steadily until the fairly general setbacks of the third. The picture in the fourth century is more varied (as we have seen it to be in Sussex), with some sites going out of use soon after 350 and others apparently surviving the troubles of the 370s and lasting into the early fifth century or even longer. The typical house here is again the corridor villa, as at Lockleys (*Fig.* 28) or Boxmoor, which sometimes extends into a courtyard type as its buildings grow around it, those at Gadebridge Park or Dicket Mead, near Welwyn, being good examples.[153] Here, as in other areas, the siting of villas on the margin of soils would suggest a fairly mixed type

28 Lockleys, Hertfordshire

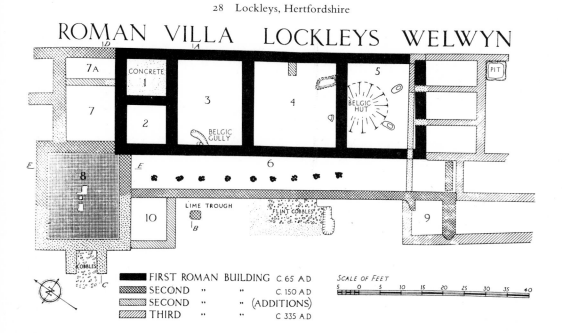

ROMAN VILLA LOCKLEYS WELWYN

FIRST ROMAN BUILDING C. 65 A D
SECOND " " C. 150 A D
SECOND " " (ADDITIONS)
THIRD " " C. 335 A D

SCALE OF FEET

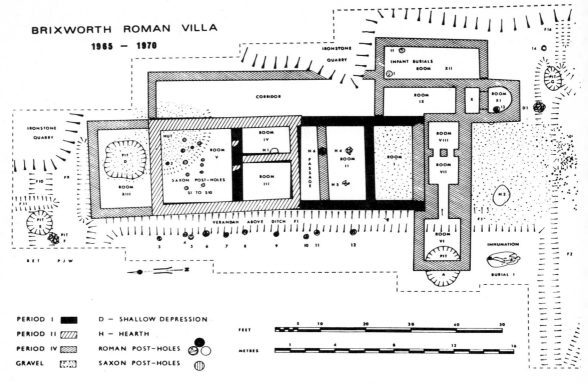

BRIXWORTH ROMAN VILLA
1965 — 1970

PERIOD I ■   D – SHALLOW DEPRESSION
PERIOD II ▨   H – HEARTH
PERIOD IV ▨   ROMAN POST-HOLES
GRAVEL ▨   SAXON POST-HOLES

29   Brixworth, Northamptonshire

of agriculture, and there are also signs of an interest in tile and pottery manufacture, particularly to the south of St Albans, where the important pottery site of Sulloniacae is situated at Brockley Hill.[154] Pottery is also the explanation, though in this case a rather more exclusive one, for the concentration of sites around Durobrivae, the centre for Castor ware.[155] The standard of luxury here is very marked, with mosaics, for example, being the rule rather than the exception, and Collingwood's picture of a flourishing industry run on a capitalist basis is supported by what we know of sites like Apethorpe, Whittlebury or Great Weldon, though recent work on such sites as Brixworth (*Fig. 29*) and Cosgrove has revealed a less lavish, more workaday side.[156] The main period of prosperity for the area was clearly the later third and early fourth centuries (though the seeds are rather earlier), and this ties in well with the growth of the British pottery industries following the collapse of the continental centres in the third-century troubles.

The comparative lack of villas in areas other than these is no doubt indicative of the level of wealth and of the degree of Romanization, though whether we can go any further towards explaining it is open to question. We shall need in due course to consider the suggestion that in this and similar parts of Britain the influence of Celtic custom and practice remained strong, and even if this is rejected there are plenty of other possibilities that might provide an answer, such as the extent of the territory associated with London, the possible existence of imperial lands, and so on. What we cannot assume without positive evidence is that the region was in any way backward agriculturally; on the contrary, as Applebaum has shown from a study of the known villas in Essex,[157] there was a marked tendency to occupy the heavier soils, or the lands along their margin, the implication being that the task of clearing woodland and extending the cultivated area was fairly energetically pursued.

The problems of ownership and tenure become more acute as we move into East Anglia proper, to the territories of the Trinovantes in north-east Essex and Suffolk, and to those of the Iceni in Norfolk, the first being complicated by the existence of the earliest *colonia* at Colchester and the second by the known estates of the client king Prasutagus.[158] A further factor, which must have had far-reaching consequences, was the great revolt of Boudicca in AD 60, in which the Trinovantes as well as the queen's own people, the Iceni, were involved; this might, for example, explain the comparative lack of Romanization, and could well have encouraged the Roman government to keep much of the territory under some kind of direct control, most obviously in the form of imperial lands. Whatever the explanation, villas are few and far between, a handful being sited to the south and west of Colchester, a few more in the northern part of Suffolk, which are perhaps associated with the nearby potteries, and a few more near the northern end of the Icknield Way. Of these we may mention the corridor villas at Gayton Thorpe and Lidgate,[159] the interesting aisled house at Exning in Suffolk,[160] and the large but not very luxurious site at Stanton Chair, near Ixworth, which Rivet has suggested may have been an administrative centre for Prasutagus' former estates.[161] It may be worth mentioning also that the site at Lidgate is on fairly heavy soil, so that the pattern detected by Applebaum in Essex seems to apply in this region also.

The territory of the Belgae, which covered most of Hampshire and Wiltshire, north Somerset and parts of Gloucestershire, was probably, like that of the Regni, an artificial creation, incorporating some of the former lands of the Atrebates and no doubt some from the Dobunni as well.[162] Within this fairly extensive area the distribution of villas is relatively simple: there are large numbers around the cantonal capital of Venta Belgarum at Winchester, with some also in the Isle of Wight, and a second concentration around Bath. From the area in between they are largely absent, in spite of the fact that this whole stretch of country (as is clear from a glance at the Ordnance Survey map of Roman Britain) was fairly thickly settled; the usual explanation is that the area might have been an imperial estate with its administrative centre at Old Sarum, and although there is little in the way of positive evidence this would at least make sense.[163] The villas around Winchester may be seen in general terms as continuing the pattern of those in Sussex, in that like them they tend to favour the southern slopes of the Downs, particularly where these are cut into by such rivers as the Test, the Itchen or the Meon. The picture generally is one of steadily flourishing establishments rather than of striking luxury, with the typical site beginning as a small aisled or corridor house like Clanville, near Andover, or Newport (Isle of Wight),[164] and developing by the addition of outbuildings into a courtyard villa in its later stages. Such, for example, are the sites at Sparsholt, near Winchester, and Stroud, near Petersfield, or (more impressively) those at Rockbourne, near Fordingbridge and Brading (Isle of Wight).[165] Signs of affluence, such as mosaics and painted wall plaster, are not uncommon, though by no means universal, and a striking feature of the area is the number of aisled buildings, either existing as villas in their own right, as at West Meon and North Warnborough, or fulfilling a subsidiary role in larger establishments, as at Brading and Sparsholt.[166] The pottery works of the New Forest, which Colling-wood long ago noted as being run on an individual small-scale basis, in contrast with the more capitalistic products of Castor ware to which we referred a moment ago,[167] were not apparently connected with any villas, though here as elsewhere a single site could change the picture radically.

Away to the west of the territory the villas around Bath are as rich and as numerous as those in any area of Britain, in keeping with the sophistication and economic importance of the city itself. They extend for up to 15 miles in all directions, particularly along the Avon to the port at Sea Mills and to the north and south along the roads to Cirencester and Ilchester respectively. Typical here are the great courtyard villas of Wellow and Pitney in Somerset, Atworth and Box in Wiltshire,[168] all on a scale to compare with the continental examples of an earlier period; mosaics are the rule, and many sites, such as Whatley or Keynsham or Newton St Loe, have several.[169] Here, clearly, there was wealth; here, if anywhere, are the final results of Romanization, with town and country linked in mutual dependence and profit. How much of this wealth was agricultural it is impossible to say: apart from the stone quarries near Bath itself, the only industries are the manufacture of pewter at Camerton and the extensive mining operations of the Mendips;[170] the latter, being under state control, were likely to be separate from the villa pattern as such, though the concentration of villas along the river Yeo between Charterhouse and the Bristol Channel would seem to suggest some kind of association. Whatever the sources of wealth, however, it is in this part of Britain that we see most strikingly that fourth-century expansion of villas which contrasts with the situation in so much of western Europe. The possible reasons for this will concern us later; our task for the moment, both here and in adjacent territories, is to record it.

Comparable to Bath in the number of villas that surround it, and to some extent also in their luxury, is the Roman town at Ilchester, which lay in the western part of the territory of the Durotriges.[171] Most of the sites that have been explored are corridor villas, though some of them, such as those at Littleton or Yeovil, had developed by their later stages into the full courtyard type with the addition of extensive outbuildings.[172] At some sites there is clear evidence of early occupation: at Catsgore,[173] for example, there is pottery and other material from the latter part of the first century. Elsewhere, as at Lufton and a site near

Ilchester itself,[174] the signs at present are that occupation did not begin until the late third century, and whatever the details on particular sites this was clearly the period of greatest prosperity for the area generally. As in the Bath region, mosaics are the rule, and some of them, such as those at Low Ham and Pitney, are justly famous.[175] The Low Ham site is near some important stone quarries, but these apart the wealth of the area was presumably in the first place agricultural; the town itself, certainly, was not particularly large or rich. Its status, indeed, is somewhat uncertain: the normal assumption is that the capital of the Durotrigan territory was at Dorchester, but there is reason to suppose that at some stage the western part became a separate unit, with Ilchester as its centre, though how this may have affected the siting of villas one cannot say. They are certainly less common around Dorchester, though one has to say that the examples we have are fairly prosperous, mosaics again being normal. Among them is the important villa at Hinton St Mary, which has yielded a mosaic with Christian motifs,[176] and there are major sites also at Dewlish, Frampton and Tarrant Hinton.[177]

Further west than this we do not need to go: with the exception of a few examples in the extreme east corner of Devon, which are presumably to be included with those of Dorset, there is an almost total lack of villas in the rest of the Dumnonian peninsula. Rivet acknowledges one example, that at Magor Farm, in the parish of Illogan, near Camborne,[178] but elsewhere the pattern is one of native sites and a low degree of Romanization. The same is understandably true of most of Wales, though the coastal plain in the south is something of an exception, with sites of some considerable interest at Llantwit Major, at Ely, on the outskirts of Cardiff, and most recently at Whitton, in the Vale of Glamorgan, where a complex series of timber and stone buildings within an enclosure ditch extended from the mid first to the mid fourth century AD.[179]

Most, if not all, of these South Wales sites were in the territory of the Silures, which probably extended over most of Monmouth and Glamorgan and parts of Brecknockshire.[180] The precise boundary between their territory and that of the Dobunni to the east of them is still unclear, but there is evidence to suggest that the latter extended beyond the Severn, and that much of Herefordshire, with Kenchester as a subsidiary centre, was part of their domain. The capital of the territory as a whole was at Cirencester, the Roman Corinium, which came to be one of the most important towns in Britain and may well in fact have been the capital of Britannia Prima in the reorganization of the late third century. Not surprisingly, the villas around it were both numerous and prosperous, among them being such sites as Chedworth and Woodchester, which, at least until the discovery of Fishbourne, were probably the most famous in the country.[181] Of the rest in the area we may mention, as representative examples, the big courtyard villas at Spoonley Wood, Tockington Park and Bisley,[182] and the corridor houses at Rodmarton, Frocester Court (*Fig.* 31) and Witcombe.[183] A further site, which will eventually assume a central role, not only in the study of this particular region, but in that of British villas generally, is the

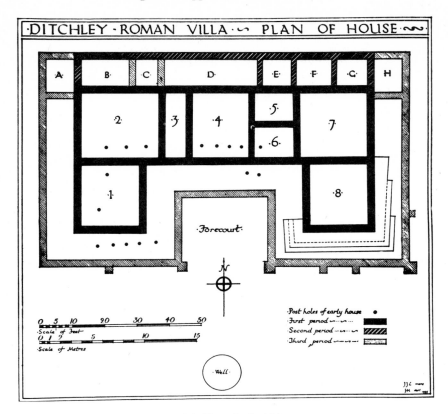

30   Ditchley, Oxfordshire

villa at Barnsley Park in Gloucestershire, where the nearest thing to a total excavation so far seen in Britain is slowly and carefully being achieved.[184] The prosperity of the area as a whole is reflected in the appointments and amenities of the various houses, particularly in the mosaic pavements, for which in the fourth century Cirencester itself was a major centre.[185] The primary source of wealth, both here and further away to the east, was presumably agriculture once again; one thinks especially of sheep, perhaps, in spite of the fact that Chedworth was not, as had once been thought, a fulling establishment,[186] though further evidence is needed before the detailed economy can be worked out with any certainty.

Particularly interesting in this respect are the numerous villas in the northern part of Oxfordshire, many of which, such as Ditchley (*Fig.* 30), Islip and Little Milton, are in ditched enclosures, and several, such as Callow Hill and Ditchley itself, are within the older circuit of the Oxfordshire Grim's Ditch.[187] Detailed work on Ditchley reveals a primary concern with grain production, but the nature of the country and the regular use of enclosures would seem to suggest that pastoral farming was also widely practised. The modest corridor house at Ditchley is certainly typical of the area, though there is a well-known courtyard

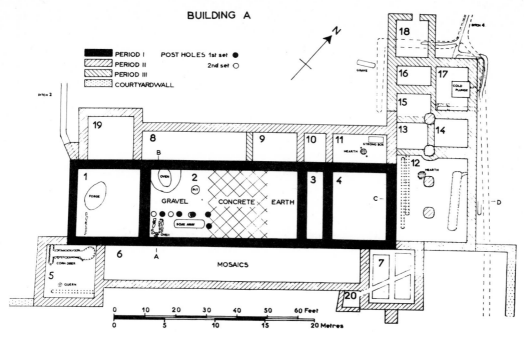

31 Frocester Court, Gloucestershire

villa with extensive associated buildings at North Leigh, on the other side of Akeman Street, and the mosaics discovered at the nearby site of Stonesfield suggest another more lavish establishment.[188]

Northwest of the Dobunni, and extending over most of Shropshire, Staffordshire and Cheshire, was the territory of the Cornovii, with its two main centres, the capital, Viroconium, at Wroxeter, and the extensive settlement attached to the legionary fortress at Chester.[189] The area seems not to have reached a very high degree of Romanization, and villas are comparatively rare; there are some around Wroxeter itself, and a few in Staffordshire, but they are absent, and understandably so, from the Cheshire Plain, where the most obvious sites are the legionary tile and pottery works at Holt. It is possible, as Rivet suggested, that some of the other industrial activities, such as the lead mines near Linley in Shropshire, may have been under military control, though it should be noted, as a possible indication to the contrary, that there are villas within the mining area at Acton Scott and Linley itself which may be associated with it.[190]

Away to the east from here lay the territory of the Coritani, which included Lincolnshire, Nottinghamshire and Leicestershire, together with Rutland and parts of Derbyshire.[191] Villas are rather more numerous here than among the Cornovii, though not perhaps as numerous as one might have thought, particularly in view of the importance of Lincoln as a centre of communications and the agricultural and other resources of the area generally. The majority of the sites are fairly modest in size and amenities, many of them consisting simply of single buildings of the aisled or corridor type; only three establishments, those at Norfolk Street, near Leicester, Southwell, in Nottinghamshire, and Scampton, five miles north of Lincoln, can be regarded as large or luxurious, on the scale of North Leigh, say, or Bignor.[192] There are, however, a number of sites which, though not lavish in their appointments, were well provided with the basic comforts, as well as the full range of farm buildings, and were clearly the centres of flourishing and prosperous estates; such, for example, are Thistleton Dyer (*Fig.* 45) and Empingham in Rutland, Winterton, in the far north of Lincolnshire, and also Mansfield Woodhouse (Nottinghamshire), Norton Disney (Lincolnshire) and Medbourne (Leicestershire).[193] The number of aisled buildings in the region is of some interest: they appear as subordinate buildings on sites like Empingham, Mansfield Woodhouse and Winterton (which, at the last count, had no less than four of them), and as villas in their own right at East Denton, Ancaster, Barholme and probably Wilsthorpe Mill (all in Lincolnshire).[194] Of interest also is the occurrence at sites like Winterton and Thistleton Dyer of circular huts – and this, in the case of Winterton certainly, at a date not earlier than AD 100; this, and the frequency of aisled houses, together with the suggestion from the evidence so far available that villas were comparatively slow to emerge in this part of Britain, seems to present a consistent, if not wholly explicable, picture.

As far as the distribution of sites is concerned, there is a tendency to favour the light and intermediate soils, particularly the sands and limestones of Lincolnshire, though a number of sites on heavier soil, such as the Keuper marl of eastern Nottinghamshire or the boulder clay of the Rockingham Forest east of Leicester, are in keeping with what we have seen in Essex and elsewhere. The nature of the economy is at present unclear: indications from some of the aisled buildings, most notably those at Winterton, would suggest fairly intensive corn production, while the existence at several sites, among them Lockington in Leicestershire, Cromwell in Nottinghamshire and Winterton itself, of ditched enclosures might argue for stock raising.[195] It is perhaps fair to say that at present the positive evidence for the latter is relatively scarce, though there may, as has been suggested,[196] be special reasons why this is so.

Once beyond the Humber there is little left of the Lowland Zone and few remaining villas. The territory of the Parisi, which corresponded roughly with the East Riding of Yorkshire,[197] included a number of examples, most of them associated with the *vici* at Petuaria (Brough-on-Humber) and at Malton. They tend to be modest establishments, comparable in many ways to those of the Coritani, and although some of them, such as Harpham, Brantingham and Rudston, had mosaic pavements, the style of those at the last-named site is such as to suggest that the level of Romanization could not have been very high.[198] We are, after all, at the edge of the civilian area: to the north and west lay Brigantian territory, which extended as far as the Irish Sea and perhaps to Hadrian's Wall; much of it was permanently garrisoned, the primary settlements were the *vici* attached to the forts, and villas were the exception rather than the rule. Of those that have been explored we may mention that at Beadlam, in the North Riding of Yorkshire, one of the most northerly in Britain,[199] and that at Castle Dykes, North Stainley, in the West Riding, which, like the similarly sited villa at Ely near Cardiff, was provided with a ditched enclosure.[200]

5

The Pattern of Agriculture
in the Western Provinces

We have tried, in the last two chapters, to see the villa in both its historical and geographical setting, and we shall begin in a moment to consider it as part of the social and economic life of the Roman world. Already, however, in interpreting its distribution in particular areas, or in assessing the effects upon it of wider historical movements, we have become involved in what is in fact its essential context, that of agriculture, and it may at this stage be useful, both as a summary of individual points already raised and as a way of preparing for what follows, to look at this context in both its Mediterranean and more northerly aspects.

For the Romans, as for the Greeks, agriculture was an honourable activity: to the respectability born of antiquity was added a belief that certain virtues and moral standards were bound up in it, and its fundamental role in the economy of the ancient world was reflected also in political theory and practice. Thus, to take a well-known example, it was utterly appropriate that when, in 458 BC, a deputation of senators sought out Cincinnatus as dictator of Rome at a moment of supreme crisis they should find him at the plough on his little three-acre farm,[1] and appropriate also that long after trade and commerce had begun to play their part in the Roman economy membership of the Roman senate was nevertheless confined to landowners.[2] For these and no doubt for other reasons we have a considerable corpus of agricultural literature, much of it written just before or during the early stages of the development of the villas, from which it is possible to obtain a fairly detailed picture, albeit in the first instance a theoretical one, of agriculture in the Mediterranean basin generally.[3] In a study of villas, of course, this is only the first stage: much of what we may call the villa area was not in the Mediterranean basin at all, so that we shall need to enquire to what extent Mediterranean practices were adapted to north-European conditions, and to what extent also this adaptation was the work of the Romans themselves, rather than the incorporation into their own system of practices already current or in the course of development in the conquered areas. There are, as one would expect, a number of problems in detail, but the overall picture is fairly clear.[4]

The influence which more than anything dominates Mediterranean agriculture, both in antiquity and in our own day, is the Mediterranean climate: consisting, at its simplest, of long dry summers and short wet winters, it imposes a basic pattern of farming practice which, though affected by varying soil quality, technical experience, or the changing economy, is in its essentials constant throughout the area. This pattern, known in other areas (such as America) where it occurs as 'dry farming', is essentially a system of making the most of what moisture is available by careful conservation and the avoidance of anything likely to reduce it.[5] The rains, when they come, are short-lived and heavy: the greatest danger is that they will run off the lands in floods, taking much of the topsoil with them, so care must be taken to keep the topsoil broken and well drained, thus guiding the water as quickly and directly as possible to the subsoil. Once there, and the young crop once established with its help, it is carefully husbanded: the soil must be kept clear of weeds, because anything growing competes with the crop for moisture, and regularly broken up to prevent the undue loss of moisture from the subsoil by capillary action. To get the benefit of the rains the staple crops of corn must be sown in autumn: spring corn was known to antiquity, but the evidence suggests that it was something of a rarity, sown only when the main crop had failed.[6] Thus any rotation system which made use of it was likely to be a rarity too. The almost universal system was the two-year one of alternate crop and fallow, the fallow year once again being devoted to the constant clearing and breaking of the soil to keep the moisture in. It is this need which underlies those features of Mediterranean ploughing which at first sight seem strange when viewed with northern eyes. The practice, for example, of ploughing the same piece of ground three, four or more times before sowing was not, as may appear at first sight, an attempt to compensate for an inferior implement, but a recognition of the need for a fine tilth to make best use of the water available.[7] True, the Mediterranean plough was, and is, a simple tool[8]: essentially a curved piece of wood for scratching the soil, its only real refinements were an iron share and a pair of pegs or boards which could be fitted to produce a ridging effect.[9] Lacking the mould board of the northern ploughs, it was incapable of turning a sod in the proper sense; but this was not what it was meant to do. The breaking up of the topsoil and the clearing away of weeds was something as easily and effectively done by a tool which scratched the ground as by one which turned over great slices of it and left it lying in clods.

Briefly, then, the sequence over the two-year period was as follows.[10] The seed corn was sown in October, after a final ploughing; during the winter care was taken to keep the growing corn free of weeds, and if necessary to thin it out, so that after the rains ceased from about March the moisture would not give out too early. Harvest came, in the western Mediterranean, in June or early July, after which the stubble was ploughed in; the burning of stubble was common, as was a period of grazing on it. The main ploughing would come in spring, from January to March, after which the land would lie fallow, though clean, until the process began again in the autumn. There were, of course, variations: in areas favoured with richer soil or wetter summers it was no doubt possible to omit the fallow year from time to time, and one must also remember that there were backward areas where a much looser system will have operated, with small plots of land being cultivated once and then left for years on end. Nevertheless, the basic simple pattern of alternate crop and fallow was widespread enough to be typical.

Corn, of course, was not the only crop, nor arable the only form of farming. The olive, which provided so many of the staple requirements of Greek and Roman life, is particularly suited to a 'dry farming' system because of its widespread root system, and also has the advantage of doing well on soils of only moderate quality.[11] The vine, the other member of the so-called 'Mediterranean triad', needs careful handling with regard to moisture, but is an obvious part of the picture in other respects.[12] The problem of moisture was solved in various ways: by allowing the vines to sprawl on the ground and so provide shade; by growing them on living trees with the same aim; or by raising clouds of dust to screen the sun. For pastoral as opposed to arable farming conditions were in some ways ideal and in others less so[13]: much of what alluvial pasture there was remained badly drained for a long time, and its use was no doubt limited by diseases in general and by such things as liver fluke in particular. The tendency was to use it for winter feeding and to rely for summer grazing (apart from limited use of the fallow and controlled grazing of growing corn to thin it out) on the rough scrub of the upper mountain slopes – in other words, to adopt a pattern of transhumance. This, of course, is linked wherever it occurs with a whole cycle of practices: the fact that animals are away from home in the summer means that the farm land is deprived of a major source of manure; this in turn makes the growing of fodder crops difficult – a problem which arises already from the long summer drought – and thus removes a valuable supply of winter food, which in turn leads back to transhumance to make up the deficiency. In other words, by pastoral farming in the Mediterranean we mean sheep and goats rather than cattle, and a concentration on milk products and wool rather than on meat.

To describe the farming pattern as briefly as this is to emphasize its simplicity, and simple it was; but it would be a mistake to regard it as primitive. There is in farming communities a collective inherited wisdom which is something apart from technological or scientific advance; the individual peasant farmer may not be aware of the technical reasons for what he does, and he is not likely to have a shelf full of manuals to refer to, but based as they are on generations of experience his methods can be said to be sophisticated in something other than the obvious sense. Nevertheless, the point should not be overstated: granted that the Mediterranean farmer may have done things that were right without exactly knowing why (such as burning the stubble, and so restoring potash and other nutrients to the soil), it is also true that there were many things that he did not do, or did only occasionally, because he lacked the scientific knowledge which might have prompted them.

Soil science is a good example: the Roman agricultural writers have quite a detailed vocabulary to describe all the different textures of soils in terms of the substances they contain, and clearly a great deal of knowledge was available on the suitability of certain crops to certain soil types.[14] Much of this could now be translated into scientific terminology and many of the precepts validated as a result, but what validated them in antiquity was not science but effectiveness in practice. It was the same lack of scientific knowledge, no doubt, which prevented any widespread development of crop-rotation schemes: the common attitude was that if a soil showed itself suited to a particular crop it should be given that crop to grow as much as possible, with the fallow year providing the necessary rest. When a rotation system seems to operate it is often prompted by something rather different from what we would expect, a crop of spring corn because the autumn one had failed, or an extra crop instead of the normal fallow because of an unusually damp summer.[15] That is to say, the aim was to exploit conditions so as to get the most possible out of the soil, rather than to nurse the soil by putting something into it. Manuring, it is true, was another matter, though as we have seen the practice of transhumance removed much of the richest potential source. To make good the deficiency all kinds of materials were resorted to: apart from human manure, about which the ancients seem not to have been at all squeamish, the droppings of poultry, pigeons and such animals as were stall fed were carefully collected, and the technical writers give detailed instructions also for the production and use of compost. There is also plenty of evidence for green manuring, that is to say the ploughing in of a crop while still green, and for the use of certain limes and marls.[16] It is worth noting that these kinds of practices, based as they were on individual experience in particular areas, will have been more varied, and in total more impressive, than they are in the agricultural textbooks, though for the same reasons the possibilities for sharing experience and thus for technical advance will, outside of the textbooks, have been limited.

The same kind of localism seems to have affected even technological progress, though this is of course part of a much larger question. The list of fairly advanced devices and systems available to Roman farming is in fact considerable, but many of them seem to have been restricted to the particular areas or conditions which gave rise to them. The reasons were complex, but the effect was to make Roman agriculture in many ways potentially advanced rather than actually so. One of the most famous examples of this is the reaping machine described first by Pliny the Elder and later in a more developed form by Palladius,[17] which seems from the examples so far discovered to have been confined to one small area, and that outside the Mediterranean basin (*Fig.* 32). The watermill too, of which some fine examples are known, was much rarer than one might have supposed;[18] the regular method of corn grinding was the hand quern, to which the Romans contributed some refinements in design rather than supplanting it by something more advanced. Why this should be so is not an easy question to answer: one factor, no doubt, will have been the ready availability, for much of the Roman period, of cheap manual labour, and another perhaps the predominance within the Roman world of the small peasant proprietor, who would lack both the capital

32   Relief from Buzenol in southern Belgium, showing the front part of a harvesting machine, or *vallus*

for such advances and also the motivation for adopting them. The result, at any rate, was that unless conditions made some sort of expedient necessary it was more convenient, even more agreeable, not to make the effort. A good illustration again is irrigation[19]: where the factors of labour, capital and adverse natural conditions all combined the standard of achievement was spectacular. The inheritance from other cultures was considerable, most notably of course from Egypt but also to a lesser extent from Carthage and nearer home from the Etruscans; but the vast irrigation systems of North Africa, or the systems of aqueducts round Rome and other Italian cities, represent a high level, not only of technological skill, but also of administrative expertise on a grand scale. Here again, however, the labour question is important, though from a rather different point of view: whereas in most cases it is the availability of labour which, one feels, inhibited technological progress, in the case of irrigation schemes it is this same availability which both prompts progress and maintains it. Indeed, the fall-off of labour, or the preoccupation of labourers with such other things as war or social upheaval, can here have catastrophic effects: the loss of hundreds of thousands of acres of arable land in fifth-century Africa as a result of a failure to maintain the water systems has rightly been quoted as an example of what could happen.[20]

The question of labour availability is relevant also to another branch of Mediterranean farming which we have so far passed over, namely the intensive cultivation of relatively small plots of land in a manner not unlike that of a modern smallholding or market garden.[21] There are many examples in Roman literature of such cultivation, from Virgil's old man of Tarentum, whose plot was unsuited to corn or vines or the raising of cattle, but whose labour nevertheless produced results,[22] to the enterprising farmer at Tabace in Africa, who contrived to grow palms, olives, vines, figs and corn all in a single field.[23] The basis of this, as of the irrigation schemes, was constant devoted attention, and each was successful only so long as this attention was readily available. In more general terms this is true of the 'dry farming' system as a whole: Columella allows four days to plough a *jugerum* (about two-thirds of an acre),[24] so that the repeated ploughing needed by even a comparatively small amount of land will have taken up a considerable amount of time, to say nothing of the weeding and other attention which was equally necessary. The fact that most ancient descriptions of paradise include a reference to the land giving of its bounties unbidden is a fairly clear indication that things in the real world were rather different; any relaxation of effort on the part of the farmer was rapidly reflected, not only in falling yields, but in more fundamental ways still – even, in extreme cases, in the virtual disappearance of the soil itself.

In these respects at least the prospects outside the Mediterranean basin were more encouraging. The unpredictability of the weather and the cooler, wetter climate, unattractive as it may have been on first experience, at least had the advantage of maintaining almost perpetual moisture in the soil and so relieving the northern farmer of one of the basic anxieties felt by his southern counterpart. It may well be that the first reaction of a Mediterranean visitor to Britain or northern Gaul was negative rather than positive. Of the three main crops in the world he knew, two, the vine and the olive, seemed not to exist, while the third, though apparently as basic here as at home, seemed less than attractive in a climate which made harvest a scramble and storage a permanent headache.[25] The greenness of the landscape may have prompted the thought that here, as in favoured parts of Italy, it might be possible to take a crop for several years on end without a fallow, but this will have seemed poor compensation for the more obvious and immediate disadvantages. As it turned out, of course, the disadvantages were not as great as may have appeared: the impression of permanent mist and overcast skies, which we find, for example, in Tacitus,[26] is not (one has to admit) a fair one, and the difficulties of a wet summer were merely a spur to greater efficiency and improved agricultural techniques. One of the more visible Roman influences on north-European farming is the improved corn-drying oven,[27] which must have gone far towards coping with the problem of storage, and the development of the scythe and a properly balanced sickle,[28] apart from the consequences which will appear in a moment, at least helped to speed the harvest itself.

But to see the north-European situation in terms of its disadvantages, real or only apparent, is to misunderstand it: it is not a Mediterranean world that has fallen from grace, but a world with its own character, and with burdens and bounties of its own. Contrasts indeed there are, but they are contrasts, not between two varieties of a single system, but between two largely separate ones. The cooler, wetter summers are a case in point: they are not merely a hindrance to harvesting on the one hand or a help to irrigation on the other, but the basis of a different farming system, with different priorities and different motives for what may often be very similar operations. Mediterranean farming, as we saw, was dominated by the need to preserve moisture, and most of the regular farming procedures are explicable in these terms; but take away the need, and the whole pattern changes accordingly. The growing crop will still need to be kept clear of weeds, but since moisture is no longer a precious commodity the fallow can be left to grow wild until the time comes to use it once again, so providing grazing for the livestock and a useful means of collecting manure for the eventual crop. Instead of ploughing to prevent weeds growing, the way is now clear to let the weeds grow and then plough them in, and the need for repeated cross ploughing no longer exists. Above all, the constant care and attention demanded of the Mediterranean farmer is replaced in the north essentially by a need to watch the weather, and instead of a fairly rigid system imposed by soil and climate we have at least the chance of flexibility.

Whether the chance was taken, and how extensively, it is not always easy to decide. The great advantage of the northern summer is that it makes possible the cultivation of spring corn, which as we have suggested was the exception rather than the rule further south. No doubt the point was well appreciated, but whether the more basic advantage – that spring corn was the key to a more sophisticated system of crop rotation – was at all extensively exploited is a matter of some debate.[29] There is some evidence, certainly, for a system based on winter corn, spring corn and fallow, and it has been claimed that the final development of replacing the fallow with a fodder crop was also achieved in some areas in the Roman period. This is not perhaps the place to consider the details of particular examples, but it may be worthwhile to look a little further at the possibilities. As we have seen, the establishment of a proper three-year system, even in areas favoured with exceptional climate or soil quality, involves a whole new pattern of farming which has to be adopted all together. The pattern starts with the need

33   Roman scythe: the Great Chesterford example has a blade of 5 feet 4 inches

for an adequate supply of manure, to be obtained, not only from casual grazing of the fallow or the growing crop, but from the quartering of animals on the farm itself for as much of the year as possible. This in turn gives rise to the problem of food, which may come from the simple three-year system in the form of a surplus of corn, or from the more developed one in the form of both corn and fodder crops. Apart from the evidence of outbuildings, the occasional finds of seeds, and the interpretation of field systems, there are one or two other items which individually make it clear that the pattern was possible, and collectively go far towards proving its existence in practice. Chief among them is the scythe already mentioned (*Figs* 33, 34): the great advantage of the true scythe (as opposed to one with the blade and handle in the same plane), and to a lesser extent

34   Roman scythes: those from the fort at Newstead are of the more common, single-handed, type

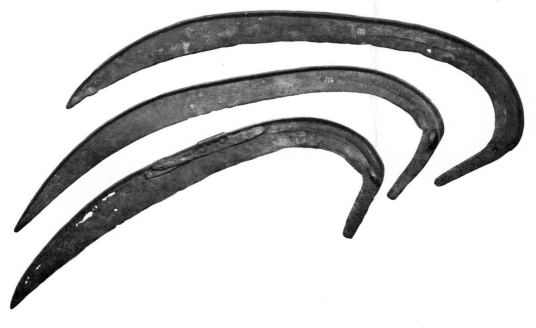

of the properly balanced sickle, was that it enabled reaping to be done at ground level rather than high up on the stalk, and it is hard to see why this should be done except to provide litter for animals, or, if we include hay as well as corn, to increase the supply of winter food.[30] The technique of well-digging too, which again is one of the more obvious contributions of the Romans to north-European agriculture, though presumably developed primarily for humans, will also have greatly assisted the quartering of animals.[31] Given all this it would be surprising, to say the least, if no advance was made beyond the two-year, crop-and-fallow pattern, and we are probably justified in assuming that the more sophisticated systems existed, even if it is not always easy to pin down the individual examples of them.

There is, however, one item for which mere assumption is hardly sufficient. Ploughing as we know it, and as already assumed in the practice of ploughing in weeds, requires an implement capable, not simply of scratching the surface and cutting off weeds at the root, but of actually turning a sod. It is true that the Mediterranean plough, as described for example by Virgil, was capable of doing this,[32] but since the effect was achieved by tilting the whole plough and moving a second time along a furrow already cut it is hard to believe that it was normal practice, and for any but the lightest soils we are probably justified in supposing that something extra in design and construction would be necessary. Two

35   Bronze model of a plough team from Piercebridge, Co. Durham

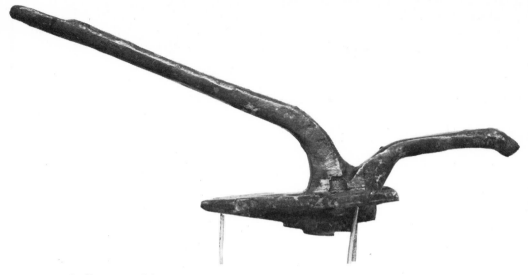

36   Bronze model of a plough from Sussex: the plough is of the 'bow ard' type

things, basically, are needed: a heavy coulter to cut more deeply into the soil, and a mould board to turn the earth over as it is cut. A third requirement is sometimes mentioned, namely the provision of wheels, but although this might seem desirable to enable the larger and heavier implement to be more easily manoeuvred, it does not appear to be essential. Wheeled ploughs are mentioned for Raetia by the elder Pliny, writing in the first century AD, and for northern Italy by Servius, the commentator on Virgil, writing in the fourth,[33] but there is no archaeological or literary evidence for them in Britain or Gaul, and one should not therefore place too much emphasis on them. Of the two things mentioned as being essential, coulters, being made of iron, survive in a number of examples; on their own, they do not prove the existence of the 'true' plough, since it has been shown that they could be used on such things as the Scandinavian bow ard, which was basically the same as the Mediterranean plough[34] (*Fig.* 36). On the other hand, the 'true' plough is impossible without them, and their occurrence is at least a first stage in proving its existence. The use of mould boards is more difficult to establish, since being made of wood they will not normally have survived; but there are some indications that they were in use in some areas in the later Roman period. They would, first of all, be a logical development of the so-called *aures* ('ears'), or ground wrests, of the Mediterranean plough, which were used to form ridges to cover the seeds and provide surface drainage.[35] They would also seem to be implied by the appearance at one or two sites in Roman Britain of asymmetrical shares, which were used presumably in combination with a mould board fixed permanently to one side of the plough.[36]

When this development might have occurred is difficult to say with certainty, though the evidence once quoted for advances in the Belgic period has now been largely discredited.[37] For Britain at any rate a later date seems likely on present evidence, and there is some support for the mid fourth century as the most appropriate period, though the small amount of material and the element of chance in its preservation make certainty out of the question.[38] For the Continent, the reference to a heavier wheeled plough in Pliny would suggest an earlier date, and the fact that the words for such a plough in most European languages are non-Latin could well point in the same direction. It is of course unfortunate that we cannot at the moment be more precise, because the implications of the heavier plough are considerable. What must be borne in mind, however, is that it would always be an alternative to the lighter or coultered ard rather than a complete substitute, and that throughout the Roman period and beyond the various kinds of plough will have existed side by side. Indeed, the evidence at present is such that unless there is definite indication of the heavier implement in a given area we would be wrong to assume its existence.

Where it does occur, of course, its possible effects, not only on farming itself but on the wider social patterns, are numerous indeed. The need for larger plough teams, for example, raises a number of crucial questions: if a team of, say, up to eight oxen was beyond the means of the average peasant farmer, are we to suppose that the heavier plough was confined to great landowners, or was there some degree of co-operation as there was in the Middle Ages? Such questions as these are perhaps more relevant to a later chapter, but there is one feature that can be dealt with here, namely the possibility, as a result of the heavier plough, of extending cultivation to the heavier loams and clays. As is well known, the tendency in the Roman period was to concentrate settlement on the lighter sands, gravels or loess of the valleys and the chalks and oolite soils of the uplands, but the work of Sir Cyril Fox in the Cambridge region, and more recent work also in Essex and Kent, has revealed a quite striking programme of expansion into soils which, because of the need for aeration, could only really be tackled with a plough that could turn a sod, and do so as a normal part of its function rather than as a temporary contrivance.[39] Detailed work in other areas, notably parts of Gaul, will no doubt improve what at the moment is only a partial picture, but there seems little doubt that the first major onslaught on the richer but heavier soils was made in the Roman period with a plough of the type described. From this end too the dating is difficult: further evidence may suggest otherwise, but it seems likely that on the Continent the process began early and petered out in the course of the third century, whereas in Britain the main achievements were made in the fourth century, with little or no activity earlier.[40] This would at least tie in with the suggested dating of the ploughs themselves, but much more work needs to be done to make this more than a provisional hypothesis.

The difficulty here, as with all the technical and other advances made in the Roman period, is to know the extent of their adoption and hence their comparative importance. Such factors as economic and social conditions, or the availability of labour and capital, can be allowed for in general terms, but other factors, such as the speed at which new techniques were likely to spread, the degree of willingness to adopt them, or the supply of craftsmen able to make the necessary implements, are much less easy to be sure about. And underlying the whole question is a serious uncertainty about the ability of ancient farmers to plan ahead, particularly in the matter of costing and general accounting, without which any large-scale changes in farming practice, at least on a voluntary basis, would obviously be impracticable. It has been argued, for example, that ancient accounting methods were designed primarily for preventing embezzlement and pilfering by officials or servants, and that a system of 'rational farming', with calculation of investments in stock and equipment, rate of profit and so on, did not appear in Europe until the work of Arthur Young in the later eighteenth century.[41] It may well be that this is going too far: the Roman theorists – Cato, Varro, Columella and the rest – are certainly cost conscious, and it would be wrong to underestimate the natural shrewdness of the practical farmer simply because it finds no expression in tidy balance sheets. Nevertheless, in a world with high interest rates and only a rudimentary mortgage system the problem of capital must have been considerable, and it would clearly be wrong to assume anything like modern standards in even the more advanced areas. Another serious problem as far as 'rational farming' was concerned was the unpredictability of harvests and the great variation in yield from year to year; this, of course, is a problem for farming in any age, but we would probably be right in assuming that in the Roman world the variations were far more extreme than now. The failure to stabilize prices, the high cost of inland transport, and the widespread exploitation of exceptionally good or bad seasons by speculators, will all have exaggerated the difficulties, but even without these there is plenty of evidence for the view that farming in antiquity was often extremely precarious. Add this to the proverbial conservatism of farming communities, and the barriers to progress might begin to seem almost insurmountable. Certainly it would be wrong to assume more than a small measure of uniformity: there will have been estates on which advanced methods and a high level of efficiency were achieved, but there will also have been areas virtually untouched by progress, where pre-Roman methods still operated. The diversity of agricultural practice in the early Middle Ages is warning enough of the dangers of generalization.

6

Villa Society and Tenure Patterns

A point which we have made a number of times already is that the villas should be seen, not in isolation, but as part of a wider social and economic framework. This is not to suggest, of course, that over the whole area within which villas occur the framework was everywhere the same, still less that it remained so throughout the several centuries of their existence. It may be that in a very basic sense they were all part of a single culture, in that they fell within the Roman Empire and were governed, at any rate nominally, by Roman administrative practice; but this, as we shall see, may not mean very much, and we are better advised, if we wish to set them in any meaningful context, to concentrate on a rather more local level. Thus in the present chapter, which is primarily concerned with social questions, and also in the next, which will deal with the more economic aspects, we shall confine ourselves largely to Gaul and Britain, since it is from these areas that the bulk of our detailed information comes. We cannot, however, remove ourselves entirely from general considerations, if only because so much of our material is itself of a general character. The broader patterns of social and economic change, reflected as they often are in particular areas and on individual villa sites, are nevertheless documented in literary and other sources of considerably wider reference. The main imperial institutions, similarly, are set out in lawbooks and other documents of an official nature, which are fairly general in their application. Such patterns and institutions will need to be illustrated from particular sites and areas, but it is doubtful whether the sites themselves would give us more than a vague and tentative picture without the more general material, which, whatever the problems involved in its interpretation, is at least direct and not the result of inference. This being so, a brief summary of what we may call the general background will not be out of place.

According to tradition the Romans were peasant proprietors. Stories such as that of Cincinnatus, to which we referred in an earlier chapter,[1] depict a society in which even prominent statesmen were content with a small family farm, which they worked with their own hands and from which they drew their basic daily requirements. Whether it was ever quite like this may well be doubted:

we know that from an early date (though perhaps not as early as the period of the kings, to which it is traditionally assigned) there was a system of social and political classes based on the ownership of land, and even if we do not accept the detailed figures provided by the sources it is clear that there was always a considerable disparity between the larger and smaller owners.[2] Even so, it was not until the enormous expansion of Rome in the third and second centuries BC, and in particular the second Punic war, which was fought on Italian soil, that fears began to be expressed for the smaller peasant farmers who had hitherto been the basis of Roman military strength. The effects of the expansion period are well known[3]: the new wealth borne of conquest was unevenly distributed, rich men had money to invest and poor men, their farms laid waste and neglected through years of campaigning, had land to sell. The great holdings thus accumulated could now be worked by slaves, who had become plentiful as a result of the wars, and were frequently converted to stock-raising as part of the same process. The dispossessed peasantry moved to the towns, and became the urban mob that we know from contemporary orators and historians. The picture, it must be said, is easily exaggerated: much was done to restore the small proprietor, either by the allotment of state-owned land (the so-called *ager publicus*) or by the settlement of citizens and veteran soldiers in new colonial foundations. The elder Pliny, writing in the mid first century AD, could claim that the great estates had been the ruin of Italy,[4] but it is doubtful whether in his day this was more than an emotional exaggeration. The fact that the writer Salvian was making the same complaint for Gaul some four centuries later[5] may suggest that it was a fashionable thing to say, and that the small farmer was in fact more tenacious. More important, even by Pliny's day and certainly later, the rise of the great estate had been largely counteracted by the increasing tendency for landowners to lease their property to small tenant farmers, the result being that, although the pattern of ownership had changed for good, the unit of tenure was much the same as ever. Pliny's nephew, writing a generation or so later about his own estates, describes a pattern which was to become increasingly common, that of tenant farmers, or *coloni*, paying for their holdings in money or produce but operating in other respects as if the farms were their own.[6]

The picture was not everywhere the same, and it was to be some time before it established itself to any extent in the provinces; even in Italy there will have been many estates which continued to be directly worked, either by slaves or free labourers, and many more in which only part was leased out and the rest retained as a unit. Nor should we assume a sharp division between the great landowners on the one hand and the small peasant proprietors on the other: the size of estates is not a subject on which we have a great deal of evidence at this period, but from what we know later of the lands attached to villas it seems likely that the whole range from large to small existed. But the basic pattern, of estates of varying size and character, some of them worked directly by the owner or by his work force and others leased to *coloni*, is fairly clear, and it is this pattern, and the developments of it, with which we shall from now on be concerned.[7]

The origins of the colonate are obscure, and need not concern us in detail. It seems that in its early stages the lease was for a fixed period, normally five but sometimes four years or less, after which the holding could revert to the owner. One can imagine, however, that it was often in the interests of owner and *colonus* alike to make the term indefinite, or at least to renew the arrangement more or less automatically, and there is evidence early on of holdings being passed from father to son on a seemingly permanent basis. Whatever the motives of the people involved, however, the tendency towards a perpetual tenure was in due course to become part of a much more fundamental process – a process whereby, to use the words of A.H.M. Jones, 'the *colonus* of the principate, a voluntary tenant of land, free to move when his lease expired, became the *colonus* of the later Empire, a serf tied to the land by a hereditary bond.[8]' The later stages of this process are illustrated by the lawbooks in clear and explicit terms: a law of Constantine of AD 332[9] provides for the chaining of *coloni* to prevent them leaving their holdings and so escaping their responsibilities, and a reference to *coloni* and their sons and grandsons in a law of AD 364[10] suggests that by this date the obligations were hereditary; by the 390s the emperor Theodosius I could decree that *coloni* in Thrace were the slaves of the land to which they were born, and had no right to leave it and go elsewhere.[11] This last enactment, as Jones pointed out, reveals that the original pretext for binding *coloni* in this way was to ensure the payment of the poll tax, probably at the time of its reorganization by Diocletian, and this is supported by the fact that 'free' proprietors as well as *coloni* were by this date tied to the place where they were registered. Indeed, by the end of the Roman period virtually the whole of society had become fossilized into what was virtually a system of castes, which affected town as well as country, trades and professions as well as agriculture, and great men as well as small.[12] Clearly, this was not a sudden transformation, but rather a gradual process, and although we are unable to trace its various stages in as much detail as we would like the overall pace and timing can be readily imagined. Jones is no doubt right to link the tightening up of the colonate with Diocletian, and it is likely in general terms that the restrictive tendencies affecting rural and other society were part of the price that had to be paid for recovery from the near disaster of the third century. But the beginnings of the process are earlier than this, and are related, not so much to legislation or other official action from above, but rather to the behaviour of the people involved.

The rise of the prosperous villa, based on the production of an agricultural surplus and the acquisition of luxury amenities, must reflect the emergence, if not of a rural aristocracy, at least of some kind of squirearchy. Who these people were, and what their origins, is not of immediate relevance, though we shall return to the question later; what matters is that the kind of pattern which these villas represent must at an early date have been to a certain extent seigneurial. In Gaul and elsewhere on the Continent such villas were well established by the Antonine period, and in some cases rather earlier; even in Britain, where the development was later and slower, they were in existence before the third-century recession. The individual estates on which such early seigneurial features can be documented are mostly imperial ones, and it is likely that they led the way to a certain extent; the best known are those of the upper Bagradas Valley in North Africa, which have yielded a series of inscriptions from the reign of Trajan onwards,[13] and where the detailed machinery of the colonate in the form of rents in kind and labour services was accompanied by what can only be called seigneurial attitudes from the *coloni* themselves as well as from the owners. What precisely the tenants of an estate near Souk-el-Khmis may have meant when, in about AD 180, they described themselves to the emperor as *rustici tui vernulae et alumni*[14] is perhaps open to question; but the tone is unmistakable, and makes it easy for us to understand how the early stages of the seigneurialization process could have been attractive to those on both sides of the colonate system. As time went on, both the attitudes and the institutional machinery were further developed: the later Empire can provide evidence, not only for labour services, but also for such things as gifts made by *coloni* to their landlord at certain times of year, and there is also the practice, referred to elsewhere, by which *coloni* and other small farmers or tradesmen attached themselves for protection to local

37 A panel from the great funerary column at Igel, near Trier, apparently showing payments being made by dependent farmers

38   Relief panel from a funerary monument at Neumagen: farmers making payments in kind

notables.[15] Not surprisingly, the law reflected and encouraged such tendencies: after 365 a landlord could intervene if a *colonus* wished to dispose of his own property, by the 390s he was given virtual immunity from legal action by his *coloni*, and in due course could prevent them, if he so wished, from joining the army, the civil service or the church.[16]

It is not our purpose, however, to sit in judgement of the system, the rights and wrongs of which have been many times debated before, but to see how its development is reflected in the villas and associated sites of the western provinces. For the legal relationship of landlord and *colonus* we need to provide physical illustration: what, we must ask, did the relationship look like on the ground, how can we tell that one site is so related to another, is there anything about the plan or size or character of a site which tells us that it belonged to a *colonus* or that it was the centre of a colonate system? It may be that, as Professor Rivet has wisely remarked,[17] a villa's land-tenure pattern is not something that lends itself to excavation, but there are nevertheless a number of ways in which the kind of relationship that we have been discussing can in principle be detected. First, we may point to areas in which larger and smaller villas, or villas and sites of a native character, are associated in such a way as to suggest some kind of inter-dependence; naturally, this is likely to be a subjective matter, and more precise evidence will be needed to convince an observer for whom the sites in question offer no such suggestion. Second, therefore, is the detection of linking evidence, or features that the sites in a given area have in common; one looks, not only for similarities in building techniques or ground plans, or even for similar patterns of prosperity and decline, since these may not be significant, but for areas where a sudden change of emphasis (for example, from arable to stock farming) affects a number of sites simultaneously, or where changes in one site, such as its extension or contraction, seem to be meaningfully related to changes in another. And third, in sites which have been carefully and comprehensively excavated, it may be possible to discover internal features which indicate their role as centres of a wider system – features, that is, which make better sense (or *only* make sense) if the sites are considered in association with others.[18] We should perhaps add a further possibility, that a system of interdependency might in principle emerge from a study of field patterns; but, as we shall see, this kind of study has yet to produce the kind of evidence we need, so that it remains a theoretical, rather than an actual, source of enlightenment. The other approaches, however, can be looked at in more detail.

Wherever a group of villas occurs within a reasonably well-defined area, particularly if one of them is larger or more luxurious than the rest, there is a natural temptation to see them as part of a single estate and to think in terms of colonate holdings. One of the earliest and most spectacular examples of this is the area around the great villa of Chiragan (Hte-Garonne), which ever since its exploration and analysis by Joulin at the turn of the last century has been an essential starting point for studies of this kind[19] (*Fig.* 39). The villa itself, both

39   The villa of Chiragan (Hte-Garonne) and associated sites

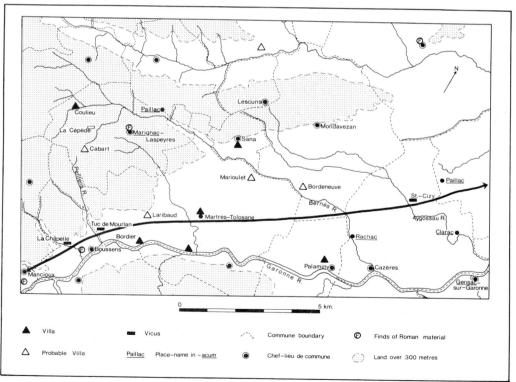

from its size (within its enclosure wall it covers some 16 hectares) and from its obviously agricultural character, must have controlled a considerable area of territory, and such is the geography of the region that the main outlines of this territory are not too difficult to establish. The villa stands on the left bank of the Garonne, and looks across the river to hills which rise rapidly to 300m and more; some 4km to the south west, at the village of Boussens, the valley narrows until it is only a few hundred metres across, providing a natural boundary which was in fact that between the two *civitates* of the Convenae and the Tolosates, in the latter of which the villa, and presumably most of its lands, were situated. With the hills to north and south providing the other boundaries, the only doubt is in the east, since the valley widens in this direction and there is no natural limit; the normal assumption, admittedly without much justification, is that the boundary lies somewhere in the region of Cazères, about 6½km away from the central villa. Within the area so defined there are at least four villas apart from Chiragan itself, together with three known village sites and numerous other places where buildings or Roman occupation material have been found. We shall, in a moment, need to look at all this in a little more detail, but simply by listing the sites and briefly studying the area in which they occur it is easy enough to convince oneself that some kind of colonate system was here in operation.

More recently the work of M. Georges Fouet on the villa of Montmaurin in the same *département* has revealed a similar pattern[20] (*Fig.* 40). Here the villa is comparable in size to that of Chiragan, there are several villas and other sites in the neighbourhood, and we have the additional advantage that the area within the central villa's control can be detected, not by geographical or archaeological considerations alone, but apparently also from documentary evidence. The group of parishes in which it lies was known from medieval times at least as Nébouzan, a name which derives from the probable estate name *Nepotianus*, and there is every possibility that this in fact preserves the outlines at any rate of the Montmaurin villa's estate. Again, we shall need to return for the details, but again the pattern of subsidiary farms seems clear enough.

There are, understandably, very few areas where we can speak with as much confidence, but both in Gaul and Britain there are plenty of villas for which we can provide both an area of operation and a series of possible dependencies with some degree of plausibility. Such, for example, is the villa of Neerhaven, in the Belgian province of Limburg, a large and fairly prosperous site which is surrounded, in Neerhaven itself and the neighbouring commune of Rekem, by at least five points at which Roman material has been found.[21] In isolation this may not seem very much, but as soon as one looks at the region as a whole it becomes a good deal more significant; for several kilometres in any direction evidence of Roman settlement is lacking, and what we have is an island of cultivation in an otherwise undeveloped tract of country. It thus becomes natural to see the main villa as the centre of operations, and to link the subsidiary sites to it as dependencies of some kind. A similar situation occurs in the commune of Draguignan (Var): in this case we have a naturally defined

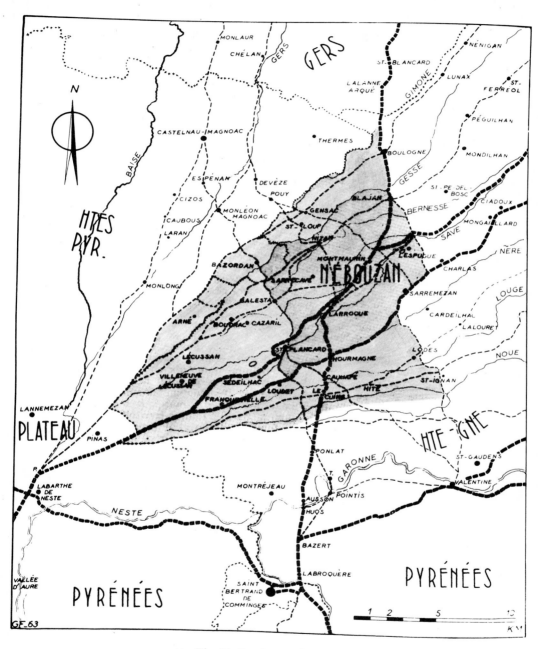

MONLAUR
CHÉLAN
GERS
GERS
ST·BLANCARD
NÉNIGAN
LUNAX
LALANNE
ARQUÉ
GIMONE
ST·
FERREOL
PÉGUILHAN
N
CASTELNAU·IMAGNOAC
THERMES
BOULOGNE
MONDILHAN
BAISE
HTES
PYR.
ESPÉNAN
DEVÈZE
POUY
GESSE
ST·PE·DEL·
BOSC
CIADOUX
CIZOS
BLAJAN
BERNESSE
MONGAILLARD
CAUBOUS
MONLÉON
MAGNOAC
GENSAC
ST·LOUP
SAVE
LARAN
NIZAN
LESPUGUE
NÈRE
MONTMAURIN
CHARLAS
BAZORDAN
NÉBOUZAN
MONLONG
SARRECAVE
SARREMEZAN
LOUGE
SALESTA
LARROQUE
CARDEILHAC
ARNÉ
BOUCHAC CAZARIL
LALOURET
LÉCUSSAN
ST·PLANCARD
HOURMAGNE
LODES
NOUE
VILLENEUVE
DE
LÉCUSSAN
SEDEILHAC
O
CAUMPE
ST·IGNAN
FRANQUEVIELLE
LOUDET
LE·
CUING
HITE
LANNEMEZAN
PLATEAU
PINAS
HTE·GNE
P.
PONLAT
ST·GAUDENS
LABARTHE
DE
NESTE
MONTRÉJEAU
GARONNE
AUSSON
FOINTIS
VALENTINE
NESTE
HUOS
VALLÉE
D'AURE
BAZERT
PYRÉNÉES
PYRÉNÉES
LABROQUÈRE
SAINT
BERTRAND
DE
COMMINGES
GF·63
1 2 5 10
KM.

40   The Medieval *pays* of Nébouzan

area – the valley of the Nartuby, bounded by wooded hills and barely 2km across at its greatest extent – crossed by a major Roman road, and containing once again a large and luxurious villa at St-Hermentaire.[22] Like Chiragan, the villa is at the southern edge of the valley, and along this and the northern edge are a number of smaller sites. We cannot, obviously, claim all of them as dependencies without more detailed proof, but we do at least have a clearly defined area with an obviously agricultural centre, and we can claim to have isolated a colonate structure at least to this general extent. Elsewhere we are less fortunate, but can still make the general claim. The commune of Chateau-ponsac (Hte-Vienne) is said to contain no less than 20 find spots of Roman settlement material, and one of these is the very large building at Buissière-Étable;[23] once again it is reasonable to suppose that some of the other 19 were dependencies, though obviously we cannot say which. One could also point to Préty (Saône-et-Loire), where a large villa on an *-acum* centre is accompanied by at least four subsidiary sites, one of them possibly a *vicus*;[24] to the two communes of Joux-la-Ville and Noyers-sur-Serein (Yonne), which contained at the last count some 23 'villas' between them of various shapes and sizes, among them the big and obviously important one at La Tête-de-Fer;[25] and to Estinne-au-Mont and Estinne-au-Val in Hainault, which again have a large central villa at La Terre-à-Pointes and at least eight sites where *tegulae* or actual foundations have been recorded.[26] In Britain this kind of study is a little less common, scholars having tended, perhaps, to concentrate on indications of dependency within the villas themselves rather than on simple geographical groupings. But much attention has been given to the probable estate of the Bignor villa in Sussex,[27] and we should also mention Applebaum's studies of the sites associated with the Newtown villa near Basingstoke, and that of West Dean in Wiltshire.[28] The Bignor villa, indeed, could well be typical of its whole region: Rivet suggested[29] that many of the 'Celtic' farms along the Downs could well be dependent on villas in the Sussex plain, and it is difficult to believe, certainly, that the two types of settlement can here have been wholly separate.

This last example does in fact raise an important point. There is a tendency in studies of this kind to look first for groups of villas rather than for a single villa and associated 'native' sites, and it is worth asking whether this is the right approach. In a sense, of course, it is not the size or character of a site that makes it a dependency, but rather an administrative arrangement, and there is no reason in principle why a quite large and luxurious villa should not be held by a *colonus*, or a more modest one be at the centre of a colonate system. There must have been many villas which started as independent farmsteads and ultimately became incorporated into larger holdings, and although there will no doubt have been accompanying changes in their internal arrangements it is unlikely that their overall character will have been radically altered.

On the other hand, and by the same kind of argument, there is no reason why the colonate system should have been restricted to villas, and the steady decline in the status of *coloni* later in the imperial period would seem to suggest that

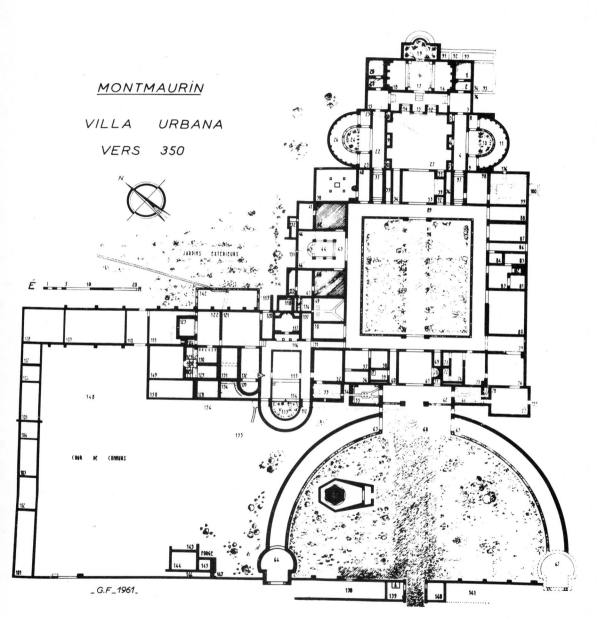

41 Montmaurin, Hte-Garonne

'native' sites, or at most fairly humble villas, might be more appropriate. If this is so, a number of other areas come into consideration – areas, that is, in which villas and 'native' sites appear side by side. With the growth of aerial surveys since the war this kind of situation has been found to be increasingly common, both here and on the Continent, and it is presumably on the basis of such surveys that progress in this direction will eventually be made. In the meantime we may mention the interest shown by a number of scholars recently in apparent associations between villas and native villages, most notably in parts of East Anglia,[30] as well as the long-standing discussion of the 'native' sites in Cranborne Chase[31] and more recently those in the Fenland.[32]

Once again, the examples from France and Belgium are more plentiful, particularly those involving villages: one of the most striking, in the sense that the dependent relationship can be proved archaeologically, is the little group of 13 dwellings at Morville (Namur, Belgium), which is linked by an aqueduct to the great villa of Anthée a kilometre or so away;[33] and there are other, though less clear, examples at La Mouthe (Sérandon, Corrèze), at Rouffiac (Aude), and elsewhere.[34] The difficulty with villages, of course, is that whereas a single isolated site either is or is not a dependency of the nearby villa, a village may well be partly dependent and partly not, in the sense that some of the dwellings in it may be part of the estate and others independent or part of another. Grenier, indeed, went so far as to remark that there was no proven example of an agricultural village, or *vicus*, in the whole of Gaul,[35] but this is a little extreme. If we feel that a given villa was big enough to have had dependencies, and if there is a village in its neighbourhood, it would be foolish to exclude that village from consideration, even if its primary character was something other than agricultural. To do so would be to suppose that dependent farmers had the habit of avoiding existing villages when setting up house, as though they had no business to belong to them, and this seems wholly unreasonable. A good example of the kind of situation we are envisaging is that of the forest of Compierre at St-Revérien (Nièvre): within this forest there is not only a villa but a large and obviously important *vicus* complete with temple and theatre,[36] and although the *vicus* would seem to be a religious centre first and foremost we are surely justified in supposing that some of its inhabitants were workers or tenants on the villa estate, and that their dwellings are to this extent dependencies. There are several examples of the same kind of thing along the lower reaches of the Seine, and in certain wooded areas of the Rhineland, that around the villa of Mayen being of particular interest.[37] It seems likely also that the ancient hut sites known as *mardelles*,[38] which appear in thousands in numerous areas of France, may in many cases have been linked in some way with villas; there are several areas, certainly, where they and villas appear together – one thinks of those around Gondrexange (Moselle)[39] and in the region to the east of Bordeaux[40] – and it is hard to believe that the two types of site were entirely separate.

The importance of native sites emerges also from another consideration, which is that a colonate system may not consist simply of a single prosperous villa surrounded by a series of more humble farmsteads, but may be something more complex. The best way to illustrate this is to look again at the sites associated with Chiragan, which, as we saw, consisted of both villas, most notably those at Martres-Tolosane, Bordier, Sana and Coulieu, and of *vici* at Tuc-de-Mourlan, Boussens and St-Cizy[41] (*Fig.* 39). The two kinds of site are clearly distinguished from one another, and there are obvious differences in standards, and what this would seem to suggest is that, if villas and villages alike were all dependent on Chiragan, we have a system, not of two levels (that is, main villa and dependencies), but of three (that is, main villa, subsidiary villas and dependencies), or in other words that the villas other than Chiragan had a sort of intermediate status. There are a number of points which seem to support this. First, the subsidiary villas are of considerable size, and two of them at least could without exaggeration be said to be luxury houses; there is no doubt that, had they occurred away from this particular area, we would have thought of them as centres of estates rather than dependencies. This leads, in fact, to the second point, which is that according to standard Roman practice an estate which was incorporated into a larger holding did not normally lose its identity; the tendency was to produce, not a unified *fundus*, but rather a *massa fundorum*,[42] and it may well be that as the owners of Chiragan extended their control through the valley this is what they did. For what it is worth, the kind of system which we are suggesting is that used by the great monastic estates of the Carolingian period, the intermediate estates being known at that stage as *fisci*, and it is tempting to suppose that this, like so much else in their administration, had Gallo-Roman origins.[43] Nor is Chiragan the only area where this pattern occurs: the secondary villas associated with Montmaurin are also of considerable size, and at least one of them (that at Ville-Rouge) is surrounded by smaller and humbler sites which could well be under its control.[44] The suggestion is, then, that in looking for evidence of colonate systems on the ground we should, while not ignoring subsidiary villas, pay at least as much, if not more attention to sites of a native or primitive character, and that where the estates in question are those of a really major villa the possibility of subsidiary centres should also be borne in mind.

All this, however, is based, not on proven connections between sites, but on simple geographical grouping, and even in areas as suggestive as Chiragan or Montmaurin we clearly need a further body of evidence before we can convince the determined sceptic. In areas, moreover, where the geographical picture is less suggestive it is only by what we have called internal or linking evidence that any reconstruction of the tenure system can even begin. To be fair, both Chiragan and Montmaurin have in fact provided evidence of this kind. At Chiragan the secondary villas are linked to the central one in the sense that its fortunes are reflected in theirs; they emerge at the beginning of its second period, which is probably about AD 100, and they reach their peak, to judge from the limited dating material, at the time of its enormous extension about the reign of Antoninus Pius; in the fourth century, when the central villa was becoming increasingly devoted to agricultural production, and working activities were encroaching on the former living quarters, a wholly new villa, that at Martres-Tolosane, was being constructed, presumably as a more convenient residence away from the bustle of the estate centre.[45] At Montmaurin the subsidiary villas begin rather earlier, develop gradually until the third century, and then after the troubles of that period are rebuilt and move into a period of notable prosperity which lasts to the late fourth century and in some cases possibly beyond. The fortunes of the central villa are very similar, the most striking change coming in the latter part of the third century, when a decision was clearly taken to phase out the administrative and working part of the site and to concentrate on its development as a luxury dwelling. The excavators saw this, no doubt rightly, as indicating at once an extension of the lands under the villa's control and a radical change in their organization, and it seems at least plausible that this was the point at which a system of subsidiary centres was set up, based on the outlier villas.[46] In both of these areas only a general picture is at present possible, and in this sense they are not perhaps ideal examples; but what they illustrate is the second kind of evidence mentioned earlier, namely the evidence within a given area of common patterns of prosperity and decline, which by linking sites together may help to establish relationships of tenure and so on of the type with which we began. A good example of the use of such evidence in Britain is again the study by Applebaum of the villas in the Basingstoke area of Hampshire.[47] As he observed, a number of sites at which occupation had ceased at some point during the Iron Age were suddenly reoccupied in the third or fourth century; presumably there was a common explanation, and it could be that it is to be found in the villa at New-town, with which the sites in question appear to be associated – in other words, that they were the holdings of *coloni*. A further example is provided by the sites associated with the Kingsweston villa in Gloucestershire,[48] and it is not difficult to think of others.

In Britain, however, the evidence most commonly quoted in this kind of enquiry is that from single villa sites – the third, in fact, of the types of evidence mentioned above. It sometimes happens that, because of its facilities, or because of the presence or lack of certain buildings, a villa can only be properly inter-preted by assuming that it was part of a larger complex, and that there were other sites in the neighbourhood with which it was connected. An obvious example is the villa at East Grimstead in Wiltshire,[49] which in spite of being fairly unremark-able in size or luxury seems in the first part of the fourth century to have had three bath houses functioning simultaneously; a similar situation occurs at Stroud in Hampshire,[50] where the bath wing was thought to be rather lavish for the modest farmstead that this was, and one's natural assumption is that the bathing facilities were intended for a larger population than the villa in either case contained. The same kind of inference can be drawn from facilities other than bath houses: the numerous corn-drying ovens at Hambledon (Bucks.)[51] suggest, perhaps, that a service was being provided for other sites nearby, which may have been dependencies of, or fellow dependencies with, the villa in question. At Ditchley (Oxon.)[52] the construction, in the early fourth century, of a large granary, representing perhaps a thousand acres of arable land, was apparently associated with the demolition and non-renewal of what had formerly been farm-workers' quarters; it seems likely, not only that there was a concentration on corn production at this date, but that the system was now to be one of dependent holdings, with the workers put out to individual farms. Inferences of this kind are bound to be subjective, and it is no use pretending that on the basis of archaeology alone a colonate system can be conclusively proved to have existed in a given area; but the fact remains that in many areas the suggestions that it did exist are strong, and given the nature of the evidence this is all that one can reasonably expect.

In assembling the evidence available we have so far omitted what might seem to be the most promising source, namely the sites and areas which formed

42   Keszthely-Fenékpuszta, Hungary

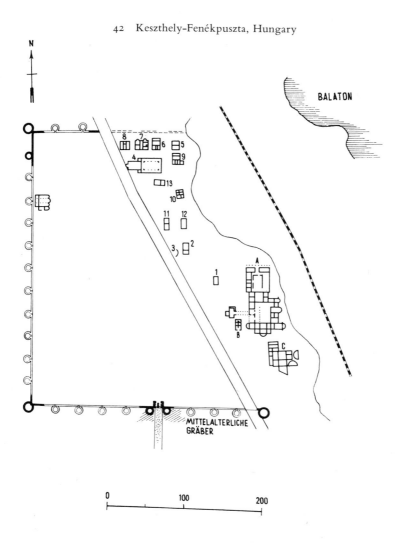

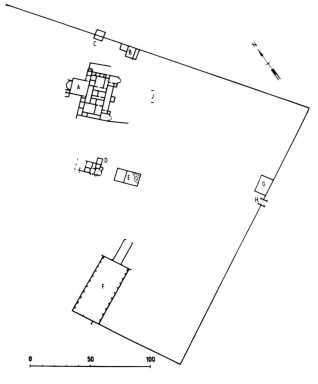

43   Parndorf, Austria

part of imperial estates. Here, if anywhere, we should be able to show what the colonate system looked like, since it is from the inscriptions relating to such estates that so much of our practical information about *coloni* is derived.[53] On closer inspection, however, the difficulty of actually identifying them, let alone describing their extent and organization, is such as to make this particular line of enquiry rather unfruitful, at least for the present. An idea of the problems involved may be gained from Dr Applebaum's summary of the evidence for imperial estates in Britain: a document from Chew Stoke in Somerset which may imply an imperial domain nearby, a number of references in the *Notitia Dignitatum* to officials responsible for imperial property, historical inferences concerning the estates of Prasutagus and Cogidubnus, and so on.[54] The same is true of other provinces: there are particular villas, like Pfalzel and Konz near Trier[55] (*Figs* 50, 51), or Fenékpuszta and Parndorf in Pannonia[56] (*Figs* 42, 43), which may well have been imperial at some stage, and inferences are sometimes drawn from such things as the royal estates of the Merovingian period, but proven examples are very few indeed. It is arguable in any case that with the ownership being vested in the emperor a system of organization based on villas is not entirely appropriate, except perhaps in cases where existing estates passed into his possession. Often, indeed, as with the native sites of the Fenland region or those of

Cranborne Chase, it is the very absence of villas which prompts the suggestion that a given area was imperial property, and that this is a reasonable line of argument is suggested by the native villages of the northern Vosges, where there is actually supporting evidence in the form of boundary stones.[57] In such areas the farmers may well have been *coloni* in the full legal sense, but their relevance to the social structure based on villas is at best a comparative one.

In all of the discussion so far we have talked of possession and ownership, and of individual owners, whether emperors or others; and in terms of Roman law, as set out in the *Digest* and in the Codes of Justinian and Theodosius, this was the general position. With the exception of land attached to the various munici- palities and certain other special categories, estates were private property and could be disposed of by sale or gift or bequest. Whether the theory was every- where reflected in practice is a question to which we shall shortly have to return, but even if we assume that it was there is much in the ownership of villas that is uncertain and much that is misunderstood. It may be, for example, that the old idea of the owners as being 'Romans' as opposed to 'natives' has now been largely forgotten, but who precisely the owners were, particularly at given periods or in given sites or areas, is still very far from clear, and a look at some of the evidence may suggest some possibilities and show where the uncertainties lie.

The fact is that only in a tiny number of cases can one attach an owner's name to an individual site, and most of the names that we have are from literary or epigraphical sources and relate to villas which are unidentified and probably in many cases unknown. In only two areas has any really systematic study of these names been made, and it is on these that most of what we know about owner- ship is ultimately based. The first is a study made in the 1930s of the villas around the Bay of Naples in southern Italy,[58] and although in many respects the situation here was peculiar to Italy and probably also to the first century there are a number of points which have a wider relevance. Of the 39 villas included in the study, some nine could be assigned to named owners: one belonged to the emperor, two to members of families prominent in nearby Pompeii, three to men whose names suggest that they, or their fathers, were freedmen, and the remaining three to men with Greek names who would be resident aliens or pos- sibly also freedmen. Of the nine villas themselves, at least five were regarded by the author of the study as being in the category of 'villas owned by absentee landlords residing only occasionally', and only one seemed to be a real farm- house with a permanently resident owner. We are, of course, dealing here with a highly desirable residential area close to a flourishing commercial and business centre, and one must not be surprised if the majority of the villas were owned as temporary country retreats by people from Rome or by prosperous business men, many of them *nouveaux-riches*, from Pompeii and the area around. Such a pattern can hardly be assumed in other parts of the Empire and at later periods, but it reminds us of at least three features for which we should nevertheless be prepared: first, that villa owners may be primarily townsmen and only secondarily farmers; second, villas may represent an appropriate and respectable, if not also profitable, form of investment for men whose main source of wealth is business of one kind or another; and third, that ownership is linked with financial resources rather than with membership of a particular social class or racial group, though of course there is a sense in which, once established, the owners of villas would come to constitute a social class by that very token.

For Britain, a list of some 26 owners has been compiled,[59] though it must be admitted that some of them are inferences from place-names, and not all of the rest appear as owners in the sources. Four of them appear in inscriptions found on villa sites, and one or two others can be linked with known centres. Granted, however, that this is a restricted body of evidence, the list does seem to be a reasonable indication of the kind of people who owned the British villas. It includes a number of Roman citizens, some of whom will have been of British descent, along with former soldiers, an official or two, and some absentee land-lords living in other provinces. As far as the range of ownership is concerned this is about as far as we can go, but there is a certain amount of evidence from particular areas which adds to the picture somewhat. Rivet's survey of known villas in fourth-century Britain[60] revealed a concentration of some of the richest sites around Bath, which as he pointed out contained a high percentage of foreign residents; and the theory of an influx of settlers from the Continent at this period is supported by circumstantial evidence from such things as religious dedications, the plans of certain villas, and the style of mosaic pavements. It may be that as more becomes known of the origins and early development of plans the nationality of individual owners may be more detectable: it has been suggested, for example,[61] that the British corridor house was an importation from Belgium or Germany, and that a number of early sites may therefore have been established by immi-grants from that area. The evidence from other provinces (one thinks particularly of Dalmatia)[62] would suggest that this is a likely pattern, with foreigners giving the initial impetus and the local population coming in at the secondary stage, but reasonable as this may be in general terms we are not yet in a position to work out the details. It seems unlikely, in any case, that as far as Britain is con-cerned we should expect a heavy influx from further afield than the northern parts of Gaul.

The mention of plans reminds us, of course, that on one aspect the villas themselves are fairly revealing, namely the relationship between the owner, or master, and the people living on the villa site itself. The typical pattern has already been referred to: a villa starts as a simple building, with master, workers and animals all gathered under a single roof; at an early stage the animals are moved into separate quarters, and the house acquires the first indications of comfort; later, with the addition of extra rooms and partitions, or with the provision of new and separate buildings, a further segregation is made between master and workers. In other words, increasing prosperity leads to an intensification of the social divisions and ultimately to the growth of an agrarian upper class. Obviously, not every villa goes through the whole process, and with those that do the pace is not always the same; but the evolution that we saw at Mayen in Germany can be matched by numerous examples throughout the villa areas. Within this general framework, however, there are two particular developments which seem to be something more than simple variations in design, and could well suggest a major modification to the picture so far presented. The first is the so-called 'hall' villa, most common in northern Europe, and the second the aisled or 'basilican' villa, which, though probably continental also in origin, is associated primarily with Britain.[63]

A 'hall' villa is one which, beginning as a large rectangular room or hall, retains this basic character even when it acquires a corridor with flanking rooms, or baths and other refinements. In this sense the villa at Mayen remains a 'hall' villa for the greater part of its history, since whatever additions and refinements are made around it the central hall with which it began remains its dominant feature.[64] (*Fig.* 5) On other sites the hall eventually disappears: at Ödheim in Württemberg a suite of baths was built inside it, and elsewhere, as at Blankenheim in the Rhineland or Parndorf in Pannonia (*Fig.* 43), it becomes submerged in later extensions.[65] In Britain it is not at all common: indeed, the sites on which it occurs, such as that at Kingsweston in Gloucestershire, have for this reason tended to be thought of as the result of immigration.[66] Whatever the truth of this may be, it does seem that, as a general rule, the early corridor villas of Britain had already shaken off the influence of the 'hall' and evolved from the start without it. Applebaum's suggestion[67] that the abandonment in Britain of the hall was in fact an abandonment of a patriarchal society, that is, of an integrated society based on kinship, in favour of one with more definite social divisions, has much to recommend it, and it would tie in certainly with the notion of immigrant landowners lording it temporarily over a native population. The implications of this for the Continent, however, would be quite considerable, because there, as we saw from Mayen, the hall retained its influence for some considerable time. Indeed, in many areas it was dominant throughout the Roman period: one finds it at numerous sites in Lorraine, for example, as at Grémecey (*Fig.* 44) or Saaraltdorf (Moselle), and in the Rhineland, as at Bollendorf (*Fig.* 22) or the villas in the *territoria* of the legionary fortress, while in areas like Württemberg it is common enough to be taken as the norm.[68] In one sense this is not particularly startling: no one would pretend that the great estate and the colonate system were universal throughout the western Empire, and the small independent family farmstead which this kind of villa seems to represent was, after all, the traditional Roman unit. But when we remember that the hall in some form or other was a feature of Celtic and German society both before and after the Romans we may well begin to wonder just how deep, in many areas, the Roman influence was. Could it be, in fact, that the social structure in these areas is not a Roman one at all, but a native one dressed up in Roman trappings?

The problems involved in aisled or basilican villas are rather more complex than this, but lead to similar questions, in the sense that a number of scholars have come to regard such sites as indications of a more indigenous society, and one in which the kinship group rather more than the social class is likely to have

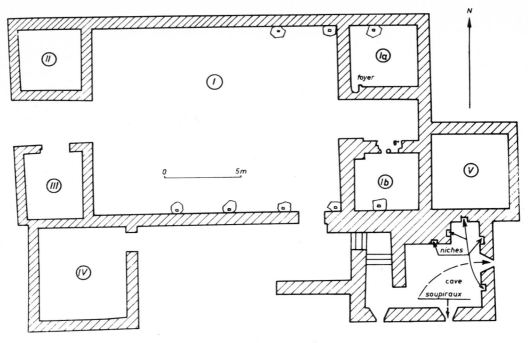

44   Grémecey, Moselle

been the determining factor. As long ago as the 1920s the German expert Oelmann[69] suggested a comparison with halls of the later Medieval period, and more recently Mr J.T. Smith has proposed that 'the aisled hall . . . served something like the same functions of court house and communal dining room on feast days as its Medieval counterpart.[70]' Essentially, the process of development is the same as that of the 'hall' villa, in that the aisled building tends to begin life as an establishment in its own right, with master, workers and stock all in together; such it was, for example, at Denton (Lincs.) or Exning (Suffolk),[71] though at both of these a certain amount of segregation was achieved by the partitioning off of aisles into separate apartments – the counterpart, perhaps, of the corridor and flanking wing rooms of the 'hall' villa. The next stage was the removal of animals, and agricultural processes generally, into new subsidiary buildings: in some cases, as at Clanville, near Andover in Hampshire,[72] the workers were apparently moved as well, as though the masters were becoming more conscious of the distinctions between themselves and the people in their employ. The logical conclusion of this process comes rather later in the Roman period, when aisled buildings appear in a subordinate role as outbuildings to villas of a more highly Romanized type, a good example of this being Mansfield Wood-house in Nottinghamshire.[73]

What is suggested, in fact, is that in all of this we are seeing a specifically Celtic aspect of the villa culture in Britain. The rise of the self-contained basilican house is seen as indicating the emergence of a native landowning class, adopting the villa as a unit but giving it their own distinctive character. On this view the early examples are inhabited and owned by kinship groups, and their appearance within the villa system suggests a recognition by the Roman authorities of Celtic practice, if not of Celtic law. The increasing segregation might then mean the gradual development of social divisions along the Roman lines, and the final appearance of the aisled building as a dependency of a more 'Roman' one would show that the kinship groups fell victim to the general process whereby the free tenant was progressively reduced to serfdom.[74] All this seems reasonable enough as a hypothesis, though not everyone would perhaps interpret each of the stages in precisely the same way; what at the moment prevents it from becoming more than a hypothesis is that the dating of the individual sites is far from certain. Applebaum's tentative scheme suggests that perhaps a third of them were in existence by AD 200 and rather more than two-thirds by some time in the third century,[75] and this would tie in nicely with the idea of an indigenous landowner class emerging, albeit a little slowly, onto the scene. But as he points out, the dating is not secure, and it may be as well, while taking it as reasonably likely that the aisled house is indeed an indication of native influence, to refrain from pressing the details too far until something more definite in the way of supporting evidence becomes available. This is not to deny that there are many sites – such as that at West Blatchington, with its associated fields arranged in a characteristically Roman grid system, or the one at Tidbury rings in Hampshire, lying within a hill-fort – which are made more intelligible on this basis.[76]

West Blatchington's fields are no doubt a special case on any consideration, but it is fair to say that much progress could be made on the subject of native influences if we could be more sure of the tenurial basis of the various kinds of field system with which villas in general were associated. The present picture, very briefly, is as follows: the fields at one time known as Celtic fields, which are predominantly but not exclusively squareish in shape, and which seem at first sight to be grouped almost haphazardly together, extended, not only over the chalky downlands where they were first observed and studied, but also over the river gravels of the Midlands and upper Thames.[77] The tendency nowadays to refer to them as 'native' rather than 'Celtic' arises from the discovery that they not only remained in use in the Roman period, but may well have been the basis of its agricultural system; indeed, in certain areas, particularly in parts of the highland zone, it was only then that they were introduced.[78] More recently, however, a certain amount of evidence has been assembled which suggests that associated with some villas were fields of a different type, which can be simply described as broad strips, extending to 600 or 700ft, and sometimes 1,000ft, in length and normally between 200 and 300ft in breadth.[79] It cannot be definitely stated that these are a Roman innovation, since strips of a similar form are by no means unknown in 'native' contexts both here and on the Continent;[80] their detailed interpretation, in any case, depends on their connection (still a matter of debate) with the possible introduction of a slice-turning plough, which falls outside our immediate enquiry.[81] But even if we regard them as 'Roman', and assume that they were widely distributed and not simply a local peculiarity, the fact remains that in the older farming areas – away, that is, from the heavier soils developed for the first time in the Belgic and Roman periods – the 'native' fields remained the dominant type, and one wonders what this may have meant as far as tenure patterns, and hence as social patterns generally, were concerned.

The fact is that without a clear guide from the layout of sites and the interpretation of field systems we are still very much in the dark about the precise social structure of the Celtic peoples before they came under direct Roman influence. The evidence, and the general outlines of what it tells us, have been neatly set out by Rivet, and we may briefly summarize what he says.[82] Society, first of all, was divided into classes, in that there were nobles, or chiefs, and commoners; but although the nobles were dominant, so that estates and houses might be said to be theirs, it does seem that essentially the ownership of land was tribal and not individual, the effect being that a chieftain might have all the outward appearances of ownership, but that the way in which the land was disposed of was governed by tribal custom. In Gaul, however, it is implied by Caesar[83] that there was private ownership as well, and this has been taken to show that, probably as a result of Roman influence at an early stage, the old relationship of kinsmen to their chief, which the Romans saw as equivalent to their own *patronus-cliens* arrangement, was beginning to be replaced by one of tenants to their landlord. In this connection Caesar's comment about the debasement of the common people in Gaul, which he associates with debt and which we can perhaps attribute to the influence of a more sophisticated economy, is very revealing.[84] That this development had not yet taken place in Britain is suggested, as Rivet says, both by Caesar's statement that the Britons were less advanced than the Gauls[85] and also by the evidence of archaeology, though it may be that the Belgic areas, where (for example) the transition from the native house to the Roman villa seems to have been comparatively simple, will have to be seen as an exception. What is suggested, in fact, is that, whereas in Gaul the adoption of 'Roman' patterns of ownership and society was well under way before the villas began, in Britain this was not on the whole the case, so that here the Celtic patterns might have been strong enough to exert an influence over the growth and character of the villas when they eventually appeared.

Influence of this kind – influence, that is, which might merely have given a local flavour to the British villa – would probably be generally admitted. It has been argued, however, that the influence was much more fundamental, and that, far from having a basically Roman system with a Celtic flavour, what we have in many parts of Britain is the very reverse. In other words (it is suggested) there were areas where, in practice if not in theory, only lip service was paid to Roman institutions, and where the social custom, and even the law, was Celtic.[86] In a technical sense, of course, it could be argued that such a situation was only possible before AD 212, when an edict of Caracalla gave citizenship to the free provincial population as a whole, and thereby brought them all under the provisions of Roman law; and, as Rivet has pointed out, one of the aims of the edict is said by the historian Dio to have been an increase in the revenue from estate duties, which could only have been achieved if property could be bequeathed and inherited in accordance with Roman legal practice.[87] Mr C.E. Stevens, however, has drawn attention to what he calls a 'Regulating Act' of AD 224, which gave a governor discretion to try cases under local law and also advised caution in dealing with it, so it was at least envisaged that in certain areas and in certain cases both Roman and native systems might exist side by side.[88] One might suppose that this would be likely only during the transitional period, while the full consequences of the grant of citizenship were being worked out, but there is evidence from the legal codes which seems to suggest that conflict between Celtic and Roman law in Britain had still not been resolved in AD 319.[89] One wonders, in any case, how far the technical position is strictly relevant; provided the people involved could comply formally with Roman administrative requirements, such as the registration of estates in accordance with the census and the paying of appropriate dues, they could well in many cases have gone on operating their own system without any conflict ever arising. Disputes between parties on opposite sides of the legal fence will no doubt have caused problems, but few will have gone to a court sufficiently high to bring them into the records; while those between parties of the same persuasion might never resort to law in this sense at all. It has been argued that even in the more fundamentally Romanized provinces there may have been a certain amount of informal jurisdiction by local notables,[90] and one can well understand this happening among people who felt the Roman machinery to be inappropriate. One could understand it too if a harassed official, confronted with an area of Celtic speakers and obviously Celtic customs of ownership and tenure, was content to get his books as straight as possible before beating a dignified retreat.

Supposing, then, that such areas existed, what effect would this have on tenure, and how would they be visible on the ground? Of contemporary evidence there is almost none, and since for the immediate pre-Roman period our evidence is of a general character only our nearest source of information is the lawbooks of medieval Wales, supported to some extent by those of medieval Ireland.[91] These, it must be said at once, are much later than the period under consideration: the codification of the Welsh laws was traditionally ascribed to King Hywel Dda, who died in the mid tenth century, though there seems little doubt that parts of them were in operation earlier than this and that with obvious reservations they can be used as at least a guide to what we might expect in the later Roman period. The detailed arguments, however, are perhaps not appropriate here: the task for us is to summarize what the patterns might have been, and then to see how far they are detectable in the distribution of villas and associated sites.

There are, in fact, two basic patterns with which we need to concern ourselves: that of the free agnatic kindreds or clans, and that of bond communities. Both have been admirably described by Professor G.R.J. Jones, and what follows is taken largely from his account.[92] The holding of a free kindred was known as a *gwely* or 'resting-place', and it was held in return for rents and services paid to the lord of the commote in which it lay; the members of the clan had holdings of land and proportional grazing rights over the common pasture, the arable being partly enclosed and partly worked on an open-field system with co-aration. A *gwely* began when the ancestor of the kinship group was granted permission to settle in a particular place; on his death the arable land was divided among his male heirs, and this continued for four generations, after which the group became proprietors of the land rather than mere occupiers. The system of partible inheritance, with land being distributed equally to all male heirs, resulted in a spread away from the original settlement (the *Hendref*), with individuals tending to hold most of their arable in newer lands on the outskirts. Heirs were encouraged to set up their homesteads on the outer edges of these lands, and the settlement pattern therefore came to be dispersed. For the same reasons, the lands of a *gwely* would often extend over several townships, and the structure of many of them was extremely complex.

The second pattern, and the second kind of tenure, is that known as *tref gyfrif*, which was associated with groups of bondmen. These people were tied to the soil, but had no heritable rights; they paid dues and services to the lord of the commote, and had temporary rights of occupation over plots of arable, which were tilled in common and reverted to common grazing when each man had harvested his own. The plots were divided equally among all adult males in the group, so that each time the number changed through death or through a boy reaching the age of majority there had to be a redistribution. This was done by a commote official, the *maer* or mayor, who was also responsible for organizing the common tillage. The unit of settlement was the nucleated hamlet, or *tref*, of which there would be several within the commote, the most important being that where the *maer* lived (the *maerdref*); this would tend to have an extensive demesne, and would also be linked to the court, or *llys*, at which the lord of the commote administered justice.

From the point of view of the Roman administrator, this second type of tenure would present fewer problems than the first. The status of the bondmen, and their relationship to their lord, were similar to those of *coloni*, and there was no reason why they should not be so described. The kinsmen in their *gwely*, however, were a different matter; in no real sense were terms applicable to the colonate system appropriate for them, and it was no doubt from them, with their joint ownership by brothers or cousins, that any conflict between Celtic and Roman law or custom would arise. For the archaeologist both types present questions which are by no means easily answered: in the case of bondmen, how far is it possible to distinguish *tref gyfrif* tenure from that of *coloni* in terms of sites and settlement distribution; and in the case of kinship holdings, how far are they detectable archaeologically at all?

One approach that suggests itself immediately is to look within the overall settlement pattern at the relationship between dispersed and nucleated sites. Stevens, basing his studies on surveys by the Historical Monuments Commission in Anglesey and Caernarvonshire, felt that in this part of Wales at least the occurrence of isolated farm enclosures on the one hand and nucleated settlements on the other could be interpreted by reference to the two types of tenure. Indeed, a study of parts of the highland zone of Britain revealed a similar situation, a broad distinction being possible between enclosed single sites and sites in 'close dispersion'; and it seemed likely that in certain 'native' areas in lowland Britain there were sites which might also lend themselves to such an analysis.[93] The problems increase, however, when we move from areas of this kind, in which individual sites can be compared with later parallels like the *raths* of medieval Ireland, into areas where the most obvious sites are the villas, whether or not they are associated with others of a more 'native' type. Here it is not so much from the settlement pattern as a whole that the answers are likely to come, but from certain sections of it, and from certain features of individual sites. As with the search for *coloni*, what we have to study is villa groups, associations between villas and native sites, and to a certain extent the layout of the villas themselves, not with the idea of foisting a given system upon them, but to see if the application of one system or another would make them more intelligible.

Bond hamlets are an obvious starting point: it is now known that nucleated village sites were relatively common in Roman Britain, and one or two of them, as we have seen, are close enough to villas to suggest that they might have been dependencies.[94] But how can we say that an interpretation in terms of bond hamlets and *tref gyfrif* tenure is more likely, or less likely, than one in terms of *coloni*? In theory, of course, there is an adequate distinguishing feature in the frequent redistribution of holdings among the bondmen, but even if this involved dwellings as well as land and equipment it is difficult to see how it would be detectable archaeologically on sites of a relatively primitive character, as these were. Applebaum, looking at the settlement pattern in the Fens, and noting the growth of nucleations from two or three huts in the first century to ten or eleven in the fourth, suggested that this was unlikely as a feature of bond hamlets and to be seen more probably as reflecting the natural growth of family groups: in other words, the criterion for bond hamlets is not a naturally evolving settlement but something which reveals what he calls 'conscious customary nucleation'.[95] What this might be, however, is far from clear, though the point is reasonable enough in principle, and it seems unlikely that a village on its own will give us the answer we require. Field patterns are a little more helpful: the evidence suggests that in their medieval form the bond hamlets were associated with an open-field system and with strips, in contrast with the free kinship groups, who tended to work a system of which enclosed plots were at least a part. If this is so, and if the pattern can be taken back to the Roman period, we have a means of distinguishing bondmen from others, and Applebaum may be right, for example, to see them at the settlement at Chisenbury Warren in Wiltshire, where a nucleated site is associated with extensive strip cultivation.[96] But here again the question is not simply whether bond hamlets are an appropriate label, but whether they are a more appropriate one than anything else, and this we cannot really say; it may well be, for example, that 'conscious customary nucleation' is as appropriate to a highly seigneurial colonate system in the fourth century as it is to bond hamlets then or later. The only other features that may help us are the *maerdref* and its associated court or *llys*, and here we may be on better ground; the suggestion already referred to, that the aisled house might serve as just such a court, is clearly an important one, and its presence inside the Tidbury Rings hill-fort, and possibly one or two other places as well, might give us a clue to where a *maerdref* might be found.[97] Other clues may come from other kinds of buildings: the appearance of temples on villas (those at Stroud in Hampshire and Thistleton Dyer in Rutland being notable examples) is seen by Applebaum as perhaps reflecting the role of a chief within a given area,[98] while Stevens has drawn attention to the isolated bath house, which may also have served as a kind of local centre.[99]

As we said earlier, however, the differences between *tref gyfrif* tenure and the

45   Thistleton Dyer, Rutland

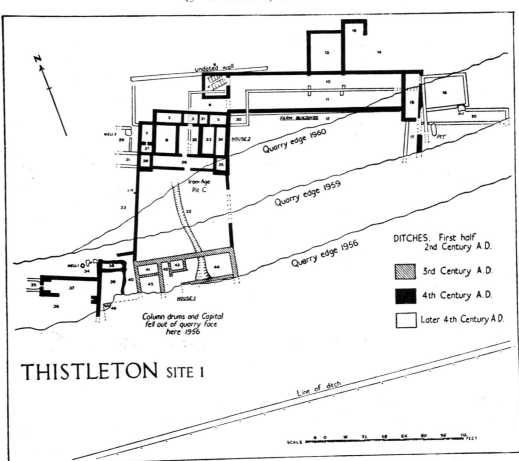

developed colonate of the later Empire can hardly have been very great – that is, from the point of view of an outside observer. Indeed, one could well imagine a situation in which they might actually become identified, with the villa owner regarding his workers as *coloni*, or at least describing them as such to an official, and the workers themselves continuing to behave as bondmen. In other words, the question which of the two they were could well be a little unreal: they might, in fact, be both. For the other main type of tenure, however – that of the kinship groups of free men – there is no such easy way out; here it is not simply a matter of the precise relationship between a lord, or owner, and his dependents, in which the differences could almost be seen as linguistic, but something much more fundamental, affecting the concept of ownership itself. This, surely, should be detectable, and its presence or absence as a feature of Romano-British society determinable, at least to some degree, in archaeological terms.

We have noted already that the settlement pattern is likely to be dispersed, and to the extent that we are dealing here with free families we are probably right to think in terms of villas as well as sites of a more native type, though clearly no hard and fast distinction can be assumed. If the later examples are any guide, the *gwely* as a unit is likely to have been both large and complex, and there is little chance of finding a complete example in the absence of documentary evidence. As far as sites are concerned we must look, presumably, for a group of villas comparable in size, and with a geographical focus rather than an actual physical centre; the tendency would be for the sites away from this focus to be somewhat later than those nearby, at least in their earliest phases. But we may, perhaps, go further: the holdings within the *gwely*, like those of the bondmen in their hamlets, were subject to periodical redistribution, and if we are right in thinking of villas in this context as well as native sites there would seem to be rather more chance of detecting it and seeing its effects. It is true that by the period of the Laws the dwellings themselves seem not to have been reallocated, or only exceptionally,[100] and it is likely also that reallotments would occur less frequently in this system than they would under that of *tref gyfrif*, in that all the brothers or cousins within a group would have to die before such a change became necessary. Even with these allowances, however, the situation of an individual *gwely* member was likely to be fairly fluid, and this can hardly have been improved by the existence of a procedure known as *dyaspad uwch Annwfn*, whereby a member who for some reason had been excluded from a distribution might lay claim to his share, either himself or through his descendants, at any time within 13 generations of the original settlement.[101] How frequent this was we are not in a position to say, but even as a theoretical possibility it must have added a note at least of uncertainty. What this seems to suggest is that for people within a *gwely* system the accumulation of capital over a long period was likely to be both difficult and undesirable: difficult, because the accumulation of land and property generally was limited by the tenure system as a whole, and undesirable because its ownership was likely to be only temporary. In other words, the system would militate to a degree against the production of a surplus, and therefore against the kind of amenities which such a surplus might make possible. If there were villas in such a context they would tend, therefore, to be fairly simple working sites, and would not evolve into richer and more lavish establishments unless the system itself broke down.

It was with such considerations in mind that Stevens put forward his theory that the extent of Celtic kinship tenure in Britain might be indicated in general terms by the distribution of patterned mosaic pavements, the point being that these are an obvious example of a fairly major capital outlay on a fairly permanent amenity.[102] Clearly, this is at best a rule of thumb, and one could hardly press it within a restricted area, but it does make sense of a number of features which might otherwise be difficult to explain. It would seem, for example, that in the eastern part of Britain – east, that is, of a line drawn from the Wash to the region of Newbury and from there to Beachy Head – the appearance of mosaics in villas is relatively uncommon, whereas in the area further west, along the Jurassic ridge from Devon to Yorkshire, they occur sufficiently regularly to be taken as normal. There are, of course, exceptions – we might expect a more Romanized pattern in parts of Kent and Sussex, for example, and Dr Branigan has argued for the exclusion also of sites in the Chilterns[103] – but the maps produced by Stevens present a reasonably clear picture and one which needs explaining. As Rivet has shown, the distribution of larger villas in the fourth century reveals a decided shift of the centre of gravity towards the west of Britain,[104] the point presumably being that in these areas the conditions were right for the establishment of large estates in a way that they were not in the areas further east. Whether this was based on a higher incidence of bondman tenure, as Stevens has argued, or simply on the absence of a well-established and tenacious social pattern in the pre-Roman period, is a question to which we cannot at present provide an answer, and it may be that the presence of large estates here is in any case less striking than the absence of them in eastern and south-east England. For this the notion of Celtic influences provides at least a plausible explanation.

It may be that we have taken rather a long time to arrive at what are admittedly very vague and imprecise conclusions; there is clearly a long way to go yet before we can speak with any assurance on social and tenurial patterns as far as Britain and the British villas are concerned. But even such an unproductive discussion can help in a number of ways: by revealing the uncertainties and outlining the possibilities, it can give us a better idea of the kind of evidence we need, and of the kind of sites that are likely to provide it; and it can also warn us against too hasty assumptions. This latter point is of some importance: even if we have lost the habit of thinking of villa owners as 'Romans' there is an inevitable tendency to think first of Roman institutions in interpreting what we find. The discovery that for the evidence we have both Roman and Celtic institutions are equally appropriate can hardly fail to be a salutary one – and one which has a relevance in areas other than that of villas.

7

Villa Economy and Investment

'The typical villa-owner', says Rivet, talking primarily of Varro and Columella and the Italian context, 'is a citizen who has invested in land.'[1] How true this was at later periods and in areas further afield we shall need to consider, but for a discussion of the economic aspects of the villa it is an appropriate point with which to begin, since it draws our attention immediately to something fundamental – the interdependence of villas and urban centres. The point itself is simple enough: the existence of towns implies an agricultural surplus sufficient to feed their population, and the market that they provide is at once an outlet for that surplus and an incentive for its production; for the farmer the surplus is a means to obtaining, not only the items of equipment which he finds it difficult to fashion himself, but some of the luxuries of which the towns have made him aware. Such a system will not arise of its own accord or in isolation, and towns and villas alike are part of something greater: they depend on relatively peaceful and stable conditions, on the existence of adequate media of exchange, on efficient communications and means of transport – on the whole pattern of circumstances, in fact, which we include in the general label of the *Pax Romana*. It is, indeed, in terms of this wider pattern that, as we saw earlier, the villa itself is most satisfactorily assessed and defined;[2] but the overall social and economic framework of which the villas form part is one to which the towns give meaning and character, and although we would be wrong to see the villas as mere appendages, the fact remains that the towns are both a necessary condition of their existence (at least, in the form in which they are familiar to us) and a major influence on their development.

The point of the quotation, however, is rather more precise: it is not simply that towns and villas were linked economically as suppliers of each other's needs, but that villas were owned, if not universally, at least typically, by townsmen – by men, that is, who thought of them as an investment and as supportive of what they considered their primary role as members of the urban community. The list of owners around Pompeii includes many whose business lay in Rome or Pompeii itself, and only a few who actually lived on the estates they owned,[3] and although it is easy enough to argue that this was a special area there is reason to believe that it was special only in degree, and that in general terms it was typical of Italy as a whole. Eventually, perhaps, we shall be able to study the origins of the villa in Italy, and to speak with confidence of the factors that brought it about; on general historical grounds, however, we would expect it to have occurred as a result of the inflow of capital from Rome's expansion in the Mediterranean, the main effects of which will have been evident from at least the mid second century B.C. If this is so, the ownership of villas as items of investment by absentee landlords would not be at all surprising, the capital being available, not to the farming community itself, but to the wealthy senators and businessmen, who needed for various reasons to invest in landed property, but were tied by status or occupation to Rome and the other Italian cities.[4] It may be that there were exceptions, and one would imagine that once the fashion was set there would be a tendency for existing farmers to try to follow suit and to turn their farms into something approaching those of their new and wealthier neighbours. But it was with the neighbours, and not with the farmers themselves, that the initiative is likely to have lain, and in the early Principate at least there is little to suggest any radical change in the picture. We must assume, then, that the typical owners at this period were the Ciceros, the Horaces and the Plinys, or their counterparts in other cities, and that the villa in its early stages was the product of the townsman's idea of comfort and convenience and only in a secondary sense a countryman's attempt to improve his way of life.

To talk of investment, of course, is to talk of villas with landed estates from which a financial return could be expected, and we can hardly concern ourselves here with those establishments, which as we said earlier were probably not very numerous, built largely as luxury retreats and providing, not a regular income, but simply the prospect of eventual capital gain. Such villas, as we know, were not confined to Italy, and we cannot dismiss them from the discussion altogether; but as consumers rather than producers of income they are clearly in a special category, and were appendages to the towns in a way that the more normal villa certainly was not.[5] More common than these, but equally inappropriate to a study of agricultural investment, were the sites which had estates attached to them, and buildings from which they were run, but which nevertheless were essentially luxury sites in the sense that not only the cost of building them but in many cases the cost of keeping them going were met from other sources.[6] It seems likely that on many such establishments the aim was simply to feed the permanent staff and to provide fresh fruit and vegetables, and perhaps the occasional delicacy, at such times as the owner was in residence, rather than the production of a really meaningful surplus. On others, perhaps, the farming element was given more prominence and went some way towards meeting the overall costs, so that it was a question simply of balancing the books rather than financing most of the enterprise. From the owner's point of view this may have been quite satisfactory: the cost of balancing income with expenditure might seem little to pay for the amenities at his disposal. For us, however, the possibility that this situation was fairly common is something of a distorting factor, since we have to allow for estates which were consciously and deliberately run at no margin or even at a loss – or, to put it another way, provided a return which was not entirely financial.

This being said, it is clear from the agricultural writers and from such individual owners as put their thoughts in writing that a financial return was the normal and primary motive. One thinks, for example, of Cato's listing of the various crops in order of profitability, as well as his eye for economy which affects almost everything he writes; of Varro's advice that specialist crops could yield a high return from estates on the outskirts of towns; of Columella's attempt to show by a costing exercise the superior profitability of vine-growing; or of Pliny's concern over the best way to restore an estate which had been allowed to decline.[7] Relevant, too, is the constant desire for self-sufficiency, reflected in Cato's famous statement that a landowner should be a seller and not a buyer,[8] though the moral element implicit in this and similar utterances may warn us against too narrow an intepretation. Apart from this kind of reservation, in fact, the impression one gets from the textbooks, at least at first sight, is one of a thorough, if not actually ruthless, concern for economy, and one wonders how far this extended outside the textbooks and into the estates themselves. How thorough, for example, were Pliny's calculations when he debated the purchase of a property adjacent to one of his own, weighing the probable economies of scale and the bargain price against the cost of the damage done by bad cultivation and the lack of suitable tenants[9]? Here as in other letters there is a natural concern for efficiency, and a desire to save on costs and avoid unnecessary waste, but the approach is careful and cautious rather than exhaustively calculating. The various items of expenditure are listed, but no figures are suggested apart from the purchase price itself; the letter asks for advice, but this can only have been very general and confined to matters of principle. It is hard to imagine Pliny, who elsewhere sells an estate to a friend below its market value,[10] making the detailed calculations that we find in the passage of Columella already referred to, in which income and expenditure are worked out in detail and the likely profit calculated over both a short and longer period.

The feeling that Pliny rather than Columella is the more reliable guide to what actually happened in practice becomes stronger in fact when we look more closely at Columella's figures, which have been shown by a whole succession of scholars to be misleading.[11] Basing his calculations on a small vineyard of 7 *jugera*, an area workable by a single vine-dresser, and assuming that the whole unit has to be set up from scratch, he calculates the short-term profit as being around 25 per cent, and the long-term profit as more than 30 per cent; but his omissions and miscalculations are such as to reduce these figures, on one recent estimate,[12] to roughly 9 and 15 per cent respectively, the suggestion being that the whole exercise was largely academic and had little or no link with practical experience. Part of the trouble, as Mickwitz pointed out,[13] was the inadequacy of ancient methods of accounting, which made it difficult to allow for such things as the depreciation of equipment or the likely replacement costs of slaves and other workers. But these are not the only omissions: Columella allows for the cost of the vines and their supports, and for that of the vine-dresser himself, but takes no account of capital expenditure on such things as buildings and equipment or of overheads such as food and general maintenance. These are not so easily explained away, and there seems to be no alternative but to regard this as what Finley calls a 'desk exercise', designed to establish a *prima facie* case, rather than a piece of professional accounting.[14] If this is so, the likelihood of any detailed costing outside the textbooks is even less, and we must assume that the villa owners, like their successors until comparatively recent times, relied on a mixture of trial and error and on personal and inherited experience.

Desk exercises, in any case, are a temptation for us as much as for the ancient theorists. Even if Columella had included all the items that a modern accountant would wish him to include, it is arguable that the real items of importance were the unaccountable ones like weather, bad harvests, and the infinitely varied local conditions. Even an argument between 9 and 15 per cent could be made entirely meaningless by a succession of poor crops or by temporary over-production elsewhere, and precisely the same expenditure might well produce less than 9 per cent in one area and more than 15 in another. It may be useful to know that the long-term return on agricultural investment in Italy was something of the order of 5–6 per cent, or was taken as such in calculating endowments and other major expenditures.[15] But the debate on the likely return from vines or olives, or on their comparative profitability, has very little meaning in absolute terms, and the fact that it continued from one theorist to another without eventual agreement suggests that it was probably of intellectual as much as practical interest. This is not to say that we should ignore it: for however much opinions may have varied about one crop or another, the basic assumptions – that farming is profitable, and that careful attention and the right conditions can lead to a sizeable return – are never questioned. What this means is that the villa, at least in its Italian context, was associated with, and could be seen as the product of, a system of market farming, and its adoption throughout the Roman west would imply that the system was similarly extended.

There will, of course, have been differences of emphasis: it was suggested at the beginning of this chapter that the notion of the villa as a townsman's investment in the country may not have been as applicable in the provinces as in Italy, and this is something that needs considering. Even in Italy, where the distinction between town and country and their respective residents was no doubt reasonably clear, the ordinary farmer can hardly have remained unmoved by the rise of villa establishments; even if the villa were the creation of townsmen it would not remain their exclusive preserve, since any landowner, townsman or not, could acquire one by achieving a surplus of production and by using it in the appropriate way. That this was so – much more so – in the provinces can hardly be doubted: here the traditions were largely rural, and towns were as much a novelty as villas; successive administrators naturally encouraged the growth of towns, both as centres of government and as models of Roman manners, and the earliest villa owners were no doubt town-based officials and investors, many of them perhaps from overseas, who might be expected to see the towns as primary. But once these town-based villas were established, the local population would be likely to adopt and imitate them just as they would any other aspect of Roman life, in which case villas could evolve within the country and on existing estates, the property of men who, for all that they might become involved in town affairs, were nevertheless countrymen in all the senses that mattered. Such, we must assume, were the men who replaced Belgic huts with villas at Park Street, Ditchley and elsewhere[16] (*Figs* 30, 46), or those who built the countless villas of modest size and standard throughout the western provinces whose origins and antecedents we have no means of knowing. Dr Branigan, discussing the appearance of villas in the Chilterns in the latter part of the first century, observes[17] that they were superior in many ways to contemporary houses in Verulamium, and remarks that a country-dwelling aristocracy may have found it easier to adopt a Romanized version of their existing environment than to move to a wholly new one; this, surely, is what one would expect. We must not go too far, however, and err in the opposite direction: simply by being the administrative centres, and the focus of all the characteristically 'Roman' institutions, the towns became the dominant features of provincial as well as Italian life; and as Jones has pointed

46   Park Street, Hertfordshire

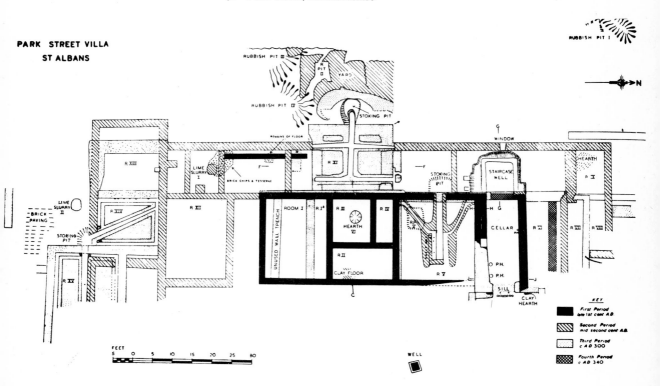

out,[18] there were many categories of people in every province who were bound by custom and even by law both to be landowners on a large scale and to reside in towns. Absentee landlords there certainly were, and a high percentage of villas were owned by them, but it is hard to believe that in Britain or Gaul at any rate this was the normal pattern. Villas and towns were linked, but the dependency worked both ways; neither historically nor economically could the towns be said to be primary.

Whatever the emphasis, however, and from whatever direction the initiative may have come, the appearance of villas within a given area implies that certain conditions existed. Economically, as we said earlier, it implies that a surplus of production is being achieved, and that markets exist both for the disposal of that surplus and for its conversion into the appropriate kinds of amenities. The creation of these conditions, and of the wider political and social ones already referred to, can no doubt be attributed in general terms to the spread of Romanization, so that the villa, by this token, is essentially a Roman institution. But, as we saw in the last chapter, it was an institution to which a decidedly local character could be given, and it is important to consider precisely what the Roman contribution was and how much of the potential existed before the Romans appeared. Did they, that is, provide the necessary techniques and abilities, or was their contribution limited to the creation of a context in which techniques and abilities already existing could be employed?

That the later Iron Age farmer could, if he wished, produce a surplus can hardly be doubted. It may be that in certain areas, where the ownership of land remained with the kinship group, the incentive to do so on any scale was largely lacking, but the evidence already cited for the growth of private ownership in pre-Roman Gaul, as well as for the appearance of social divisions on something approaching the Roman pattern, would suggest that this was by no means universal.[19] Scholars have pointed, for example, to the comparative ease with which Caesar fed his troops in Kent on his first invasion, as well as to Strabo's statement that grain was exported from Britain to the Continent in the reign of Augustus, both of which imply an ability to farm for profit on a considerable scale.[20] The known achievements of the Belgae, even without the introduction of the heavier plough and the first steps towards the exploitation of the richer valley soils, are evidence in the same direction, as is the accumulation of wealth by Celtic chieftains generally, of which their tombs bear witness. And what is suggested by such general indications as these is confirmed directly when we come to consider the actual improvements in agricultural technique that the Roman conquest brought. It may be that Jones's forthright statement, that 'no changes in agricultural methods are recorded under the Roman Empire'[21] is based too narrowly on literary evidence and a little harsh at that, but the list of skills available for the first time in the Roman period, though by no means negligible, is not so great as to suggest a revolution, at least at the practical level. The pattern, indeed, is one of improved efficiency, and of better and more readily available tools, the effect of which was to make certain practices more easy and more widespread, rather than the introduction of a radically different system.

The point is well illustrated by Professor Hawkes's analysis of the sites in Cranbourne Chase, and in particular that at Woodcuts, where the evolution of a single farmstead of native type can be studied from the early first to the late fourth century.[22] In its earliest phase, which began a generation or so before the Claudian conquest and continued to the mid second century, the farm was worked by the traditional methods familiar to us from Little Woodbury and other Iron Age sites, and the main indications of Roman influence are the appearance of samian pottery and evidence for the requisitioning of corn. The real changes came in the second phase, which ran from soon after 150 to the early years of the fourth century; three enclosures were added for stock, a well was dug, and corn-drying ovens provided. Of these, the first is probably the most significant, in that it implies the wintering of stock on the farm itself, though the well is part of the same picture since the provision of an adequate water supply was clearly necessary if animals were to be kept through the winter in any numbers. The effect of wintering the stock in this way, if not its actual purpose, was to make available a supply of manure which could be used to improve the yield of corn and other crops; this would naturally be helped by the improved facilities for drying corn, and no doubt also from better storage. How far these possibilities were exploited we cannot say; whatever surplus they may have produced was not employed for any detectable purpose, and the site remained a 'native' one throughout its history. Nevertheless, the changes themselves, as well as their possible effects, were very considerable – sufficient, certainly, for the emergence of some kind of villa had the necessary motivation been also present – and there is no doubt that their introduction represented something of a breakthrough as far as the economy of this particular site was concerned. But in what sense were they 'Roman', a benefit conferred on the site by its incorporation into the Roman orbit? Enclosures for wintering cattle were hardly a Roman invention; the notion once current that pre-Roman farmers regularly slaughtered a large proportion of their stock each autumn has now been shown to be an exaggeration, and there is no lack of sites, such as that at Figheldean Down in Wiltshire,[23] where the system detectable at Woodcuts was already in operation to a certain extent. The reason it was not more widespread, or its advantages more fully exploited, was not a lack of knowledge so much as an inability to cope with the practical difficulties involved, which were essentially those of providing sufficient food and water. In this respect the digging of wells was an obvious advance, as was the introduction of the large two-handled scythe (*Fig. 33*), which by cutting close to the ground assisted greatly in the collection of hay for fodder.[24] But useful as each of these must have been, it can hardly be said that either was strictly essential for the successful wintering of cattle, which would seem in fact to be a Roman innovation only in the sense that with the help of such Roman refinements it was now a more feasible system.

The same could be said of other refinements, and of the other effects of these ones: the digging of wells, by making the settlement pattern to some extent independent of natural springs and streams, could lead to an extension of the cultivated area, while the large scythe, in addition to its use in the cutting of hay, will certainly, as Applebaum points out, have speeded the reaping of corn – a benefit indeed in the changeable weather of Britain and northern Europe.[25] The general improvement in tools, and the introduction of new ones such as the iron spade, the rake and the harrow, will have contributed in similar ways, the effect in most cases being to ensure that techniques and systems already known but restricted in use could become more generally available. To say this is to go just a little further than Collingwood's assertion[26] that Romano-British agriculture was largely an extended version of that evolved by the Belgae, with the Romans merely providing a political framework and the necessary economic stimulus.

Of what, then, did the stimulus consist, if not of farming systems or radically new techniques? In general terms it is easy enough to define: richer markets, most obviously those provided by the towns and through them by areas further afield; improved communications, without which the markets would be less effective; and a proper financial system, with facilities for banking, for credit and the raising of capital, together with a standard and reliable currency. These were obviously basic, and will need our further attention. But there was also another factor, one which at first sight would seem to have a deadening rather than a stimulating effect, but which may in fact have been sufficient to jerk a province, in economic terms, from one way of life to another: the demands of the Roman government, in taxes and levies in kind, upon a newly conquered territory.[27] Woodcuts, as we said, shows evidence of levies in corn, in the form of a marked decline in the number of storage pits in the first century of Roman rule;[28] it may be that this decline is explicable by other means, but even if it were, the levies themselves are known from literary evidence and the point can be illustrated from other areas. It is generally thought, for example, that the purpose of the Car Dyke, which links the Fens with the river Trent, was to carry the levies of corn and cattle and other commodities to the armies of the north,[29] and Applebaum has argued that the increased production of oats in Britain, particularly in northern areas, was prompted by their use in the army as horse fodder.[30] The amounts involved in supplying the British armies are really quite staggering: the figure produced by Rivet[31] is something in excess of half a million bushels of corn alone, which would effectively swallow up the produce of about 100,000 acres of arable land. Britain was no doubt exceptional in having a particularly large garrison for which it alone could be responsible, but other areas faced similar demands, albeit at a more manageable level: in Gaul, for example, the needs of the Rhine armies would be met largely from eastern and northern districts, though the pressures will have eased when the policy of an advance to the Elbe was abandoned, while in Africa the whole process will have begun rather earlier, with demands being made from the date of the conquest onwards for corn for the cities of Italy. Whatever the amounts involved, however, the point in all these areas is the same, that the need to produce a surplus in order to satisfy official requirements was a valuable stimulus to the local farmer simply because it revealed to him that a surplus was perfectly possible – a surplus which, moreover, could well be largely his when the pressures eventually eased. It says much for the Roman administrators, and for the resilience of the British farmers in particular, that these pressures produced a positive and beneficial response; typical of this could well be Woodcuts itself, where in the period when a proportion of the produce was apparently being removed elsewhere there was still enough of a surplus for the purchase of samian pottery.

The situation is admittedly rather different in the later Empire, and there is evidence to suggest that at least from the third century the level of taxation was high enough to be a serious burden for farmers in certain areas. Lactantius, referring to Diocletian's reform of the census system, explicitly states that the excessive demands involved had caused land to be abandoned by its cultivators so that it had reverted to scrub,[32] and similar complaints are by no means uncommon. As Jones has pointed out,[33] the burden of taxation in the Empire had always fallen very largely on agriculture, simply because it was predominantly upon agriculture that the economy as a whole was based, but the build-up of complaints as well as the considerable evidence for lands gone waste would suggest that by the early fourth century or thereabouts the demands were becoming intolerable. There are, of course, other factors to which the large-scale abandonment of land could plausibly be attributed: the general insecurity resulting from the third-century invasions, the decline in numbers of the agricultural population, even the exhaustion of the soil. But, as Jones has rightly argued,[34] none of these is sufficient to explain the phenomenon in all the areas in which it occurred, including as they do both Egypt and Africa and areas far removed from the imperial frontiers, and there seems no alternative but to take the complaint seriously and to see the taxation as having a harmful effect. Precise figures are difficult to obtain: the only explicit documents are from the sixth century, and although they reveal a dangerously narrow margin between the rate of tax and the likely return from rents it is doubtful how far they can be used for an earlier period or for areas outside Egypt and Italy, from which they come. It seems probable, however, that margins had been narrowing for some time, and with a shortage of labour as well the abandonment of less productive lands would be inevitable. It has also been suggested by Applebaum[35] that not only the level of the demands but the increasing requirement of payment in kind may have had an adverse effect on farmers in some areas by compelling them to concentrate on crops for which their land was unsuitable, to the detriment of other branches of agriculture. It may be that in Egypt and other more prosperous areas land remained an attractive item of investment, but if Jones is right in his suggestion[36] that the deserted lands referred to in the sources could have represented as much as 20 per cent of the total the problem is hardly negligible.

All this, however, is part of the general decline of the villa, to which we shall return in a later chapter; our present concern is with what we may call the normal villa economy, and with the factors behind its success. Not least of these was the availability within the Roman context of wider and more lucrative markets, which as we said were associated primarily with the rise of urban centres. Markets of the local rural type are a feature even of subsistence economies, and must have existed long before the Roman period; as Finley points out,[37] there were few items that the average peasant farmer could not produce for himself, so that the size and importance of such centres will not have been very great, but it was no doubt through them in the first instance that the wider trading contacts of the pre-Roman period were established. As local markets, they will certainly have continued under Roman rule, although for the large-scale movement of goods over long distances the new towns and the improved communications by land and water will have provided a more convenient system; a very high proportion of trade, after all, will have remained local, and markets dealing with an area of, say, 10–15 miles radius will have served as the basic and most immediate centres.[38] Many of them will no doubt have continued on their

47   Mosaic from Tabarka, in Tunisia, showing some out-buildings, olive trees and vines

48 Mosaic from Tabarka, in Tunisia: further out-buildings and livestock

pre-Roman sites, at crossroads or near local religious centres, often perhaps in the form of temporary gatherings with little in the way of permanent buildings; a site which is often quoted as an example of such a centre is the temple site at Woodeaton, near Oxford,[39] where coins and other metal objects have been found over a wide area, suggesting fairly intensive activity without any actual occupation. There would, one imagines, be a tendency in the long run for these sites to attract more permanent settlement, so that in some cases a *vicus* might eventually appear; alternatively, an existing *vicus* might well become a local market centre. Unless there was an extensive use of coin as a medium of exchange, which seems unlikely in this sort of context, we may not be able to identify them with any certainty, but there is no lack of examples of *vici* at road junctions, river crossings and so on which would fit the bill. Professor MacMullen has drawn attention to the phrase *vicus et nundinae*, which occurs in inscriptions from

Numidia, and refers to a study by Oelmann of sites of a similar character in Germany;[40] one could also point to the villages studied by de Maeyer in Belgium, such as those at Vodecée, Tourinnes-St-Lambert and elsewhere.[41] In addition, as MacMullen also reminds us, a market could be held on a private estate, though whether in this case it might be sited in an actual villa rather than a dependent village is perhaps a little doubtful. Wherever they were held, however, their increasing importance in the Roman period is likely on *a priori* grounds and in some areas well attested; there is evidence from Spain, dating to about AD 300, of people travelling from one such fair or market to another,[42] and a number of inscriptions from Italy provide lists of market days at various centres within an area, suggesting that there were people who moved systematically from one to another throughout the year.[43] Such practices, if at all common, would provide an important link between these local markets and those with wider connections.

With the rise of the larger urban centres, however, one begins to talk, not of markets in the sense of places where buying and selling occurred, but rather of *a* market, that is to say a demand for agricultural products on a large scale and at a fairly constant level. The effect of this was not only to extend the system that had existed earlier but to change its emphasis and character. The extensions are plain enough: geographically, a wider area was now available to the individual producer in that the towns were of necessity linked with centres further afield, to which they were connected both physically by the Roman road system and socially by the movement of various groups of people from district to district; with this was associated an extension to the range of goods available in exchange, since the towns, both by their more cosmopolitan character and by the sheer size of the market they represented, encouraged a whole host of commodities and services, both locally and from further afield, which would not before have been economically viable. Just as important, however, if not more so, was the change of emphasis which was brought about by the existence of large numbers of people engaged on non-agricultural activities, for which a large and continuing supply of agricultural products was essential. What this meant for those with extensive holdings of land was the possibility for the first time of growing for profit on a major scale, since their produce could now be disposed of in large quantities at major centres to people who could not supply it for themselves. Instead of large estates worked mainly on a peasant economy and valuable largely as capital, the way was now open to the achievement of a financial return from land and the accumulation of the kind of wealth that gave rise to the splendid villas familiar to us both here and on the Continent. For the more modest owner, too, the change will have been considerable, in that the incentives were now more evident: whereas in the past he might well have waited until the need arose for some item of equipment before collecting some spare produce to take to the market to exchange for it, he could now regard the production of a surplus as being something to aim at on a regular basis, with the prospect either of exchanging it for goods and services or of converting it to cash for future use. That the incentives evoked a response is shown by the transformation throughout the western provinces of the Iron Age hut into the small, still primitive, but unmistakeably Roman farmhouse – the emergence, in fact, of the villa itself.

Economically, then, the villa and the town are part of a single system, in the sense that neither could fully exist without the other. To illustrate this in general terms one has only to look at the distribution of sites in almost any area that has been reasonably well explored. There is, as has been noted,[44] a special problem with *coloniae* and certain other centres, but generally speaking the picture is fairly constant: a concentration of villas associated with a radial pattern of roads, with a town at the centre of the pattern. One thinks, for example, of the sites around Poitiers or Amiens in France, around Mons or Tirlemont in Belgium, or Bath and Ilchester in Britain.[45] In each case it makes little sense to see either town or villas as primary, or to see the one as governing the distribution of the other in a largely one-sided manner; rather should we see each as depending on the other, and the system as one and not two. What is more difficult, however, is to illustrate this in more detail and in rather more concrete terms: obvious as it may be that Chedworth, say, is linked with Cirencester, or St-Priest-sous-Aixe with Limoges,[46] the task of proving this archaeologically or of showing in more than a vague outline the relationship that existed between these and neighbouring villas and their respective towns is at the moment largely beyond us. Part of the trouble, obviously, is that, as with the links between villas and their dependencies, we are dealing to a certain extent with something that is not directly discernible in archaeological terms; but it is also true that the detailed links between villas and towns have not so far been as intensively studied as other aspects, and we are therefore restricted to a small number of areas where at least a start has been made.

One such area is that around Trier, where the work of Dr Edith Wightman has revealed in some detail what had earlier been recognized only in general terms.[47] The city itself is in the fertile centre of the region, and it is here that one of the main concentrations of villas is to be found. As one would expect, the fortunes of city and villas are linked at every stage, most noticeably in the recovery of the fourth century, when, as we saw, the rebuilding of farms and the construction of new ones occurred on a larger scale than in almost any other area on the Continent, part of the reason undoubtedly being the emergence of Trier itself as one of the western imperial capitals. Grenier, indeed, saw this as explaining the existence of major villas as far away as Lorraine, though clearer dating of sites like Téting and Rouhling is needed before we can take this as proven.[48] A similar linking of fortunes between town and country is visible to some degree at Verulamium, where Dr Branigan has begun the task of relating sites in the Chilterns to the development of the city itself.[49] There is, as we saw, a difference of pace in the early stages, with the villas at first developing faster and the city outstripping them in the Antonine period, but apart from this the broad history of both is the same, with third-century decay and fourth-century revival and the final breakdown of the system at some date early in the fifth century.

Neither here nor at Trier can we be more precise about links with individual sites or markets in actual commodities, but there is one area where something more is possible, and where the way to future discoveries of a similar nature would seem to be indicated. The study of certain types of mosaic pavement in Roman Britain has led to the suggestion that at least four centres of mosaic production can be identified, all of them apparently in urban centres, and all of them supplying work to a number of neighbouring villas.[50] The largest and most important was probably located at Cirencester, and its main product, which Dr David Smith describes as 'a distinctive and exclusive type of Orpheus mosaic', occurs at villas in Gloucestershire and Oxfordshire, with outliers in Wiltshire and Somerset as well. The others were at Brough-on-Humber in east Yorkshire, at Dorchester in Dorset, and at Water Newton in Huntingdonshire, the products of this last centre being spread over a wide area of the eastern Midlands. What is of interest here is not only that we have an actual commodity by which villas are linked to an urban centre, but that a fairly clear idea can be gained of the area covered. With the exception of the centre at Brough-on-Humber, which seems to have been a very local one, a distance of up to 30 or 40 miles between workshop and customer was fairly normal; what this means, presumably, is that workmen would travel out from the centre and live on the site until the work was finished, so that in this sense there is no obvious limit to the distance they might travel except for their personal convenience. What governed the distance, in fact, was probably not the willingness of the workmen to travel but rather that of the customer, with whom the initiative would lie in the first place, and who would naturally go to his local supplier unless his requirements were very special. It seems likely that a similar system will have operated for similar crafts, such as those of stonemasons and the painters of wall decorations, with the higher quality work being distributed over wider areas, and as the techniques for studying such things grow more advanced it should be possible to point to further examples. As far as more portable items are concerned, the evidence at present is somewhat inconclusive, with some products (such as flue tiles) seeming to enjoy a fairly wide distribution, and others (such as pewter) a rather more restricted one.[51]

For the efficient movement of materials, and much more for that of breakable or perishable goods, an adequate communication system was essential: in this sense a villa away from a road or river network, if not actually a contradiction in terms, is likely to have been a rarity. In the Roman context one naturally thinks first of roads, and their impact economically was of course enormous, but from the point of view of markets and of the interchange between town and country, there were definite limitations. Goods travelled slowly, whether by road or by other means, and such things as foodstuffs, unless preserved in some way, would be strictly limited in their distribution. More important, road transport was expensive, largely because of the need to feed the draught animals as well as the drovers. Jones's famous calculation,[52] based on figures in the Price Edict of Diocletian, that a wagon-load weighing 1,200lbs would double in price in 300 miles, is a useful rule of thumb as well as a valuable reminder that transport in bulk over long distances was an expensive luxury rather than an everyday facility.

Water transport was very much cheaper – a similar calculation reveals that a shipment of grain from one end of the Mediterranean to the other would cost as much as carting it by land for 75 miles[53] – and as far as commerce was concerned it seems likely that the river and canal networks were if anything more important than that of the roads, which were built in the first instance for administrative rather than commercial reasons. Finley points out[54] that the great attraction of Gaul in the eyes of Roman writers was not its roads but its many navigable rivers, which not only provided a natural system of communication throughout the country but made access between the Channel coast and the Mediterranean a much more practicable proposition; and we have already noted the Car Dyke in Britain as essentially a means of transporting goods from the producers to the consumer armies.[55] Whether this kind of consideration had much effect on the siting of individual villas is perhaps open to doubt: few villa owners would be in a position to use long-distance transport at all regularly, and for most of them the produce available for market would be perishable and therefore disposed of within a fairly restricted area. This said, however, the obvious savings to be had from water transport could well have acted as a secondary influence on the pattern of settlement, and it is hard to believe that rivers like the Thames or Severn in Britain, or the Moselle, the Rhine and the Gironde in Gaul, to name but the more obvious examples, were of only marginal interest to those whose estates lay near their banks.

In this as in all the matters so far discussed relating to the economy of the Roman villa, we have taken the nexus between town and villa as fundamental, the assumption being that the towns were vital, both for providing a market for surplus produce and for making available the particular goods and services which gave the villas their character. That this was generally so seems fairly certain, but it is worth for a moment considering if a villa might in fact exist independently of a town and still remain a villa. It has, after all, been suggested[56] that in the later Empire there was something of a move to the villas, with the apparent aim of making them and their estates more self-sufficient, and if it was possible in this way to lessen their dependence on nearby towns it may in theory have been possible to remove the dependency altogether. The two questions can perhaps be dealt with separately: is there evidence of a desire for self-sufficiency at this date, and would a condition of self-sufficiency in fact be possible?

The notion of a 'flight to the villas' was linked by Collingwood, and by others since, to the great resurgence of villas in fourth-century Britain, and to the increasing burdens imposed by successive emperors upon the *curiales*, or city aristocracy; the suggestion is that, finding these burdens intolerable, such people abandoned their city houses and responsibilities and went to live permanently on their country estates. There is evidence, certainly, of widespread complaint against the taxes and official duties involved, and constant legislation was needed to keep the system working. It may well be that, as Jones has argued,[57] the problems have been exaggerated, and that the *curiales* were merely, as it were, taking a cut in their income rather than having to draw on their capital; but the question is not whether their situation really *was* intolerable, but whether it seemed to them to be so, and the flight to the tax havens in our own day, which is in many ways comparable, should remind us that feeling poor is a very relative matter. Such a consideration would also go a long way towards meeting Rivet's point[58] that the enormous expenditure in fourth-century Britain on the rebuilding and extension of villas is evidence, not of an impoverished aristocracy, but of a relatively rich one, though one has to admit that in such a context the complaints and avoidance of duties already referred to would seem to make little sense. More important, perhaps, is his further point that the towns of Britain, unlike those of Gaul, remained comparatively prosperous, the implication being that there were people (though not necessarily the owners of the newly extended villas) who continued to shoulder the burdens; in other words, there is no support from this quarter for a flight from town to country. Nor is there much, as far as Britain is concerned, for the growth of self-sufficiency; much was undoubtedly changing, both socially and economically, and it is possible to argue for such things as the decentralization of estates or an increasing concentration, in some areas, on cereal production, and in others on pastoral farming, but there is little or nothing to suggest that part of the aim of such changes was to rid the villas of their dependence on towns or other outside sources. Applebaum points to the example of the Purbeck marble industry, which by the later fourth century served an area much reduced from what it had earlier been;[59] but even if it could be shown that this was the result of economic pressures generally rather than a simple loss of confidence in the durability of the product, one could still quote examples, such as that of New Forest pottery,[60] where no such shrinkage took place, and without more detailed evidence we can hardly claim one situation rather than the other as being more typical. What we would need, in any case, is not evidence from outside the villas but internal evidence, such as the establishment on individual sites of kilns and furnaces and workshops – the signs, in fact, that owners were beginning to make their own equipment instead of obtaining it from elsewhere – and at the moment such evidence is not particularly common.[61]

The situation on the Continent is rather different, in that there the towns were more permanently affected by economic and other troubles, and also in that the villas (with the exception of certain areas) were less spectacular in their recovery than those in Britain. Indeed, as we have seen already,[62] the tendency was for the agricultural work to be emphasized and the working parts of the villas to be extended, often at the expense of the luxury apartments of an earlier century – in other words, for a more intensive pattern of farming, without, apparently, the production of a disposable surplus on such a scale as before. Whether this means a move towards self-sufficiency is not at all clear, though it could presumably be argued that the surplus was now being used to maintain a larger staff of non-agricultural workers and craftsmen. An interesting site in this connection is that at Liffol-le-Grand in the Vosges *département*, where at a comparatively late date, and as part of a general shift of emphasis, a pottery kiln was inserted into the corridor of a hitherto large and luxurious villa.[63] How common this sort of thing was it is hard to say, since the chances of getting such striking evidence within the villa itself can hardly be very high; there may have been something like it at Rouhling (Moselle),[64] where tools for a wide range of crafts and other activities were found, and where work buildings were still being repaired in the second half of the fourth century, but this is a site dug 70 years ago and the dating is not secure.

Here, as in Britain, the evidence has yet to be assembled, but there is enough in general terms to suggest that the conditions on either side of the Channel were not necessarily the same. The pressures which, on one view, provoked a migration of farmers from northern Gaul to Britain in the later Empire[65] could well have led the ones who stayed behind to seek a measure of economic independence as an alternative means of survival. Self-sufficiency was, after all, an old and respectable doctrine: it was certainly popular with the agricultural writers, and Cato's observation, already referred to, that a *paterfamilias* should be a seller and not a buyer, is only one of many along similar lines.[66] For most periods and most areas the question of whether it was ever achieved is probably largely academic; the availability of local markets and urban centres will normally have removed the incentive to try it.[67] But what might have happened if towns declined and markets ceased to function is worth considering, if only to form an impression of what the end product may have looked like and thus of the evidence that might reveal it. It seems likely, for example, that the sites most able to achieve this independence would be those at either end of the scale – the small ones, in the sense that their needs from outside would be fairly restricted in any case, and the larger ones, in the sense that with them the provision of workshops and private 'industries' might be economically viable. In the first case one could well argue that at this rather primitive level the label 'villa' may no longer be strictly applicable, while of the second it could be maintained that sites as large as this (one thinks of Chiragan, say, or St-Ulrich) are virtually towns in their own right, in the sense that economically their function is roughly the same. A fuller discussion of this and related questions is more appropriate to later chapters than this, though it must be said at this stage that any theory along the lines so far suggested is likely to involve, not only a weakening of the link between town and villa, but an extension to the meaning of the word 'villa' itself which to some might well be unacceptable.

The mention of private 'industries' gives rise to a further question and a further possible extension. Granted that on many villas, if not the majority, there were workshops of one kind or another, were there sites at which industrial activities were not merely a sideline, or a matter of repair and maintenance, but something more important? Was there such a thing, in fact, as an industrial villa? What is envisaged, presumably, is an establishment which owed its existence, not to the production of an agricultural surplus, but to the profits derived from iron working, say, or pottery manufacture, or some other industrial undertaking. The villa itself might differ very little from other, more normal, sites: even its work buildings might be largely agricultural in character, in the sense that the people living and working within it would still require to be fed, so that the true nature of its income might be evident from sites in the surrounding area and from its relationship with them as much as from its own layout and character. Whether this makes it easier to accept as a villa, or on the contrary makes a new category necessary to contain it, remains to be considered.

That such establishments existed there seems little reason to doubt. The notion of industrial villas has, admittedly, lost favour somewhat in Britain since Richmond explained that the so-called fulling operations at Chedworth were in fact nothing of the kind,[68] and it is true that few sites have yet been discovered which are industrial in that particular way. Applebaum, indeed, in a section devoted to villas with particular kinds of specialist activities, can point only to a possible malting establishment at Woodchester and the temporary use of Darenth for what has been claimed as another fulling mill.[69] Nor, if we confine ourselves to actual villa buildings, can many examples be found in areas other than Britain. The villa of Anthée in Belgium[70] (*Fig.* 21), which is often quoted in this connection, is probably the best we have, in that its numerous outbuildings included several devoted to bronze working, and its subsidiary village at Morville was clearly part of the same activity; it has, indeed, been suggested that the enamelled bronze ornaments discovered on the site were actually manufactured there and that this was part at least of the villa's function. But, as the original excavators were careful to observe, the presence of numerous querns and stone-masons' tools is evidence that other activities went on as well, and the task of weighing their relative importance in the villa's economy is by no means easy. A clearer indication, both here and at other sites, can be gained from a study, not of the villa itself, but of its immediate context: Anthée, like many sites in this part of Belgium, is in an extensive iron-working area with little in the way of decent arable land, and even without its extra quota of workshops it would be an obvious candidate for a list of industrial villas. Chastres-lès-Walcourt in the same province is another example;[71] again the surrounding land is not particularly fertile, there are numerous ironworking sites in the area, and a nearby Roman road is paved in iron slag. Equally common, on both sides of the Channel, are villas in pottery-making areas: that at Banassac-la-Canourgue (Lozère),[72] for example, described by its excavators as a prosperous site in a not very prosperous region, is best explained in terms of the pottery kilns nearby, and Dr Wightman has drawn attention to similar sites at Speicher and Herforst in Treveran territory, which, as she says, were industrial sites in the sense that they probably belonged to the men who controlled the potteries.[73] The villas around the town site of Durobrivae, the centre for Castor ware, are an obvious, and often quoted, British parallel, and Rivet has drawn attention to the concentration of villas around Farnham in Surrey, which again is a pottery-making area.[74].

That sites of this kind should exist is not, after all, surprising; even in terms of agriculture the differences between one villa and another could often be striking, simply because regions differ from one another in the fertility of their soil and the kinds of crops for which they are suited. It is by no means uncommon for villas to specialize in a particular crop or a particular branch of farming, and most provinces can provide examples. In Africa one thinks of the farms devoted to olive production, in Gaul of the sites around Bordeaux or in the Mâconnais which must, one feels, have been involved in wine;[75] in southern France as a whole, in fact, there are plenty of villas where quantities of *amphorae* have been found, and the export of wine along the rivers that one suspects at sites like Auterive (Hte-Garonne) is actually depicted on a sarcophagus at the villa of Fayence (Var).[76] Even in Britain, where it would seem to have been a matter of emphasis rather than of monoculture in any developed sense, one can point to villas where corn was intensively cultivated, such as Hambledon, or where cattle were probably primary, such as Spoonley Wood or Thistleton Dyer.[77] Among the more exotic examples elsewhere we may mention the site at les Stes-Maries-de-la-Mer, on the southern edge of the Camargue, which in so remote a position could only be associated with some kind of maritime activity,[78] or that at Berthelming (Moselle), which has yielded wood-working tools in some quantity and may have used the nearby Sarre as transport for its timber.[79] The difference between these and industrial villas is really very slight: iron and clay, one could argue, are just as much natural products as timber, and villas might just as reasonably be based on them as on any of the more normal items. Like timber, and like any agricultural product, they have to be worked and processed at the places where they occur, and a villa could just as well be supported by groups of smiths and potters as by groups of dependent farmers. The vast majority of villas were no doubt agricultural sites, but to insist on agriculture as a defining characteristic is surely to go too far.[80]

All this, however, is very general: we have talked of the various kinds of villa economy, of the types of activity on which they were based, of their links with towns and the means of distribution, but of the detailed economy of individual villas we have said very little. How far is it possible, of a given villa site, to calculate the size of its estate, to say whether this activity was more important or more profitable than that, or whether its activities in general were subsidized by income from some other source? Granted that a rise or fall in prosperity can be readily diagnosed, can we give any analysis of its causes, not by reference to wider historical patterns, but by studying that particular site in its own immediate context? Before attempting to answer such questions it may be as well to be clear about our ignorance, because there are major areas for which information is not only lacking but unlikely to be forthcoming. We do not know, for example, what it would cost to build a villa, or to maintain and administer it for a given period of time; even the price of estates that we have are few in number, exceptional in size, and unrepresentative in place and period.[81] As we have seen already, the likely financial return on a given crop or a given size of farm could be calculated only within wide and unhelpful limits, and was certainly variable from one region and one period to another. If we were told that on a certain villa the annual yield from the arable was so many hundred bushels, we could not even say with any confidence what its value would be, let alone whether the profit would pay for this mosaic, or that set of wall paintings, or that extension to the bath block. For questions of profit and loss, of income and expenditure, we are limited inevitably to general observations; anything more than this can be based only on tentative inference from such aspects of a site which seem to be significant.[82]

What we can do, and what we are doing with gradually increasing assurance, is to identify buildings and to ascribe their functions to them. Gone are the days when villa reports were merely 'a day in the life of a Roman', with detailed descriptions of residential wings only and imaginative reconstructions of what went on in each of the various living rooms. Increasingly nowadays attention is given to outbuildings, and efforts made to understand their use, the aim being to provide an answer, if possible, to the kinds of questions raised a moment ago. With the help of the ancient writers on agriculture, and by using comparable material from military sites, it is now possible to identify barns and granaries, and the quarters of various kinds of animals – even, tentatively, to distinguish between those housing cattle and horses, or to calculate the number of animals a given building might hold.[83] Such studies are clearly important; only through them, and by the further refinement of the associated techniques, can any detailed understanding be gained of the working of individual establishments. There are, however, limitations, and however precise and detailed our studies become there will still be unknown quantities and margins of error hard to avoid. So long as these are recognized there are major advances still to be made; what is worrying is that they may be only partly recognized, and therefore be given less weight than they deserve, the result being that our understanding, though apparently deeper, will be less securely based.

The point can best be made by considering an imaginary example. Suppose on a given site the granary, byres and stables have been identified with a fair degree of certainty. To leave the site with the general comment that it was based on a combination of stock rearing and arable farming is unsatisfactory, and the possibility occurs to us that more detailed calculations are possible. We begin with the granary: its dimensions on the ground are available, the thickness of the walls is an indication of its height, and we therefore work out its capacity, with suitable allowance for error. Taking an average figure for the likely yield per acre, we can work out the amount of arable it represents. Turning to the byres, we calculate the number of oxen they housed, and by working out the area of land they might be expected to plough we provide ourselves with a cross check on the calculations from the granary. We may even be tempted to calculate the annual yield of manure, and make inferences about the acreage that it might benefit or the kinds of crops it might make possible. Faced with discrepancies between one set of figures and another, we might make further inferences: if the amount of corn suggests a higher acreage than the available teams could plough, we suggest that it was grown elsewhere and collected here, or that some of the ploughing was done by people from other sites; if the discrepancy is the other way round, and there is less corn than we would expect, we conclude that it was taken elsewhere as part of dues or a levy of some kind. Inferences such as this lead us into social questions and thus to further kinds of speculation. No one, of course, would make such inferences, and indulge in such calculations, without emphasizing the uncertainties with which they are associated. To return to the granary: we do not know whether it was designed for an average crop or for an exceptional one, and therefore how often it was full; we do not know what proportion of the crop would be retained for the next year's seed, and therefore what proportion the granary might represent; we cannot be sure (though we could, in theory, discover) whether the corn was stored in the grain or in the ear, or what system of rotation was in operation, and hence what fraction of the arable was under corn at any one time. With byres and stables there are similar, though perhaps less serious, uncertainties: apart from the general question of whether farmers ever read from manuals, there are the more particular ones, such as whether a farmer builds quarters for as many animals as he has, as many as he may have, or as many as he can afford to house, and so on. All such uncertainties are obvious enough, but what is less immediately clear is that they multiply one with another; the margin of error over the capacity of the granary leads to a wider one over the calculation of the arable, and so to a wider one still at the next stage of the argument, with the result that one either qualifies one's statements at every point or adopts a range of figures which would cover almost anything. Statements can be made, and have been made in this and other chapters, on the basis of calculations of this kind, but the uncertainties that lie behind them, and the difficulties inherent in making them, should not be underestimated.

A further danger, which applies to social questions as well as to economic ones, is that we see the occupants of villas in ideal, and therefore unreal, terms. The 'typical Roman' of a century ago, progressing through the various stages of his bath before entering his dining room to be waited on by his slaves and attendants, is tending to give place to the 'typical owner', working his estates with all the shrewdness, if not the technical expertise, of his modern counterpart. The notion that people may go on doing things, not because they have worked out the profit in detail, but merely because such things have always been done, or that changes may be made, and buildings begun or discontinued, with only a general awareness of the long-term effects, seems not to be considered. In many reports, again, there is far too rigid a distinction drawn between owner, bailiff and dependents: a decline in material standards is taken as an indication that the owner is gone and the bailiff left in charge, or even that the owner has abandoned the site altogether and left his dependents to manage as best they can – as though it were impossible for people to come down in the world as well as rise, and as though there were certain standards which were always and everywhere appropriate to owners, and others which were not.[84] To say that we need to be flexible in such matters is reasonable enough, but it adds a further degree of uncertainty to the kind of calculations we have been considering, and to the more general statements of which they form the basis.

8

The Fourth Century
and Beyond

Constantine died in AD 337, having ruled as sole emperor of East and West since 325. His achievements, whether of his own initiation or on the basis of earlier work by Diocletian and others, were enormous, but they were not to last. The events and processes of the fourth century, at least from about 350 onwards, bear a distressing resemblance to those of the third, and once again we are faced with the question of what happened to the villas – the main difference this time being that the answer is at once more difficult and immeasurably more important. This being so, a somewhat longer look at the problem will be in order.

The main sequence of events can be briefly summarized.[1] Early in the 350s a force of Franks and Alemanni, prompted no doubt by the struggle between the emperor Constantius II and the usurper Magnentius, broke into northern and eastern Gaul across the Rhine. Destruction was widespread (the sources mention 40 towns laid waste), but there is reference also to the occupation and use of town and country,[2] and it seems likely that this was a bid for land on which to settle rather than the kind of raid for booty that had been the pattern a century earlier. In spite of initial successes against them by the future emperor Julian, the invaders were to prove a problem until at least the 380s, by which time there seems to have been a tacit acceptance on the part of the Romans that their settlement was to be permanent. Whether, as has been suggested,[3] the regularly spaced villa sites that one encounters in various parts of Alsace and Lorraine are to be connected with this must remain doubtful, but it is a possibility that some such attempt was made to regularize the situation. If so, it was only partially successful: trouble broke out again on numerous occasions, and a sign of the general insecurity was the reappearance of the peasant brigands known as *Bagaudae*, who were more or less endemic in Gaul from now on.[4] In Britain, too, there were problems: the mid 360s saw pressure from Saxon raiders in the south and from Picts and others in the north, and order was with difficulty restored by Theodosius, the father of the future emperor.

Already, however, the signs of something far more serious were beginning to appear. By early in the 370s the tribes to the north of the Black Sea were coming under increasing pressure from the people known as the Huns, and this was to lead before long to further invasions across the Roman frontier. In 376 a force of Goths and others broke through the Danube defences and eventually defeated the emperor Valens at the battle of Adrianople; for a time they remained in Illyria, and their leader Alaric was given the title *magister militum*, but they were soon to threaten again. In 406, while they were pressing south, a great wave of invaders came across the Rhine in the region of Mainz and swept westward and southward right through Gaul to Spain. St Jerome, in a famous letter,[5] provides us with a list of the invading peoples and of the towns and provinces through which they passed, and even allowing for exaggeration and the effects of literary style it is hard to find an area of any size which may have gone unscathed. Having over-run the whole of north-east Gaul as far as the Seine, the invaders – Vandals, Suevi, Alans, Burgundians and others – advanced by two main routes, the first due south by the valley of the Rhône and into Provence, the second south westward through the basin of the Loire and on to Bordeaux and Toulouse. By now the Goths in their advance had moved into Italy, and in 406 the unthinkable happened. Rome itself was sacked.

Eventually the dust settled, and the new situation gradually became more clear. The movement through Gaul had no doubt left some groups of settlers in its wake, but the main body of the invaders established themselves in Spain, very little of which could now be regarded as part of Roman rule. To Spain also came many of the Goths who had recently gone into Italy, and the same people (by now distinguished as Visigoths) were settled extensively in Provence and Aquitania as well. To the north east the Franks, who had put up a resistance to the new invaders, began to assert themselves once more. In Britain, now officially abandoned by Rome in the aftermath of Alaric's invasion of Italy, things remained confused: the Saxon and Pictish raids continued, and were to lead eventually to a migration of refugees across the Channel and to the settlement of Armorica in the 440s. Before this, however, there were movements elsewhere: in 429 the Vandals, who had joined in the main invasion of 406 but had subsequently formed themselves into a separate group in Spain, crossed over into North Africa, where they were able in due course to set up an independent kingdom. With this, and with the other Germanic kingdoms in Gaul and Spain, the western Roman Empire now survived in little more than name. No matter how wide her nominal authority, it was only in certain pockets of territory that Rome could still be said to rule, and this by courtesy of the nearest Germanic people, who might at any time withdraw the facility. Thus it was that when Attila and his Huns invaded in 451 they were repelled, not by the armies of Rome, but by the earlier Germanic invaders, with whom, in spite of the temporary recovery of Africa and parts of Italy under Justinian, the future was now to belong.

The effects of all this on life in the western provinces, and on that of the villas in particular, are at first sight all too obvious. The lamentations of poets and preachers leave little to the imagination: to Jerome's description already referred to, we may add such things as the poem of Orientius, which talks of the whole of Gaul on one great funeral pyre, and provides the striking hexameter: *Mors, dolor, excidium, strages, incendia, luctus.*[6] Even allowing for exaggeration, the amount of evidence of this kind is very considerable, and it would be foolish to argue that the invasions were anything less than a disaster. On the other hand, our own generation has seen disasters on a similar (and, arguably, much greater) scale both in Europe and further afield, and our knowledge of the way in which peoples survive and economies and political systems are rebuilt should make us look very carefully at what might appear at first sight to be a total and final destruction. Indeed, the evidence from the third century, in which a similar disaster was followed by large-scale revival and reconstruction, should also warn us against an over-hasty judgement. We know the provincial population, and we know, in general terms, what their likely response would be. We know something also of the invading peoples, and however unsuited to their way of life the villas may have been there are two points which it is as well to bear in mind: first, that at this period their primary desire seems to have been to find land on which to settle; and second, that even in the first century, if we may believe what Tacitus tells us, they were not without some measure of agricultural knowledge.[7] It would be wrong also to think of them as overwhelming in sheer numbers: the inability of the imperial forces to cope with them was a much more complex matter than simple numerical inferiority.[8] If this is so the *prima facie* evidence may prove to be misleading, and an answer is still to be found to two fairly crucial questions: how extensive was the damage, and how permanent were its effects?

The danger of jumping to conclusions, and of imposing preconceived ideas upon the archaeological evidence rather than letting it speak for itself, has already been pointed out.[9] Burnt material in villa buildings, even when it can be shown to be part of a destruction and not simply the result of domestic or industrial processes, should not be tied to a particular invasion unless there are strong indications that this is so. The amount of timber in even the most lavish villas would make fire a constant hazard, and the risk would be very much increased if, as seems likely, they were inhabited for any length of time at a reduced economic level. Dr Webster's observation that there is no villa in Britain whose total destruction can be attributed with any certainty to the invasion of 367 is in this sense most important, not because it proves anything positive, but because it increases the possibilities.[10] As he goes on to point out, there were many sites which continued to be occupied in some form or other after 367, and unless it can be proved otherwise we should expect the same to be true after the invasions of the early fifth century, both here and on the Continent. The possibility is (and this is what we need to consider in more detail) that the decline and fall of the villa was linked to a general economic and social collapse, and that the invasions, apart from aggravating the situation and constituting as it were a last straw in many cases, were largely secondary in their importance. The evidence, as one would expect, is poor in both quality and quantity, but it may be that its meaning is now beginning to become more clear.

The reoccupation of villas at a lower, or at least a different, economic level is familiar to us from the late third and early fourth century in Gaul, and the pattern is very similar in Britain after the troubles of the 360s. The evidence is again conveniently summarized by Dr Webster.[11] Bath-houses cease to be used, as at Lantwit Major or Lullingstone, either because of the difficulty of maintaining them or because, being solidly built, they were an obvious source of materials for more essential work.[12] Hearths and corn-drying ovens invade the former residential areas, as at Whittington Court or Great Wymondley,[13] presumably because it was more convenient to move into rooms for which there was no longer any use than to rebuild the less solid outbuildings in which such things had earlier been housed. The same is probably true of such things as burial customs: in more prosperous times a villa might have had its own little cemetery at some distance from the house, but as the standards began to slip the practice arose of placing the dead in an abandoned corner of the buildings. This, at any rate, is a better hypothesis than the fanciful explanations current a generation or two ago, in which the villa inhabitants were seen as stoutly defending their property against the invader and dying in the attempt. The whole question of burials on villa sites is one to which we shall need to return, but except in a minority of cases their relevance to the actual invasion period would seem to be very slight. Otherwise, it is a question of general delapidation: mosaics work loose from floors, and are swept aside and replaced by concrete patches; parts that fall down are sealed off by blocking up doorways or corridors; rooms are subdivided by rough partition walls. Sometimes these things are done in a relatively tidy fashion, sometimes not, but the signs in most cases are unmistakeable.[14]

What is true of Britain in the late fourth century is true also of Gaul in the early fifth. The villa at Berthelming (Moselle)[15] was partly rebuilt after a destruction at about this time: the new walls were constructed in a rough and ready manner from pieces of tile and other débris, and the date is perhaps suggested by the appearance in association with them of a coin of Theodosius II (AD 408–50). The occupation, if such it was, may only have been temporary: the building contains burials of the seventh century, by which time its use for residential purposes would seem to have ceased. A similar pattern appears at Anthée (Namur, Belgium),[16] where the excavator reported Frankish material, mainly pottery, and suggested that the villa was used as a temporary shelter during the invasion period; one or two of the rooms had apparently been modified at a very late stage, but the report provides no details. One of the central rooms at Montmaurin (Hte-Garonne)[17] contained a hearth of crude construction, with food remains and part of a barbarian belt, and there were wooden huts above a late destruction layer at Beaucaire (Gers) and Colleville (Seine-Maritime).[18] At Pujo (Htes-Pyrénées)[19] there was an interesting situation, in that part of the villa ruins were used as a cemetery and the rest, to judge from the post-Roman pottery and other material found there, retained as living quarters. Fifth-century material suggesting occupation is also beginning to appear in Britain: to take a recent example, the four post-Roman phases at Latimer in Buckinghamshire, which are apparently based on timber buildings of a Germanic character, could well prolong the history of the site to the mid fifth century or even later, and there is similar, though at the moment less clear evidence at a number of other sites.[20] It is possible, of course, that these sites, and the others like them that are increasingly beginning to appear, are indicative of nothing more than casual squatting, either by travellers or by people temporarily homeless in a troubled period. But the evidence is equally consistent with the idea already suggested of villas continuing to function, albeit at a fairly debased level, in a period of economic and social failure. By the early fifth century most of the western mints had ceased production, and even if coin had been available it is arguable that it would have been of little practical use to people working at subsistence level and hoping at best for self-sufficiency. Pottery and other household objects would in such a situation be retained and repaired, or replaced by local manufacture; very little would be thrown away or left behind when people moved elsewhere. In other words, the evidence for occupation is likely to be both scanty and difficult to date, and while it would clearly be rash to base a theory of long-term survival upon it there is equally no justification for setting it aside as being insignificant.

We should eventually be able to speak with more assurance about these later phases of our villa sites, as the appropriate material becomes more plentiful and the techniques for dealing with it are further developed. Already, on the basis of Mrs Hawkes's work on the buckles and belt fittings of the period, Dr Webster has been able to outline a theory, admittedly very tentative, about the possible situation in parts of lowland Britain.[21] His suggestion that in particular areas some kind of rural life based on the villas could well have continued for at least two centuries after 400 is at the moment based on very little positive evidence, but it is an idea which has seemed attractive to scholars at various times and there are signs that at long last it may soon be properly tested. In recent years, in addition to the work on belt fittings and similar items, there has been a reassessment of the evidence of coinage in relation to the later phases of Roman sites, as well as the first stages in the identification and interpretation of pottery in the immediate post-Roman period.[22] Work in these fields, together with the increasing interest in Dark Age studies inspired, amongst other things, by Professor Alcock's excavations at South Cadbury and elsewhere,[23] should ultimately give us some at least of the evidence we require. Across the Channel, the position as far as archaeological evidence is concerned is roughly the same. It has long been common for scholars to assume that some villas survived for a considerable period after the great invasions, and claims have been made from time to time for particular villa sites.[24] As in Britain, material evidence has until recently been scarce and only imperfectly understood, but the advances already made in the study of jewellery, and to some extent also of pottery, will no doubt make the position clearer before too long.[25]

It must, however, be said that the kind of survival that we have so far been talking about is hardly on a very spectacular scale. The continuation of rural life based on the villas is something rather different from the continuation of the villa system, if by this we mean the whole economic framework of which the villas formed a part. The mere fact that some kind of rural life continued is hardly surprising, and if the villas played some part in this it may not mean very much, particularly if they were in a ruined, or at best delapidated, condition. The survival that is meaningful is the survival, not of objects, but of the institutions to which the objects belonged, or in the case of the villas some part at least of the villa system. At the moment this is not at all what the archaeological material would seem to suggest.

But archaeology, as we have had occasion already to remind ourselves, is only one of our sources, and it so happens that what it at present tells us is at variance with, and in some respects actually contradicted by, our other kinds of evidence. Before attempting to resolve the disagreements we shall need to look at this alternative material so as to discover, if possible, precisely what it implies. There are two main areas to be considered, that of the literary descriptions of villas and that of place-names in -*acum*; ultimately, as we shall see, they lead in the same kind of direction, but for the moment we can deal with them separately.

The practice of describing villas and their estates, which we saw as something of a literary convention from perhaps the time of Augustus onwards,[26] continued well beyond the period with which we have so far been concerned. The best known example is the description by Sidonius Apollinaris of his own estate at Avitacum[27]: by now we are well into the fifth century, the Visigoths are firmly established in southern Gaul, and yet here in the region of Clermont-Ferrand a man who had himself opposed the Gothic advance enjoys the amenities of a villa as lavish, if not more so, than that of the younger Pliny more than three centuries earlier. Here there is no sign of financial stringency, no hint of insecurity, the baths have *not* been closed down, and all the trimmings of the classic villa are still very much in evidence. The houses of other people in other places were apparently equally flourishing: Sidonius mentions the property of Consentius, near Narbonne, which he describes as *agris aquisque, vinetis atque olivetis . . . amoenissimus*, and also the villa of Burgus, the home of one Pontius Leontius at the confluence of the Garonne and Dordogne rivers, which again had all the amenities of the best fourth-century houses.[28] Another Leontius appears in a poem of Fortunatus, owning two estates near Bordeaux and a third, called Praemiacum, which provided not only corn but excellent fishing as well.[29] That this sort of thing was not confined to one area is shown by the description, also in Fortunatus, of the villa of Nicetius, bishop of Trier, where not only the house itself but also a flourishing agricultural system seems to have survived – and this in the mid sixth century.[30] We are, of course, dealing for the most part with poetry, and some allowance must certainly be made for conventional literary motifs; but it is surely inconceivable that descriptions of this kind, some of which are in considerable detail, can have been wholly imaginary. The assumption must be that the villas in question existed, and the absence in the descriptions of any suggestion that they were exceptional must also be significant.

There is, of course, an obvious problem: none of the villas here mentioned has yet been satisfactorily identified on the ground, in spite of our having a good deal of archaeological and topographical detail, and in some cases also a name. Burgus is the most promising so far, in that the name survives at Bourg-sur-Gironde and a villa has been found within a kilometre or so of the modern village[31]; but there is no excavation report, the identification is based on a very cursory examination of the parts above ground, and no explanation has so far been offered as to how the name was transferred from the villa to the village. In other cases the finds are scanty or non-existent: Praemiacum is probably Preignac (Gironde), and Avitacum is almost certainly Aydat (Puy-de-Dôme), but neither has so far provided anything like the luxury establishment we would expect.[32] In other words, the advocate of survival and continuity is faced with a double problem: not only is he unable to offer an excavated example, but worse still, he cannot locate the examples whose survival is apparently well attested. Either he must abandon the literary evidence altogether, or find some way of explaining the apparent contradiction between it and the archaeology.[33]

Before addressing ourselves to this problem it will be as well to look at the other kind of 'survival' evidence, that of place-names in -acum, because as we shall see a similar difficulty arises here. The main facts about these names have already been given[34]: their use as estate names is well attested in the literary and documentary record, and although as we saw an individual example must always be handled with care there would seem to be no reason why the main body of them should not be seen as having originated in this way and therefore as having at some stage been connected with actual villas. The point that we now have to face is that the names themselves have survived, and survived in their thousands, and there is at least a possibility that their survival is indicative of something more fundamental, namely the survival of the villas to which they were attached. To argue from the one to the other without further evidence would of course be very rash: the reasons why place-names persist or fail to persist are far more complex than this. On the other hand, it would seem to be reasonable to suppose that if a name continued through the troubles of the invasion period and beyond then something also continued to which it could be applied. It is this possibility that we need to consider.

There are now quite a lot of villas appearing at sites with attested -acum names. There are at least four, for example, in the area around Melun to the south east of Paris (*Fig.* 49): one on the farm of Mauny in the commune of Limoges-Fourches, another on the site of the *ancien manoir de Genouilly* at Crisenoy, a third on the farm of Pouilly-Gallerand in St-Germain-Laxis, and a fourth in the village of Savigny-le-Temple.[35] This last example is the most typical: in the Gironde *département* there are a number of villages (Frontenac, Loupiac, Plassac being among them) which have -acum names and villas underneath then,[36] and the same is true of Grépiac (Hte-Garonne), Moissac (Tarn-et-Garonne) and a number of other places.[37] The archaeological material is never entirely satis-

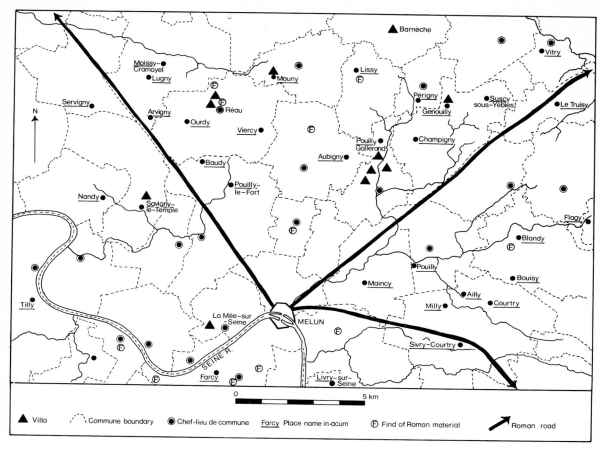

Villa labels and place names on map:

Barnèche · Vitry · Moissy-Cramoyel · Lugny · Lissy · Le Truisy · Servigny · Réau · Arvigny · Périgny · Suscy-sous-Yebles · Ourdy · Viercy · Genouilly · Champigny · Baudy · Aubigny · Pouilly Gallerand · Nandy · Savigny-le-Temple · Flagy · Pouilly-le-Fort · Blandy · Tilly · Pouilly · Bouisy · Maincy · La Mée-sur-Seine · Ailly · Courtry · MELUN · Milly · SEINE R. · Sivry-Courtry · Farcy · Livry-sur-Seine

▲ Villa   〜 Commune boundary   ◉ Chef-lieu de commune   F̄a̲r̲c̲y̲ Place name in-acum   Ⓕ Find of Roman material   ➤ Roman road

49   Names in *-acum* and villas north of Melun

factory; the sites have been built on, many of those in villages are actually under a church, and the chances of the upper levels being reasonably free of disturbance are more or less nil. But this, as we shall argue in a moment, is what in fact continuity means, and it would be unreasonable to expect much more; and even with what we have, the idea of a connection between *-acum* name and villa and of some kind of continuity between villa and village would surely not be unreasonable.

But we do need rather more than this. The link between villa and modern village might well be very tenuous, enough to preserve the name but not enough to be meaningful in the way that we have been suggesting. More important, what of the thousands of *-acum* names at which no villa sites have been recorded? In many cases there have been finds of Roman material, and it is likely that a survey on the ground would produce many more, but there would still be far more names without evidence of Roman occupation than with. We referred a moment ago to the villas with *-acum* names in the area around Melun: more significant in many ways is the area just to the west of this, the area in the southern outskirts of Paris which we earlier used as a sort of test area for the genuineness of names of this form[38] (*Fig.* 4). Here, it will be remembered, there were 33 such names for which reasonably secure documentary evidence could be provided, most of them now the names of villages or hamlets. Yet in the same area only three possible villas have so far been discovered: two of them admittedly can be plausibly linked with names in -*acum*, but even so the discrepancy between the two kinds of evidence is very striking.[39] The same thing happens in almost any area one chooses: a study of the region around Conques in the Rouergue revealed some 58 probable -*acum* names and only half-a-dozen probable villas, and studies in the Mâconnais and near Bordeaux produced the same result.[40] This is in fact a phenomenon which has often been pointed out: Albenque's work on the *département* of Aveyron reveals that, while in some areas -*acum* names far out-number villas, in others they are scarce and villas rather more numerous,[41] and our general survey of France in an earlier chapter contains a number of similar examples. The problem, in fact, is very similar to that presented by the literary evidence: we have the names of villas which we have reason to believe may have survived, and we know roughly where they are, but we cannot actually locate them. The choice in both cases is fairly clear: either we abandon the literary evidence and what would seem to be the implications of the place-names, or we provide an explanation of the discrepancy between this evidence and that of the archaeology. The second alternative would seem at least to deserve con-sideration.

The problem is that we have so far been unable to find something that we have reason to believe existed, and unless we are prepared to admit that we are mistaken our only course is to suppose that we have been looking in the wrong place or even for the wrong thing. This is not so naive a suggestion as may at first appear: we know from what happened in the third century that the survival of a villa could be a very slow and painful affair, and that what finally emerged at the end of the troubles was often something rather different from what had existed before. The actual invasions of the late fourth and early fifth centuries were probably no greater, and perhaps even less, than those of the third, but the accompanying economic and social upheaval was this time much more lasting, and it therefore makes sense to ask ourselves precisely what we would expect a villa to look like if it did survive into the late fifth or early sixth century. Until we have some kind of picture in our minds we can hardly know what to look for, and unless we can imagine something of the process of survival we may not know where to look.

There are two developments for which a certain amount of evidence exists, and which would seem in any case to be likely; each of them has been suggested at various times, but neither has so far been given its full weight. The first is fortification, the second nucleation.[42] The first can be most vividly introduced by looking again at some of the literary examples quoted earlier. The villa called Burgus, for example, even has a name which suggests a stronghold rather than a country house; it is no surprise to find it described as *alta spectabilis arce*, and as having walls and turrets strong enough to resist attack.[43] Similarly, the long description of Nicetius' villa begins with lines suggesting a citadel:

> *Mons in praecipiti suspensa mole tumescit*
> *Et levat excelsum saxea ripa caput;*
> *Rupibus expositis intonsa cacumina tollit*
> *Tutus et elato vertice regnat apex.*

'The mountain rises sheer with mass suspended, and the rocky bank lifts high its head; the summit rears its shaggy pinnacles above the bare rocks, and reigns secure with lofty peak.'

Later we are told that it was protected by 30 turrets.[44] This is no doubt an extreme case, and it may be that it was built after the invasions rather than surviving through them, but it would be surprising if villa owners made no effort at all to protect their property and ward off attack as far as possible. We know that this happened in potentially dangerous areas: the use of the word *castellum* to indicate a rural centre in Africa is well known, and whatever it may have implied

50 Pfalzel, Germany

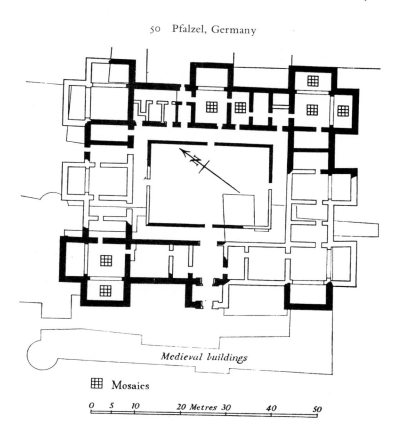

Medieval buildings

⊞ Mosaics

0   5   10   20 *Metres* 30   40   50

on the ground a glance at sites like the olive farms of the Gebel in Tripolitania will show how appropriate the word was[45] (*Fig.* 14). In the northern provinces too there are examples of fortification in areas close to the frontiers: the second-century site at Kuttolsheim (Bas-Rhin), which consists of a square building with circular towers at each corner, makes little sense in military terms and is probably a fortified farm.[46] Clearly, if this kind of thing happened in dangerous areas we can reasonably expect it to have happened in dangerous periods: a good example of what this might have produced is provided by the site at Pfalzel, near Trier, a villa begun in the mid fourth century, and clearly designed with defence in mind[47] (*Fig.* 50). The ground plan is square, around a central courtyard, with projecting rooms at each corner; there is one main entrance only, and no windows or doors at ground floor level. This is obviously something different from villas of the classic kind, and Dr Wightman's comment[48] that Sidonius's Burgus must have looked rather like it is reasonable enough.

Very similar to Pfalzel in its general plan is the villa of Sümeg in the Lake Balaton area of Pannonia: here there is an enclosure wall also, and the site is in any case at a strategic point near the crossing of a marsh. More striking still, and recalling the 30 turrets of the villa of Nicetius, is the site at Keszthely-Fenékpuszta in the same area (*Fig.* 42): the fourth-century enclosure wall is liberally supplied with bastions and turrets, and the large number of buildings inside it, most of them also of fourth-century date, may well indicate a gathering together of dependencies in a troubled period. It may be significant that on both these sites abundant post-Roman material has led the excavators to suggest that occupation continued into the medieval period.[49] Protection on this scale was no doubt exceptional; Pfalzel, as its name may suggest (it is probably *palatiolum*, a little palace), was almost certainly an imperial property, which would make the need greater and the necessary finance more available. Other owners might try other means, such as the provision of earthworks or other defences, or might simply choose a naturally fortified site when rebuilding their farms after the invasion period. Something like this may have happened at St-Gervais in Switzerland, where the enclosure of a medieval manorial centre lies round a villa site,[50] and it is also worth noting that two of the most promising 'continuity' sites in France are at l'Isle-d'Abeau (Isère) and l'Isle-Aumont (Aube), both of which, like the 'Isle' of Ely, are on eminences in an otherwise flat country.[51] In other words, if this kind of process was at all common we could well have a situation in which villas persisted, not in the form that we are used to, but in a form which came to resemble more and more a medieval château, a tendency which would be accentuated by changes in building techniques and materials as well as by changes in social custom and usage. Survival, in fact, would have meant evolution into something else, and if we are seeking evidence for survival it is this something else that we must look for.

Why, however, should it be so difficult to find? The answer to this may lie in the second of our two probable developments, that of nucleation. As is well known, the word *villa* changed in meaning from the Roman to the medieval

period, beginning as something like 'farm' and ending as something like 'village'.[52]
Exactly when the change took place it is difficult to say, but the change itself is
surely suggestive. A similar process occurred with *-acum* place-names at a very
early stage, so that in Gregory of Tours, for example, many such names are clearly
applied to what have become fairly sizeable villages,[53] and it therefore seems
possible that during, and as a result of, the unsettled invasion period villas began
to turn into villages by gathering around themselves the houses belonging to the
local peasantry as well as their own dependencies. There is an analogous social
process, after all, in the tendency during the later Empire for people to attach
themselves for protection to a prominent local person, often no doubt a landowner,[54] and it would not be surprising if this kind of thing were reflected in a
physical attachment also. Again, the African provinces provide a likely parallel:
one of the *Agrimensores*, writing in what appears to be an African context, tells
how in the provinces people tended to collect in villages around the local villas,[55]
and although a corruption in the manuscript prevents us from knowing whether
this made them look like municipalities (*municipiorum*) or fortifications (*muni-
tionum*) the general picture is clear enough.

Supposing then that a villa survived and developed in the ways we have
suggested: what would it be like, and what would be our chances of finding it?
If we were able to look in, say, the seventh century the chances are that it would
still be fairly easily visible. What we would look for would be a village of perhaps
a few hundred people, grouped round a manor house, which would itself be in
some form of fortified enclosure; the manor house would still retain much of its
Roman structure, though this would be to some extent concealed by the later
accretions and delapidations. To look at the same site now, however, would be
to look at something very different. Even if there were little or no expansion of
population, the effects of building and rebuilding over the centuries would be
considerable. The chances of finding much still remaining of the original manor
house would in most cases be negligible, and the fortifications would be likely
to exist, if at all, only as variations in ground levels or as a pattern of streets. The
most prominent feature would probably be the parish church, which might well
be within the old fortified area and be linked, through its predecessors, with the
manor house itself. The original villa might still come to light, but there would
be little chance of a full-scale excavation with all the levels available for study
and the site's whole history open to investigation. The most one could hope for
would be a mosaic in the churchyard, or Roman material appearing in building
operations or road works; the evidence would be fragmentary, the site confused
and disturbed, and the study of any post-Roman phase, difficult enough on any
site, would here be next to impossible.

What we need to realize is that this kind of evidence is not a matter for dis-
appointment, but rather something to be expected; indeed, if it were less fragmentary and less disturbed we would need to be suspicious. The fact is that the
sites which are not disturbed by later settlement are by definition the ones which
did not persist beyond the Roman period; the longer and the more successfully

they persisted, the less easy they would be to discover and explore. In this sense it is rather pointless going through the major reports looking for evidence of post-Roman occupation; the reason that they *are* major reports, with plans, detailed stratification and so on, is that they are of sites away from later settlement. They are, in fact, the dead sites: because there are very many of them they prove that very many villas failed to survive beyond the Roman period, but this is all. Whether there were other sites which did survive is a question to which they can give no answer one way or the other.

This said, the archaeological evidence we have for survival is really quite considerable, and is increasing in volume year by year. The discovery of Roman material under churches or in churchyards, for example, is very common on the Continent, and not at all uncommon in Britain.[56] We have already referred to the sites at places like Frontenac or Moissac which have a villa under the church and an *-acum* name as well, but there are scores of places which, though lacking the name, can provide the villa and the church. Such, to name but a representative sample, are Ornézan (Gers), Penol and St-Romain-de-Jalionas (Isère), Sion (Hte-Savoie), St-Léon-sous-Vézère (Dordogne), Néoules (Var), Mazères-sur-Salat (Hte-Garonne), Bernex (Geneva, Switzerland), Böckweiler (Kr Homburg, Saarland), and Konz (a possible *-acum* name) at the confluence of the Saar and Moselle[57] (*Fig.* 51). It may be, as we shall argue later, that in some cases the coincidence of church and villa is brought about, not by the survival of the villa, but by its transformation during and after the invasion period into a kind of religious site. This would appear to have happened, for example, at Montcaret

51   Konz, Germany

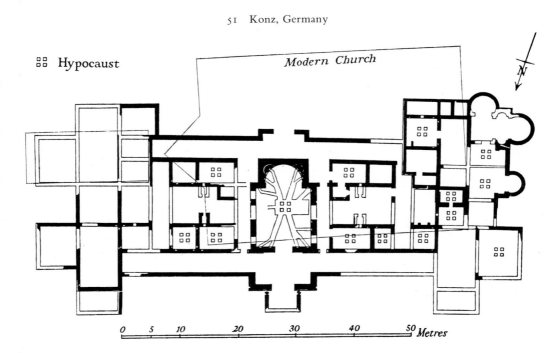

□□ **Hypocaust**   *Modern Church*   N

0   5   10   20   30   40   50 Metres

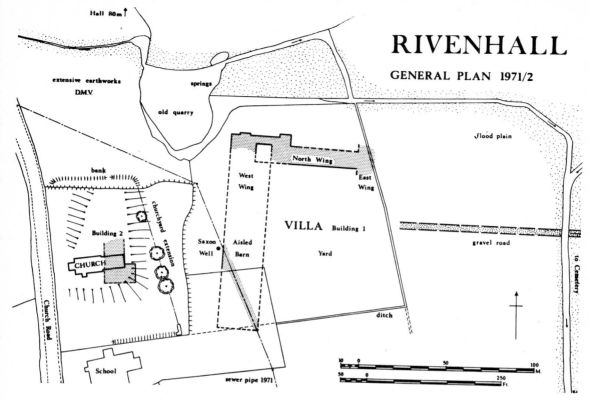

52 Rivenhall, Essex

(Dordogne) (*Fig. 56*) and Martres-Tolosane (Hte-Garonne), where churches are built, not only on the site of villas, but on their actual foundations, and where the sites are used at an early date as cemeteries;[58] whereas at Montfort-sur-Argens (Var), where the farm of les Espelluques contains a ruined medieval church and a villa site as well, the survival in some sense of the villa would seem more likely.[59] In most cases the evidence is fairly fragmentary, and there are few sites where we can be confident that the one process rather than the other has occurred. But whatever the process, the sheer number of sites where church and villa both appear can hardly be ignored. Apart from villas, there are examples of Roman buildings and other material beneath old village centres in many areas, some of which could be equally important: the church at Espaon (Gers) is on an artificial mound, apparently surrounded by ditches of some kind, and beneath it is a Roman occupation layer containing tiles, bricks, fragments of marble slabs and a good deal of pottery; the combination of all this and the old name for this part of the town (Magnonac, a probable *-acum* name) suggests something very much like what we were imagining a moment ago.[60]

The suggestion, then, is that at the end of the Roman period a number of villas continued to exist, the proportion presumably varying from one area to another, and evolved gradually as the centres of nucleated villages, which were ultimately to supersede and largely obliterate them. Possibly only a few survived in anything like completeness; most will have gone through a period of decline, many may have been temporarily abandoned and reoccupied later, or destroyed and rebuilt. But whatever the degree of continuity, it was sufficient in hundreds, perhaps thousands, of cases to ensure the survival of the original estate name. This is not the survival of the villa system, if system there ever was, and it is not even the survival of the villas if by this we mean villas in their familiar second- or fourth-century form; but survival on a large scale it was, and if it can be established on more secure and more abundant evidence its repercussions are considerable.

There are a number of areas in which the outlines of this process may well be visible, and it may be useful to look at them briefly so as to gain some idea of how the kind of survival we have been talking about affected whole districts as opposed to individual sites. A useful starting point is provided by the observations of M. Raymond Agache on the results of his aerial surveys in the Somme basin in northern France[61] (*Fig.* 19). As he points out, the great majority of the villa sites visible from the air are in open country away from modern settlement, and this, combined with the fact that the modern settlement in any case consists of nucleated villages rather than dispersed farmsteads, would at first sight seem to suggest a complete discontinuity between the Roman and post-Roman periods. But this, he argues, is a false impression, since it remains possible that many of the modern villages in fact have villages underneath them. His main argument for this is that many of the villas which are now in open country are actually underlying deserted villages; indeed, it is almost normal for deserted villages in the area to have villas under them,[62] suggesting that in these cases the break in continuity came comparatively late. This, clearly, is a situation which is rather more amenable to archaeological investigation, and one hopes that evidence on it will soon become available.

The apparent discontinuity between villa sites and villages here is similar to that between villa sites and -*acum* names in many areas, and it may be that Agache's hypothesis will apply much more widely. Is it likely, for example, that the villages with -*acum* names in the southern outskirts of Paris, to which we referred earlier, and which outnumber known villas by about 20 to one, represent a fairly massive survival of villa estates in this part of Gaul? A closer look at the map may well suggest that it does[63] (*Fig.* 49). In one section of the area, along the Roman road south eastwards from Paris to Melun, there is a whole series of attested -*acum* names: Moissy, Lugny, Servigny, Arvigny, Ourdy, Viercy, Baudy, Pouilly, Savigny, Nandy. Most of them are a few hundred metres from the line of the road, as villas tend to be; they occur at remarkably regular intervals of between 1,500 and 2,000m, giving each a 'territory' of something like 350 hectares. To claim them all as villa sites may well seem rather rash, but only by making this kind of assumption can we make any real sense of the Roman settlement pattern. The excavated sites that we have are apparently random in their distribution, with no obvious relationship to the road network or to natural conditions; add in the *-acum* names, however, and a coherent pattern immediately begins to emerge, with settlement related to roads and sources of water, and a broad distinction becoming apparent between cleared and forested areas. Coherent too is the area's subsequent history: the road continued to exist, the villas along it survived until they were taken over by the villages to which they gave rise, and the end result was that names and boundaries became permanent.

A similar picture emerges from another area, again in the northern part of Gaul, where one might have expected the upheavals of the invasion period to have been particularly acute. The area in question is at the eastern edge of the province of Hainault, in Belgium[64] (*Fig.* 53); its boundaries are formed, in the north, by the upper reaches of the Sambre between Thuin and the frontier with France, and in the east and west by two of the Sambre's tributaries, the Biesme and Hantes respectively, while along its southern edge ran the great Roman road from Bavai to Trier, visible now not as a major route but simply as a series of country lanes and parish boundaries. As in the area south of Paris, *-acum* names and

53   Names in *-acum* and villas in the Hainault province of Belgium

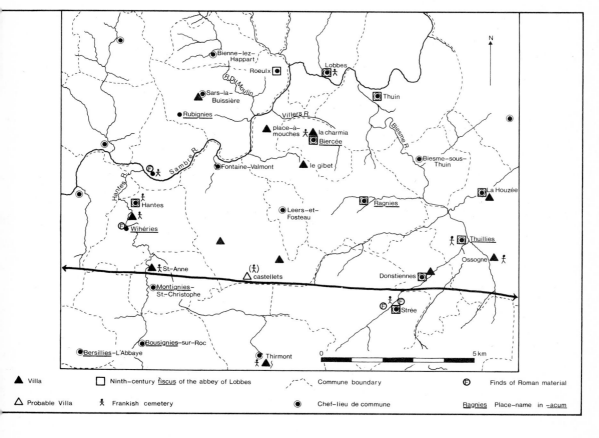

▲ Villa

□ Ninth-century *fiscus* of the abbey of Lobbes

⌐⌐ Commune boundary

Ⓟ Finds of Roman material

△ Probable Villa

⚘ Frankish cemetery

⊙ Chef-lieu de commune

Ragnies Place-name in *-acum*

villa sites are largely separate, the -*acum* names being situated at fairly regular intervals along the river valleys, and the villas being associated primarily with the Roman road. Here again it is only by taking the -*acum* names as having once been villas that one can make full sense of the settlement pattern, because although the pattern of known villa sites is easily explained in relation to the road it seems hardly likely that the Roman exploitation of the area would have been confined to the poorer soils that this involves and would have left the more attractive soils of the valleys wholly untouched. A more reasonable solution is to take the -*acum* names as villas and to assume that river valleys and road alike were settled. In due course the road went out of use and the sites along it became derelict, while those along the rivers were able to survive and so their names were preserved. The fact that the known Frankish cemeteries of the area are all along the rivers must point in the same direction. It may be that we can go a little further: in at least two places we have a situation where an -*acum* name has survived as that of the modern commune centre, and where two or three villa sites are grouped around it but some distance away. One of these is the village of Thuillies, which appears as Tiwiliacas in the ninth-century *Descriptio* of the estates of the abbey of Lobbes;[65] here there are three sites, at la Houzée, some 2km to the north east, at Donstiennes, about the same distance to the south west, and Ossogne, about 1½km to the south east. The same kind of thing occurs at Biercée, where again three probable villa sites are grouped in roughly the same way at some distance from the centre. What precisely happened at such places can hardly be stated dogmatically, but it seems plausible at least that we have here an indication of that tendency towards nucleated settlement to which we referred earlier and which was perhaps one of the ways in which successful villas persisted and 'turned into' villages.

Clearly, this kind of study needs not only to be repeated in other areas, but also to be thoroughly tested by excavation and topographical survey,[66] and it would be foolish to pretend at this stage that the large-scale survival of villas is anything more than an attractive hypothesis. But even the limited work that has so far been possible is enough to suggest that the hypothesis does at least make sense of what might otherwise be confusing and often conflicting evidence, and it is only by forming the hypothesis in the first place that we become aware of the kind of evidence we need as well as the limitations of what we have. And if it should prove to be right, or even partially so, the implications could well be considerable: for attached to the villas were people – people who were part of a complex system of social and economic relationships. It is worth remarking that the increasingly seigneurial character of these relationships is now well documented, and from the point of view of the medievalist this kind of development becomes notably more important if there is a chance that some of it survived the invasions than if it were abolished by them.[67]

9

Villas, Churches and Monasteries

It was suggested in the last chapter that the history of the villas during and after the great invasions was complex and likely to have varied considerably from one area, and one site, to another. At one end of the scale a very large number fell victim to the invaders or to the adverse economic conditions and ceased to exist, while at the other end a small minority may have survived more or less intact. For the rest, possibly a majority of the total, fortunes will have varied: some will have been temporarily destroyed or abandoned and later reoccupied, others will have struggled through but at a lower economic level, while others still will have changed their character completely. It is with this last group, which has so far not been taken into account, that the present chapter is concerned: with the sites, that is, which, though they continued as sites and as centres of activity, nevertheless ceased to be villas even in the broadest sense and assumed a totally different function. We shall be considering, in fact, the process whereby villas survived, no longer *as* villas, but as religious centres, as cemeteries, chapels or monasteries. The process is, in some parts of the Roman west, extremely common, and although in some ways it takes us outside the study of villas *per se* it has, as we shall see, a very real bearing on the question of what happened to the economic and social system of which the villas formed a part.

The most convenient point with which to begin is the practice, apparent from the end of the Roman period onwards, of using villa buildings as places of burial. This is extremely common in France and Belgium, where there are literally hundreds of examples, and frequent also in the Rhine and Danube provinces. In Britain, though by no means unknown, it is relatively rare,[1] and the question naturally arises of why this should be so. From the evidence available from Gaul, where examples can be found to cover most of the racial groups, it would seem that the practice was not confined to a few Germanic peoples, or indeed to Germans as opposed to Gallo-Romans, and it seems likely that the disparity between Britain and the Continent is not explicable solely in racial terms, though whether we can offer an alternative explanation of, say, a historical or religious nature is by no means certain. Surprisingly, the practice itself has not attracted a great deal of attention, in spite of a growth of interest in Dark Age cemeteries both here and on the Continent. Until fairly recently burials on a villa site were more often than not dismissed in a brief appendix or noted simply as *des sépultures de l'époque barbare*, without any further comment; indeed, the fact that during the last two decades their occurrence would appear to have become more frequent might even suggest that in some cases they were not reported at all.[2] Even now, when they are treated in some detail, the reasons for their appearance are rarely discussed.[3]

We must, of course, be careful to confine our attention to sites which are properly meaningful, that is to say, where the coincidence of villa and burials is not simply accidental. The appearance of a cemetery, not in the villa itself, but merely somewhere near it, may not be very significant, and even where the connection seems very close it is often as well to be cautious. The villa at St-Hermentaire (Draguignan, Var)[4] lies under an extensive cemetery, but an examination of the site as a whole suggests that this is largely fortuitous. The burials are late (the earliest probably tenth-century), and their focus is not the villa itself but a medieval chapel some 30m away. What presumably happened was that having started around the chapel the cemetery gradually spread outwards until it finally encroached on the villa, which had long since gone out of use and may well by this time have been largely invisible. A similar case of 'accidental' continuity is at Escolives (Yonne),[5] where a villa of average size and luxury was found to contain more than 50 burials arranged in rows obliquely to the main axis of the buildings. But 200m away to the east is the present church of Escolives, which is said to have contained the relics of the (possibly fifth-century) St Camilla. The presence of the relics gave the site its attraction as a burial ground, and eventually the burials spread to the villa; from their distribution it is clear that the villa buildings were compley disregarded. Granted, however, that this kind of situation may sometimes (perhaps more than sometimes) occur, there are nevertheless scores of sites which are not so easily explained. There are a number of cases, for example, where burials are placed in orderly fashion within a villa's rooms – in other words, where the building is recognized *as* a building and allowed in some measure to govern the cemetery's arrangement. More often, admittedly, the villa is treated not as a building but simply as a suitable locality, but here again it may be said to have been chosen rather than chanced upon, and the reasons are worth exploring.

Oddly enough, it has sometimes been assumed that the presence of burials in a villa is an indication of continued occupation. At Berthelming (Moselle)[6] some 24 burials of the sixth to eighth centuries occurred in the ruins of what appears to have been a fairly prosperous villa; the corners of rooms, the foundations of walls and so on were used to provide one or more sides for the rudimentary coffins. Yet in one of the earlier reports the excavators argued for continuous occupation of the site beyond the invasion period. At Pompogne (Lot-et-Garonne)[7] a cemetery of the seventh and eighth centuries overlay a range of mosaic pavements: 'on acquérait ainsi', says the report, 'l'indication fort précieuse d'un habitat permanent depuis l'antiquité'. In a very general sense, of course, this may be right: 'occupation' may not be the word to use, but it can at least be argued that there was continued (if not continuous) use of the sites in question, by people who lived somewhere near and regarded it as their own. And even occupation may not be wholly out of the question: we saw earlier[8] how in the general collapse of the invasion period things like burial practices could easily become more lax, and there seems no obvious reason why people should not have placed their dead in the more luxurious sections of villas for which they had no further use, while they themselves lived on in the less lavish but more manageable parts. How long this kind of situation may have lasted we can only guess, but it can hardly have been other than temporary, and in the long term we must surely work on the assumption that the presence of burials and occupation in any meaningful sense are mutually exclusive.

Why then were villas so used? What was it about villas that made them seem appropriate, even in their ruined state, as places of burial? The reasons may well have been complex, and it may not therefore be necessary to choose any one explanation to cover all examples. The fact that the practice was not confined to Germans as opposed to Gallo-Romans will at least remove the idea that it was intended as a sort of insult to the monuments of an alien culture;[9] but we still need to decide whether the reasons were religious or secular, that is, whether the villas were seen as in some sense holy places or simply as places away from the normal activities of life. To help us decide, it may be best to look at one or two individual sites in some detail, to see if any explanations suggest themselves or common features appear.

The villa of St-Aubin-sur-Mer, in Normandy[10] (*Fig.* 54), is essentially a corridor villa of a type which is common all over the northern provinces. Its date, in this form at least, is the period after the invasions of AD 275, when a large central living room was given the characteristic portico and flanking rooms at either end, and a bath block established a few metres away to the north. Modifications occurred throughout the fourth century, and the rough character of the latest of these suggests that there was something of a decline in standards towards the end of the Roman period. The site was eventually destroyed by fire, perhaps in the early part of the fifth century, and there is no evidence that it was subsequently lived in. The burials, of which there are close on 50, were scattered apparently at random in and around the main building and the bath block. There were no sarcophagi: the bodies were protected by slabs of stone arranged around them, and there was an almost total absence of grave goods. A coin of Constantine, apparently in association with one of them, led an early excavator to suppose that they were perhaps fourth century, but in later reports this was wisely abandoned and their date remains uncertain. Their most obvious feature is their comparative disregard for the villa buildings: their orientation along an east–west axis is roughly that of the villa, but is presumably the result of religious practice; there is no orderly grouping, and where burials come into contact with parts of the building they are normally placed on top of wall footings rather

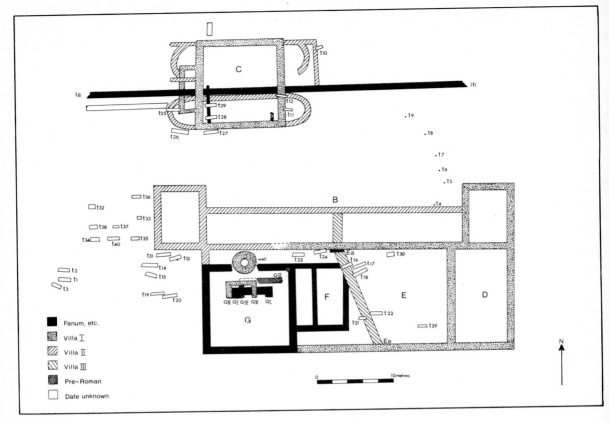

Fanum, etc.

Villa I

Villa II

Villa III

Pre-Roman

Date unknown

54   St.-Aubin-sur-Mer, Calvados

than inside rooms. Indeed, the overall appearance is not unlike that at St-Hermen-taire, except that here there is no external site to explain the burials and that the villa must therefore in some sense be the focal point.

A possible explanation for this lies in the early history of the site, which was not agricultural at all but religious. Indeed, the earliest building on the spot was a small temple of Celtic type, dateable perhaps to the second century AD but overlying an even earlier structure which could well be pre-Roman and which may, as has been suggested, have been linked with a series of *menhirs* now sub-merged in the sea.[11] The temple was destroyed, probably some time in the third century, and it was upon its ruins that the villa was built, the shrine itself being incorporated in the main living room, and the new bath block being constructed along its northern enclosure wall. On the site of the ruined *cella* a small chapel was built, containing a large cult statue of a seated female figure, most of which has survived, and in its north wall a well was dug, either for everyday use or perhaps for some religious function. In other words, the site retained something of its religious character, even if its overall purpose had changed. But not for long: towards the end of the fourth century the cult of the goddess was violently ended. Her chapel was destroyed, this part of the building became a kitchen, and her statue was broken and thrown down the well, though whether this represents the appearance of Christianity or an invasion we cannot say. The point, in any case, is clear enough: in spite of its changes of fortune and character, this was a site with strong religious associations, and even if this was not the only reason for its use as a cemetery it seems very likely that it was a strong contributory factor. It is well known that in the fourth century the followers of St Martin, having destroyed a pagan sanctuary, would frequently replace it with a Christian one on the same site,[12] and it may well be that a similar kind of thinking operated here.

At the opposite end of France the villa of Arnesp (Valentine, Hte-Garonne)[13] is one of the great palatial villas of southern Gaul. Its central feature is a courtyard, some 40m square and surrounded by a colonnade, around which the main residential wings are grouped. In the centre of the southern side is an ornately decorated entrance hall, which is approached by two successive courtyards, each comparable in size to the central one and each flanked again by colonnades; the whole thing is fronted by a monumental entrance some 40m across. Most of this was dug in the 1950s, though parts had already been explored in the nineteenth century and there have been smaller digs more recently. At least two phases are discernible, separated apparently by a destruction midway through the fourth century, the later phase being of inferior quality in building and decoration and indicating, no doubt, the kind of decline in standards with which we are familiar elsewhere. According to a preliminary report of excavations in 1949–50 a number of burials of the 'barbarian' period were found in this main

55 Arnesp, Valentine, Hte-Garonne: diagrammatic representation of the religious quarter

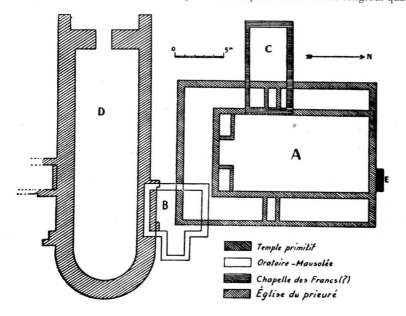

Temple primitif
Oratoire –Mausolée
Chapelle des Francs(?)
Église du prieuré

building, but no details are given and they do not appear on the published plans.

More important than the main building for our purposes, however, is an area some 50m further south, which served the religious needs of the house, at least in its later stages (*Fig.* 55). Here there are no less than four buildings superimposed one upon another, each with its associated burials, the series as a whole providing a fairly clear illustration of the kind of processes which at St-Aubin-sur-Mer could only be guessed at. The earliest building is a small temple, rectangular in plan, and dateable to the second quarter of the fourth century; it was dedicated to Jupiter, and a dozen or so incineration burials were found immediately beside it. At some time during the same century it was destroyed or dismantled, and a mausoleum, with associated Christian burials of the late fourth and early fifth centuries, was constructed partly on its ruins. The church at Valentine nearby contained an inscription referring to one Nymfius, who has been thought to be the villa owner at this period, and it seems likely that the inscription came in fact from this building. With the arrival of the Visigoths in the area in about AD 418 the mausoleum was not destroyed but used by the invaders for their own dead; one of the burials of this period, that of a woman, contained a belt buckle with the bird's-head ornament characteristic of this people. A further change, however, came in the sixth century, when a new chapel was constructed on top of some of the Visigothic burials; the excavator, M. Georges Fouet, attributes this to the Franks, and there are contemporary burials to support this. Finally, and on the same site, there is the medieval priory of Arnesp, which appears in documents from the sixth century onwards, and is again accompanied by burials.

The contrast between this and the residential part is really quite striking. With a site as large as this it would be foolish to base much on an argument from silence, but to date there is no evidence of occupation of the main house beyond the Roman period. Indeed, the palatial character of the site would tend to discourage this, one imagines, and what evidence we have of the later phases is, as we said, indicative of a certain decline. We seem to have a situation, therefore, in which the villa itself declined and went out of use, while its religious quarter went on and developed. There are, of course, differences between this and what happened at St-Aubin: here it was an actual shrine, there the memory of one that attracted the burials; here, because the shrine was in existence, the burials were arranged in obvious relation to it, whereas there the shrine was in ruins and perhaps no longer identifiable, and the burials were simply placed on or near the site. But if we take the two sites together a reasonable hypothesis does emerge: that in the general decline and abandonment or destruction of a villa its religious associations could well refuse to die, and that even if their physical existence was interrupted or ceased altogether they could still attract attention and respect.

A third site, which takes this hypothesis a little further, is that of Montcaret (Dordogne)[14] (*Fig.* 56), a lavish villa once again but only partly dug and that mostly in the 1930s. We need not go into all its phases, which were clearly numerous: suffice it to say that the villa was founded in the first century AD, was destroyed, presumably in the raids of the 270s, and subsequently rebuilt. It was

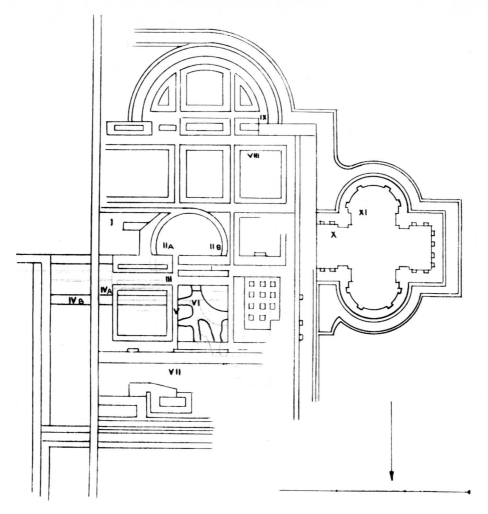

56   Montcaret, Dordogne

planned throughout on a lavish scale, with all the refinements so characterstic of these great southern houses, and although the excavated part is not the whole of the site it is clearly the central and most important section. Concentrating as they did on the luxury apartments the early excavators were hesitant about calling it a villa at all, but later exploration, as well as the uncovering of sites like Arnesp and Montmaurin, make it almost certain that it was.

As at Arnesp, there are signs of a decline in luxury in the later Roman phases, though at present the evidence is only slight; there is, however, clear evidence that these later phases ended in a destruction, dateable probably to the early years of the fifth century. Whatever the circumstances, the site was quickly once more in use, if not in occupation; pottery of the fifth and sixth centuries is abundant, and there is a building dateable to the sixth century under the apse of the present church, which stands, in any case, precisely on the villa site with exactly the same orientation. Inside the church are pre-Romanesque capitals, one of them probably of the seventh century and one perhaps of the fifth, and just to the north is a mosaic pavement, said to be Merovingian, which is presumably to be connected with this or another early building. The position of the sixth-century building, as well as its plan, make it quite clear that its purpose was religious. Details of the associated burials are hard to come by, but they appear to be scattered all over the villa, being placed on wall foundations and even dug out of mosaic floors. A large number of them are said to be Visigothic, and it may be that the sixth-century building, which is apsidal, is Visigothic too. It has indeed been claimed that there are burials here of all the main invading tribes; if this is correct the continuity of use at Montcaret is about as complete an example as we are likely to get, and it is all the more annoying that full details of the burials are not given in any of the reports so far. There is mention also[15] of a continuous coin series from the Roman period to the eighteenth century; once again, for want of details, this is not as helpful as it might have been, but there does appear to have been a quite remarkable continuity. Between the sixth-century apsidal building and the present church (which itself goes back to the twelfth century) there was at least one other religious structure, and there may well be more material awaiting discovery in the as yet unexcavated parts of the site.

To this extent the development is fairly clear: a villa, destroyed at the end of the Roman period, is used almost immediately as a religious centre and begins a new and successful existence. The pattern is similar to that of Arnesp in some ways, but different in others; there the post-Roman development was confined to a small outlying part of the villa, whereas here the whole of the central block is involved; there the existence of a Roman shrine provides an obvious explanation for what happened, whereas here the motivation is far less clear. As earlier commentators realized, the springs now present on the site are hardly enough to support the idea, once current, that this was a spa or bathing establishment; it is possible that the villa contained a shrine of some note, but there is little evidence so far of its existence, let alone its location. On a site like this such lack of evidence is hardly conclusive, but it does at least allow us to consider another possibility, which is that the attraction of the building was not its previous function but simply its shape. Its excavator, Formigé, remarked that several parts of it, especially the central rooms in the block to the left of the published plans, are very similar in form to the early Christian basilicas, and that their obvious suitability for conversion into a church could well have made them attractive to the successive occupants of the area. Clearly, this is not an idea that can be tested by reference to one site alone, and we shall need to return to it later to see if it makes sense in other contexts. For the moment, we may simply observe that the logical jump from sites with religious associations to those with religious possibilities and appearance is not an enormous one, and that for communities who, for various reasons, came to believe that churches were a necessary complement to their cemeteries the existence of buildings adaptable to the purpose could well have been something to be welcomed.[16]

The coincidence of villas and churches has, of course, already arisen in the last chapter, but as part of a different process. The situation there envisaged was that a villa might survive the invasions *as* a villa, and subsequently acquire a church as part and parcel of acquiring a nucleated settlement; here, on the other hand, we are suggesting that a villa might cease to function as such and, rather than acquiring a church, actually become one. Whether the two processes can actually be distinguished archaeologically is perhaps an open question: if either were successful over any length of time the natural result would be the growth of a village, which could well in due course eat away the evidence until the exact relationship between one phase, or one building, and another could no longer be established. These, certainly, are problems with which we shall need to contend; but for the moment we should perhaps look at a rather larger sample of the evidence, to see if the change from villa to church is plausible, and to what extent the sites which we have chosen as representative are really so and not mere aberrations.

In keeping with them, certainly, is the villa at Martres-Tolosane (Hte-Garonne),[17] one of those mentioned in the last chapter as being built for the first time in the fourth century. Its history as a residential site appears to have been short, with a major destruction coming at the very end of this century or the beginning of the next. About the same time the first tombs appear, and these are quickly followed by a Merovingian chapel, dating perhaps to the mid fifth century, built directly on the villa ruins and with the same orientation. This was apparently rebuilt a century or so later, and was succeeded in due course by the eleventh-century church which is still on the site. A very similar sequence occurs at Erôme (Drôme),[18] where the church of the former priory of Notre-Dame-de-la-Mure lies exactly on top of a villa, the ruins of which contained nearly 90 burials and two successive early churches built on its actual foundations. At Ste-Colombe (Gironde)[19] (*Fig. 57*) a villa with Merovingian burials in its ruins lies under the thirteenth-century church, which is built on precisely the same alignment; here there are so far no earlier religious buildings, and the break between villa and church has yet to be filled, but the overall picture is suggestive. It is a picture, moreover, which with minor variations is repeated many times elsewhere. At Moissac (Tarn-et-Garonne)[20] a large hypocaust was discovered beneath the floor of the church of St-Martin, together with burials of the Merovingian period, while another church of St-Martin at Noroy-lès-Jussey (Hte-Saône)[21] was found to be directly above a villa site, with burials, again of Merovingian date, inserted in the Roman levels. A similar sequence appears at Izaux (Htes-Pyrénées),[22] where the villa was destroyed at the end of the fourth century, used as a cemetery from some time in the fifth, and succeeded in due course by the chapel of Notre-Dame-des-Barthes. At Callas (Var)[23] a small ruined chapel is superimposed exactly on one of the buildings of a large villa, the walls of which it preserves to a height of some 2–3m; in this case, as at Arnesp, the building to attract attention was a small shrine or mausoleum, though to date

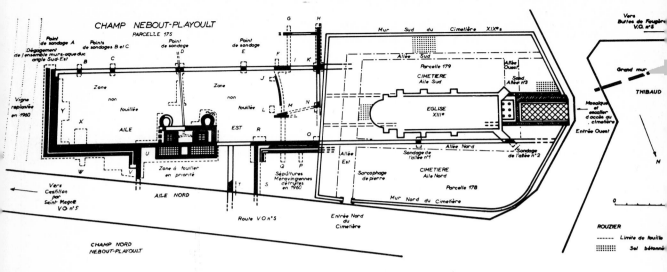

57 Ste-Colombe, Gironde

there are no early burials. The chapel of St-Étienne-de-Candau at Les Angles
(Gard),[24] on the other hand, is surrounded by burials from the fifth century
onwards, and lies above a probable villa; there are remains of a hypocaust, and
pottery from the second to the fourth century. And so the list continues: at
Villecroze (Var)[25] there is a villa below the church of St-Pierre-du-Cimetière,
with burials of both the Roman and Frankish periods, and at Puységur (Gers)[26]
a villa with burials and architectural fragments which suggest a Merovingian
religious building. The triple coincidence of villa–burials–church is in fact so
common that any further insistence on its significance would seem to be unnecessary: for the record, we may note that it occurs at Flayosc and la Roquebrusanne
(Var), at Prusly-sur-Ource (Côte-d'Or), at St-Symphorien (Vannes, Morbihan),
Bouxières-aux-Dames (Meurthe-et-Moselle) and Trinquetaille (Arles, Bouches-
du-Rhône) – to name but the more obvious examples.[27] It is worth noting also
that on many of the sites here mentioned there is little or no modern settlement,
so that we are dealing frequently with deserted villages or isolated chapels. In
other words, it is thanks only to a break in their development at some point in
the Middle Ages that we are able to see the early stages in any detail, and one
can only speculate on the number of sites there may be where a more successful
history has made such a study impossible.

One very noticeable feature of the sites so far referred to is that the original
villas were in most cases fairly large, and this is presumably of some importance.
Even in a ruined state they would still, one imagines, be quite impressive, and a
certain feeling of solemnity about them could well have added to their convenience
and attractiveness in other respects. The majority of our examples also are from
the more southern parts of Gaul, with none from the larger villas of north-east
France or the Rhineland. Evidence from that quarter is not entirely lacking – one

could cite the villa at Morken, near Cologne,[28] which underlies a medieval church in a manner very similar to the one at Ste-Colombe, and there may well be other examples to add when M. Agache's many sites in the basin of the Somme have been explored[29] – but it is certainly much less plentiful than that from further south, and it is clear that impressive ruins on their own were not enough. Presumably where such ruins *were* used we are justified in assuming a plentiful and reasonably flourishing population, but it would be rash without further evidence to suppose that their non-use implied the contrary. Nor can we yet speak in terms of particular Germanic kingdoms, though the evidence from Arnesp and elsewhere might suggest that the Visigoths (for example) were perhaps more ready to adopt such sites than other peoples. Uncertainty of this kind, however, should not be allowed to obscure the main point, that the sequence itself of villa–burials–church is fairly common.

Occasionally, a site other than a villa is given the same, or similar, treatment. The Roman site at Aynard (Cortevaix, Saône-et-Loire)[30] was probably some kind of *vicus* associated with a river crossing, but again there are burials and eventually the church of St-Jean-St-Martin; while at Montferrand (Aude),[31] a site to which we shall return in a moment, the precise nature of the Roman buildings is still uncertain. Nor should this surprise us: whatever the sites may have been originally, it was as ruins that they came into use as cemeteries, and as such, presumably, that they were chosen.

The suggestion so far is that an important reason for choosing them was their religious associations, in the form of earlier temples and shrines, or their religious possibilities as prospective churches or chapels. We shall see in a moment that there could, and must, have been other reasons, accounting perhaps for a majority of the known examples, but before looking at them we can perhaps pursue the religious aspect a little further. An idea which we mentioned in passing in connection with the site at Montcaret was that the central part of the villa may have been converted into some kind of basilica, or at least may have suggested the plan of a basilica to the people who used it, and whatever we may decide about Montcaret itself the idea has something to commend it. There is, at Tác-Fövenypuszta in Pannonia[32] (*Fig.* 58), a large peristyle villa which seems to have been used for just this purpose in the early Middle Ages; its northern range has a large room of just the right size and shape, with a smaller and similar room on either side, and one can easily understand how its use as a church could have come about. Such a conversion would be particularly appropriate in Pannonia, where it is not uncommon to find villas, such as those at Sümeg or Donnerskirchen,[33] with basilicas attached to them. What the excavator had in mind for Montcaret, perhaps, was a basilica standing on its own, such as the fourth-century one at St-Bertrand-de-Comminges,[34] a building some 40m in length with an apse at its eastern end and burials of the post-invasion period. How common this kind of site was it is difficult to say, but there are certainly a number from the Rhineland, most of them rather smaller than this one and on the whole less carefully constructed. One of the most interesting examples is the so-called Grabkapelle

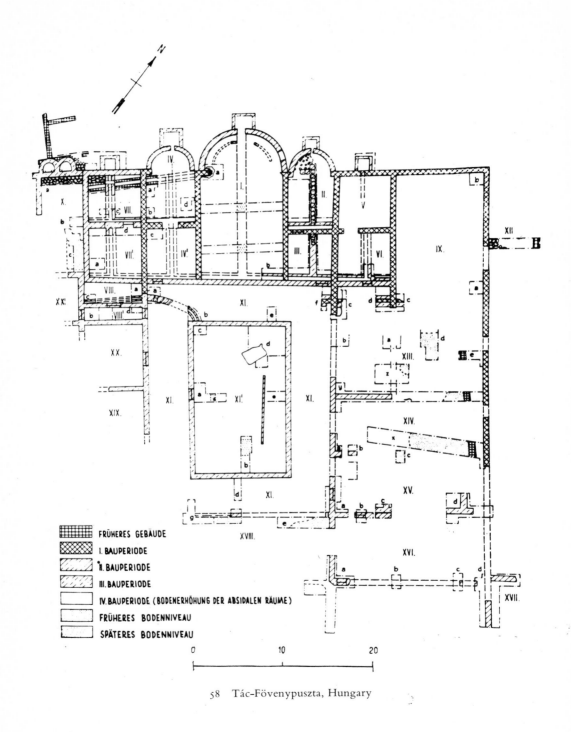

FRÜHERES GEBÄUDE

I. BAUPERIODE

II. BAUPERIODE

III. BAUPERIODE

IV. BAUPERIODE (BODENERHÖHUNG DER ABSIDALEN RÄUME)

FRÜHERES BODENNIVEAU

SPÄTERES BODENNIVEAU

0   10   20

58   Tác-Fövenypuszta, Hungary

in Trier,[35] which is about 17m long, has an apsidal end once more, but burials of the Roman period rather than later; it is worth noting that this little building would fit very nicely into Montcaret, its apse coming under the large semi-circular room at the southern end of the main block. The orientation of these early churches is not always the same, though there is a tendency naturally towards an east–west axis, and if this is so there is no reason why villas, which are normally orientated in accordance with rather different considerations, should necessarily be disqualified from use. And once we begin to look at villa plans the possibility does begin to look more reasonable. Essentially what these churches consist of is two main sections – a nave, as it were, and a chancel – the smaller being frequently semicircular or semihexagonal in shape, and the overall dimensions being something like 12 by 20m. In dozens of villas in Gaul and Britain and Germany these specifications are met by what are normally called dining rooms, the great central rooms, often covered with mosaics, which are so notable a feature where they occur. One finds them in the Rhineland, as at Konz or Odrang, in Lorraine, as at Téting, in the large villas of the south of France such as Montmaurin or Chiragan, and in sites like Cadeilhan-St-Clar (Gers), Chateau-renard (Loiret) or La Chapelle-Vaupelteigne (Yonne).[36] They occur also in Spain, as at Cuevas de Soria (*Fig.* 13) in Britain, as at Lullingstone, and in Pannonia, as at Parndorf (*Fig.* 43) or Csúcshegy.[37] At Sana (Hte-Garonne)[38] a room of this kind is the central feature of a villa in which burials are found in large numbers, and although we cannot always link rooms and burials as closely as this there are enough examples to make the idea plausible. It is worth noting also that a room with an apsidal annexe is a very common feature in villa bath blocks, St-Aubin-sur-Mer being a good example, and it is surprising how often the burials on a site tend to group around this very part. Clearly this is not something to press too strongly, and unless the practice can be more fully documented it would be wiser, perhaps, to see the shape of rooms as simply a contributory factor in the choice of sites rather than as a primary influence.

Before we leave the point, however, there are one or two additional sites which may shed a little more light. At Montferrand (Aude)[39] (*Fig.* 59), for example, there is an intriguing building containing just the kind of room that we have been considering: it is about 17m long, with an apsidal east end, and inside and around it are burials of the late fourth century onwards. The dating is by no means certain, though it is thought that the building began in the fourth century, was destroyed sometime in the fifth, and then re-used until perhaps the seventh; some of the burials are clearly associated with the earliest phases, but some are laid on top of the ruined walls, suggesting that the building itself was not repaired after the fifth-century destruction. What exactly the building was is not at all clear; not far away from its western end is a small bath block, and the two are obviously parts of a larger complex of which at present we have no more than a section. It could equally well be a villa or some kind of sanctuary, and has even been claimed as Elusio, the residence of Sulpicius Severus mentioned by Paulinus of Nola at the end of the fourth century (which, incidentally, would

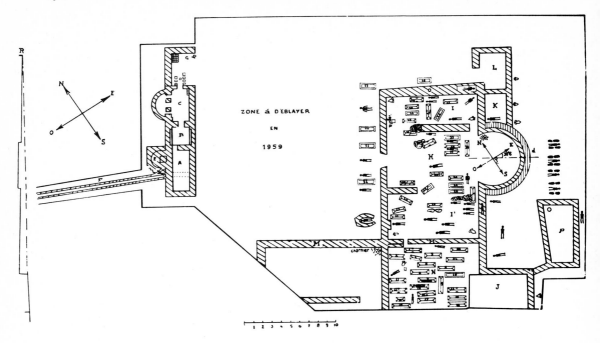

59   Montferrand, Aude

be very helpful if we could prove it, since Elusio was said to have a chapel containing relics). For our purposes it is precisely the uncertainty that is of interest: we are, after all, considering the possibility that villas, or parts of villas, might have become churches, and a site which could very well be either must surely be taken seriously. Montferrand is the most striking site of this kind, but there are others: at St-Ambroix-St-Hilaire (Cher),[40] for example, a Roman building of some kind was converted into a sanctuary, and although its dating, and that of its associated burials, has not been fully worked out, it is an obvious parallel; its size is roughly the same as the central part of Montferrand, though it lacks the apsidal end, and the note in *Gallia* quotes as comparative material the early basilicas from the Rhineland to which we have already referred.

The question of ground plans arises in connection with another process for which there is rather better documentation. Grenier, in the course of discussing St-Ulrich and the great villas of eastern Gaul, remarked that in many cases the general layout was similar to that of early monasteries; and he pointed out that villas and monasteries do occasionally coincide.[41] There is, in fact, quite a lot of evidence in support of this, and together with that already quoted it does provide considerable support for the theory of religious continuity with which we are at present concerned. Grenier, perhaps, with St-Ulrich as his main example, was thinking of something like the celebrated ninth-century plan of the monastery of St-Gallen in Switzerland,[42] but there is no need to go so late for an illustration or to such major sites. Much more striking, both for its date and its size, is the site at Ain-Tamda in North Africa,[43] where we have what is in fact a fifth- or sixth-century monastery but which could easily, so far as its plan is concerned, be taken as a fairly prosperous villa. The central feature is a church, about 25m long, with an apse at its northern end, which very much resembles Montferrand, and adjoining this on its eastern side a large courtyard surrounded by rooms of various sizes serving as living quarters. Essentially, as the excavator points out, it is a villa, and there is no reason, after all, why this should be surprising. St Augustine was taught at a monastery in Lombardy called Cassiciacum,[44] which to judge from its name was at one time a villa, and when in due course he came to found a monastery for himself he did so on his own estates, presumably in an existing villa building.[45] Cassiodorus, similarly, in describing his own foundation at Vivarium,[46] makes it clear that once more a villa was being converted to religious use. Sulpicius Severus, on becoming a Christian, retired to a monastery in southern Gaul with the name Primuliacus,[47] again suggesting a villa originally. All these are cases of conversion without an intervening break caused by abandonment or destruction, but there would seem to be no *a priori* reason why a ruined site should not be put back into commission and similarly converted. Whatever the process in a given case, however, the number of villas which appear under monasteries is significantly high. A few, such as Moissac (Tarn-et-Garonne),[48] are in our list of sites underneath churches, and they can be added to more or less at will: apart from St-Ulrich, which has a monastery overlying the central *atrium*, there is an example at Eschau, south of Strasbourg, another at Loupiac (Gironde), and a third at Kergollet (Landebaëron, Côtes-du-Nord), while at Sorde-l'Abbaye (Landes) the coincidence is so close that the villa's bath wing serves as the actual foundations for what is now the abbot's residence.[49]

Occasionally the literary sources offer a brief glimpse of the process itself and of the motivation behind it. An account by Gregory of Tours of a religious foundation by St Senoch contains the following passage:

> For he found . . . the walls of ancient buildings, which he cleared of rubble and made fit once more for habitation. He found there also an oratory, where it was said St Martin had frequently gone to pray. This he constructed with special care; he built an altar, prepared a shrine there to receive the relics of saints, and invited bishops to come and give it their blessing.[50]

Oddly enough, we can provide an almost exact illustration of the passage in archaeological terms from the celebrated site at Ligugé (Vienne),[51] which touches on our discussion at so many points that it is worth considering in detail. The plan of the villa here can only be partially established because of the very precise use of many of its walls as the foundations of later buildings, but it was clearly a reasonably prosperous one without being obviously luxurious. The excavation reports contain little in the way of finds or detailed dating material, but they state categorically that this first building was destroyed, without however suggesting a date or a destroying agent. Upon its ruins was built an impressive structure, semicircular, or strictly speaking semidecagonal in shape, with an overall diameter (to judge from what we have) of between 25 and 30m. In form it is essentially a chamber surrounded by a cloister or colonnade, and it is orientated exactly on the cardinal points of the compass; from this, and from the fact that it lies in the grounds of the abbey of St-Martin-de-Ligugé, one of the most ancient religious houses in Gaul, the excavators deduced that it was in fact a *martyrium* of St Martin, and there would seem to be no reason to disagree. The building in this form, to judge from architectural remains and associated pottery, is probably of the late fourth or early fifth century, and it lasted for only a short time before being deliberately (and perhaps ritually) destroyed. A large trench was cut across it, parallel to its diameter, and two burial pits were dug into its longest side; both of these features are dateable to the fifth century, the former by pottery in its filling and the latter on the basis of funerary practices, and it seems likely that the Christian monument, if such it was, was destroyed by a pagan community. Eventually, in the sixth century, the Christian element returns: a basilica was built immediately to the west of the *martyrium*, and within it were found some 30 Merovingian burials, one of them bearing an inscription with the first explicit reference to St Martin. A further enlargement came in the seventh century, and from this point the continuity with the present monastery seems to be complete.

By now we have perhaps said enough to support the idea of a religious element in the history of villa sites during and after the great invasions. In a sense, of course, it should not surprise us: the role of religion in the survival of Roman towns is already well documented and agreed upon, as is the adoption by the early church of numerous *civitas*, *pagus* and even parish boundaries.[52] But even if we grant that the sites so far referred to are representative of a sizeable minority of the total number, there still remain many hundreds of examples of which they clearly are not. It may be that the placing of burials is itself a religious act, but since in the majority of cases the use of a ruined villa as a cemetery does not lead to any further development, religious or otherwise, we need to look again at the motives behind the practice, which we have learned already may be somewhat different from its results.

The motives suggested by those who have actually dug this kind of site are admittedly mainly religious: Salin,[53] for example, suggested that villa ruins were chosen because they contained the necessary material for constructing the rudimentary coffins, so common particularly in the early cemeteries, and even claimed that there might be evidence for a kind of rubble ritual associated with some of them. The difficulty here, however, as with all the religious explanations, is that the detailed religious or ritualistic practices may well have been actually suggested by the ruins rather than being the reason why the ruins were chosen, and it may be safer to leave this line of enquiry and think of more secular, more practical motives. One of the simplest suggestions, but one which may well be right, was made many years ago by Linckenheld in connection with a villa at Gondrexange (Moselle)[54]: the attraction of ruins, he said, could well have been that they made the land on which they stood quite useless for agricultural purposes, so that by using them as cemeteries the local people could ensure, first, that their dead were not likely to be disturbed, and second, that they would not diminish the area available for farming. Whether we could ever prove this suggestion it is hard to say, but if it were true its implications would be considerable indeed: it would imply, for example, that farming land was valuable, that what land there was was mostly under cultivation, that apart from the villa sites themselves there were few derelict areas. We are talking, of course, of districts where there was a reasonably sizeable population, indicated indeed by the existence of the cemeteries, and there were no doubt great tracts of territory which were largely depopulated at the end of the Roman period and only reclaimed much later; but it seems likely that where some sort of population remained, or perhaps returned fairly quickly, the dereliction of farm land was by no means as extensive as the villa ruins might otherwise have suggested. Just as in an earlier chapter a decline in living standards was not infrequently linked with an intensification of agricultural activity,[55] so here the disappearance of a villa building might well be linked with something very similar. As in so many other respects, the villas provide us with meaningful information only when they are seen as part of the overall social and economic pattern to which they belong.

Notes and References

Abbreviations

Antiq. Journ.—Antiquaries Journal
Arch. Cant.—Archaeologia Cantiana
Arch. Journ.—Archaeological Journal
C.I.L.—Corpus Inscriptionum Latinarum
Cod. Just.—Codex Justinianus
Cod. Theod.—Codex Theodosianus
Econ. H. R.—Economic History Review
E.H.R.—English Historical Review
J.R.S.—Journal of Roman Studies
P.B.S.R.—Papers of the British School at Rome
Rev. Arch.—Revue Archéologique
T.B.G.A.S.—Transactions of the Bristol and Gloucester Archaeological Society
V.C.H.—Victoria County History

Chapter 1

1. The problem is not confined to students of the villa: for similar difficulties in defining the manor of medieval England, see F.W. Maitland, *Domesday Book and Beyond* (1897), 107–28
2. cf. the entry in Lewis and Short's *Dictionary*, which translates *villa* as 'country house, country seat, farm, villa': i.e. the word itself has to be used to indicate the lack of precision
3. *Heauton Timorumenos*, 731–2
4. Livy, ii. 62, 3
5. Cicero, *Pro Roscio Comoedo*, 12, 33
6. *Epodes*, i, 29
7. *C.I.L.*, viii, 11824
8. Apuleius, *Apologia*, 67, 11. cf. Columella, *De Re Rustica*, i, 6, 21; Cato, *De Agri Cultura*, iv, 1, etc.
9. cf. Varro, *Res Rusticae*, iii, 2, 6
10. *Digest*, 1, 16, 211
11. cf. Varro's remark (iii, 2, 6) that what matters

is not size or luxury but an economic function; he does not at this point define the function further as being agricultural
12. As suggested by J. Harmand, *Rev. Arch.*, 28 (1951), 155–8, and followed by (for example) Haverfield in his *Romanization of Roman Britain* (4th ed., 1923)
13. cf. Caesar, *De Bello Gallico*, iii, 29; v, 12; Varro, *Res Rusticae*, iii, 1, 3; Virgil, *Eclogues*, i, 69, etc. The point is made by A.L.F. Rivet, *The Roman Villa in Britain* (1969), 181–2
14. As observed by W.H. Manning, *Antiquity*, 36 (1962), 56–8
15. R.G. Collingwood, *The Archaeology of Roman Britain* (1930), 113; I.A. Richmond, *Roman Britain* (2nd ed., 1963), 109
16. cf. Manning, op. cit. (Note 14), with Rivet's criticisms (*The Roman Villa in Britain*, 177, n. 2); phrases such as 'regularly built in masonry, or less commonly in the first or second centuries of wood', though accurate enough as part of a definition, are of less help when one is confronted with an individual site to which a label has to be attached
17. *The Roman Villa in Britain*, 177

Chapter 2

1. cf. A.L.F. Rivet, *The Roman Villa in Britain* (1969), 209
2. R. de Maeyer, *De Overblijfselen der Romeinsche Villa's in Belgie* (1940)
3. E.B. Thomas, *Römische Villen in Pannonien* (1964); cf. O. Paret, *Die Römer in Württemberg,* iii (1932), 27 for an estimate of about 800 villa sites in Württemberg at that date
4. See the brief surveys below, pp. 52–66
5. An interesting study of the villas of Gaul from this point of view is that of J. Harmand, *Les*

origines des recherches françaises sur l'habitat rural gallo-romain (1961)

6. For the question of ownership generally, see below, pp. 133–4

7. The evidence is conveniently assembled by S. Applebaum, in *The Agrarian History of England and Wales*, ed. H.P.R. Finberg, I. ii (1972), 87–107; see also below, p. 137

8. Barnsley Park: see the interim reports in *J.R.S.* and *Britannia*, and also *T.B.G.A.S.*, 86 (1967), 74–87. Montmaurin: G. Fouet, *La villa gallo-romaine de Montmaurin (Hte.-garonne)* (1969)

9. For a further discussion of this point, see below, pp. 176–7

10. A particularly striking example is that of M. Reusch, who by patient fieldwork in the immediate neighbourhood of Sarrebourg (Moselle) in the early 1900s, located no less than 99 villas: cf. his brief report in *Ann. soc. hist. et arch. Lorraine*, 24 (1912), 302–40

11. For England, see in particular *A Matter of Time: an Archaeological Survey of the River Gravels of England* (R.C.H.M., 1960). In France, the most notable work of recent years has been that of R. Agache in the basin of the Somme, the results of which are summarized in his *Archéologie aérienne de la Somme* (1964), and *Détection aérienne de vestiges protohistoriques, gallo-romains et médié-vaux* (1970)

12. *Rev. Arch.*, 19 (1892), 322f.; the mosaic is illustrated in M. Rostovtzeff, *Social and Economic History of the Roman Empire* (2nd ed., 1957), Plate XXXVI. cf. also H. Stern, *Gallia*, 9 (1951), 22–30

13. African examples are frequently used as illustrations to more general works: a good selection may be found in Rostovtzeff, op. cit. (last note), Plates LVIII, LIX, LXIII, LXXVII, LXXIX and LXXX

14. cf. T. Précheur-Canonge, *La vie rurale en Afrique romaine d'après les mosaiques* (1961)

15. Précheur-Canonge, Planches III, III bis; cf. Rostovtzeff, Plate LXIII, 2

16. Précheur-Canonge, Planche IV; cf. Rostovtzeff, Plate LXXIX, I

17. Zliten: S. Aurigemma, *I mosaici di Zliten* (1926); cf. Rostovtzeff, Plate LIX. Oudna: Précheur-Canonge, Planche I; cf. Rostovtzeff, Plate LXIII, I

18. Rostovtzeff, Plates VIII, 1–2; IX, 2

19. Stabiae: Rostovtzeff, Plates VIII, 3–4; IX, I. Rome, etc.: M.A. Levi, *Roma Antica* (1963), 48f.

20. Rostovtzeff, Plate X, I

21. cf. K.D. White, *Roman Farming* (1970),

Fig. I, opp. p. 56

22. The fullest publication is in E. Espérandieu, *Receuil général des bas-reliefs, statues et bustes de la Gaule romaine* (1907, repr. 1966), vi, 437–60

23. A selection of the Arlon reliefs is given in Rostovtzeff, Plate XXXVII; for a more comprehensive coverage, see Espérandieu, v, 211–84, and for the harvesting machine cf. M. Renard, *Technique et agriculture en pays trévire et rémois* (1959)

24. cf., for example, Rostovtzeff, Plates LVIII, 3; LXI, etc.

25. On all of these, see W.H. Manning, *J.R.S.*, 54 (1964), 54–65

26. The most comprehensive account, with bibliography of earlier work, is that of K.D. White, *Agricultural Implements of the Roman World* (1967)

27. As can be clearly seen from a study of the different 'reconstructions' of villas: compare, for example, the severely functional German model of Köln-Müngersdorf (A. Grenier, *Manuel d'archéologie gallo-romaine*, ii (1934), Fig. 292, p. 815) with the standard Stockbroker's Tudor so dear to British artists

28. Rostovtzeff, Plate XIV, 2

29. Though cf. the apparent attempt at perspective on the very late mosaic from Carthage, illustrated by Rostovtzeff, Plate LXXX, 2

30. Such a study is in fact readily available in W.E. Heitland's *Agricola* (1921), which covers the Greek and Hellenistic as well as the Roman world

31. Loeb edition by W.D. Hooper and H.B. Ash (1934)

32. Edited by Hooper and Ash (1934), with Cato; cf. also Bertha Tilly, *Varro the Farmer* (1973)

33. Oxford Text by R.A.B. Mynors (1969); Loeb edition by H.R. Fairclough (1935); translation by C. Day Lewis (1966)

34. Loeb edition by F. Granger (1931–4); translation by M.H. Morgan (1960)

35. Loeb edition by H.B. Ash, E.S. Forster, E. Heffner (1941–55)

36. Loeb edition by H. Rackham, W.H.S. Jones, D.E. Eichholz (1938–63)

37. Teubner edition by J.C. Schmitt (1898)

38. Teubner edition by C. Thulin (1913); cf. also F. Blume, K. Lachmann, A. Rudorff, *Gromatici Veteres* (1848–52)

39. Teubner edition by H. Beckh (1895)

40. Loeb edition by M. Heseltine (1913); edition of the main episode, the *Cena Trimalchionis*, by W.B. Sedgwick (1925); translation by J.P. Sullivan (Penguin, 1965)

41. Oxford Text by R.A.B. Mynors (1963);

Loeb edition by W.M.L. Hutchinson (1921, 1927); translation by B. Radice (Penguin, 1963)

42. *De Herediolo*, 20–3

43. *Epodes*, i, 16, 1–15

44. For a plan based on the description, see p. 305 of the Penguin translation

45. *Epistulae*, ii, 2

46. id., *Epistulae*, viii, 4; *Carmina*, 22; Fortunatus, *Carmina*, i, 18, 19, 20; iii, 12; x, 9, etc.

47. *Cod. Theod.*, ed. T. Mommsen (1905); *Cod. Just.*, ed. P. Krueger (1877); *Institutes*, ed. J.B. Moyle (2nd ed., 1890)

48. Ed. T. Mommsen (1870)

49. *C.I.L.*, xi, 1147 (Veleia); 1455 (Ligures Baebiani); cf. the extensive discussion of these documents in R. Duncan-Jones, *The Economy of the Roman Empire* (1974)

50. *C.I.L.*, viii, 25902, 14428, 10570, etc.; see the references given in Note 13 of Chapter 6

51. *Gallia*, 21 (1963), 393 (Vernais, Cher); F. Wagner, *Fundstätten und Funde in Grossherzogtum Baden* (1908–11), 114 (Wössingen)

52. *Gallia*, 20 (1962), 541–5 (Mantoche, Hte-Saône); *Mém. Comm. Antiq. Côte-d'Or*, 20 (1933–7), 98–106 (Lamargelle)

53. Less certain: cf. Grenier, op. cit. (Note 27), 286–91

54. *Gallia*, 17 (1959), 276 (Vallangoujard, Seine-et-Oise); ibid., 16 (1958), 266–80 (Guiry, Seine-et-Oise)

55. cf. J. Harmand, op. cit. (Note 5), Chapter iv

56. *Gallia*, 26 (1968), 525 (Cintegabelle, Hte-Garonne); O. Paret, op. cit. (Note 3), 363 (Remmigsheim, Württemberg)

57. F. Wagner, op. cit. (Note 51), 46 (Messkirch)

58. *Arch. Journ.*, 6 (1849), 14

59. *Bull. soc. arch. Gers*, 64 (1963), 171 (Roquelaure); *Gallia*, 23 (1965), 338 (Concarneau)

60. *Ann. soc. hist. et arch. Lorraine*, 16 (1904), 259 (Rouhling); F. Wagner, op. cit. (Note 51), 133 (Geisslingen)

61. *Gallia*, 28 (1970), 281 (Champigneulles, Meurthe-et-Moselle); ibid., 25 (1967), 255 (Pierrefitte, Deux-Sèvres)

62. For a vivid illustration, see the inscription from Veleia referred to in Note 49

63. The significance of the names was first recognized by H. d'Arbois de Jubainville, *Recherches sur l'origine de la propriété foncière et les noms de lieux habités en France* (1890); for the linguistic questions, cf. F. Falc'hun, *Les noms de lieux celtiques* (1966), esp. Chapter i

64. For a useful summary, see A. Grenier, op. cit. (Note 27), 914–18

65. Sheet XXIII. 15 (Corbeil–Essonnes)

66. A. Nicolai, *Bull. et mém. soc. arch. Bordeaux*, 53 (1936), 55–126; 54 (1937), 50–153

67. *Digest*, I, 16, 211

68. A. Albenque, *Les Rutènes* (1948), 114f.

Chapter 3

1. Of the many works of general interest on the history and administration of the Roman Empire, one may cite: M.P. Charlesworth, *The Roman Empire* (1951); Fergus Millar, *The Roman Empire and its Neighbours* (1967); J.P.V.D. Balsdon, *Rome: the Story of an Empire* (1970), from all of which references to earlier and more specialized topics may be obtained. For the policies of Augustus and his immediate successors, see *Cambridge Ancient History*, x (1952)

2. cf. A.L.F. Rivet, *Town and Country in Roman Britain* (2nd ed., 1964); id., *The Roman Villa in Britain* (1969), 189–98. On relations between the army and the civilian population, see P. Salway, *The Frontier People of Roman Britain* (1965); I.A. Richmond (ed.), *Roman and Native in North Britain* (1958)

3. *Agricola*, 19, 4

4. For the effects of military demands on British agriculture, see Rivet, *The Roman Villa in Britain* (1969), 189–98, and below, p. 152

5. Dio, 62, 2

6. The standard general work dealing with, as it were, the philosophy of Romanization is still that of A.N. Sherwin-White, *The Roman Citizenship* (2nd ed., 1973). For works relating to particular provinces, see F. Cumont, *Comment la Belgique fut romanisée* (1914); F. Haverfield, *The Romanization of Roman Britain* (4th ed., 1923); T.R.S. Broughton, *The Romanization of Africa Proconsularis* (1929), and Chapters 4 and 5 of Rivet's *Town and Country in Roman Britain* (2nd ed., 1964)

7. *C.I.L.*, xiii, 1668; cf. the summary by Tacitus in *Annals*, xi, 24

8. *Agricola*, 21, 1

9. *Epistulae*, x, 23–4, 37–40

10. cf. ibid., x, 37, where something like $3\frac{1}{2}$ million sesterces were spent on an unfinished aqueduct; Trajan's reply, in the next letter, urges Pliny to find out if there has been any corruption

11. For Seneca, see above, Note 5; for Florus and Sacrovir, Tacitus, *Annals*, iii, 40

12. op. cit. (Note 6), 46

13. *The Roman Villa in Britain* (1969), 177

14. *Bonner Jahrbücher*, 133 (1928), 51–152; the villa is discussed at length, with illustrations,

by Grenier, *Manuel d'archéologie gallo-romaine*, ii (1934), 784–95, and there is a more recent study of the surrounding area and subsidiary sites in *Bonner Jahrbücher*, 163 (1963), 317–41.

15. Park Street: *Arch. Journ.*, 102 (1945), 21–110. Ditchley: *Oxoniensia*, 1 (1936), 24–69

16. Lockleys: *Antiq. Journ.*, 18 (1938), 339–76. Brixworth: P.J. Woods, *Brixworth Excavations*, i (1972); cf. *Britannia*, 3 (1972), 322. Hambledon: *Archaeologia*, 71 (1921), 141–98, with Fig. XIII, opp. p. 141

17. The evidence in each case is a series of postholes along the front of the house: see, most clearly, the Brixworth plan in *Britannia*, 3 (1972), Fig. 7

18. Haccourt: *Archaeologia Belgica*, 132 (1971), 15–32, with Fig. 2, p. 18. Cadeilhan-St-Clar: *Gallia*, 11 (1953), 41–67, with Fig. 2, opp. p. 48

19. *T.B.G.A.S.*, 77 (1959), 23–30

20. For a further discussion of such sites, see below, p. 146

21. Chiragan: L. Joulin, *Les établissements gallo-romaines de la plaine de Martres-Tolosanes* (1901). Montmaurin: G. Fouet, *La villa gallo-romaine de Montmaurin (Hte-Garonne)* (1969). For the Italian parallels, see R.C. Carrington, *J.R.S.*, 21 (1931), 110–30, and the description by the younger Pliny of his own villa at Laurentum (*Epistulae*, ii, 17)

22. *Jahrb. der Schweiz. Ges. für Urgeschichte*, 48 (1960–1), 95–103; cf. *Helvetia Archaeologica*, 1 (1970), 38–40

23. Fishbourne: B. Cunliffe, *Excavations at Fishbourne, 1961–1969* (1971). Eccles: interim reports in *Arch. Cant.*, *J.R.S.* and *Britannia* since 1962; most recent plan, *Arch. Cant.*, 85 (1970), Fig. 2, opp. p. 56

24. The reference is, of course, to the first paragraph of the *Decline and Fall of the Roman Empire*

25. For investment by Romans in the provinces, see above, p. 35 ; cf. the remarks below, p. 88 on the development of villas in Dalmatia

26. Haccourt: *Archaeologia Belgica*, 132 (1971), 15–32, with Fig. 2, p. 18. Montcaret: *Congrès arch. France*, 192 (1939), 182–95; for plan, see *Gallia*, 9 (1951), Fig. 1, p. 115

27. Guiry: *Gallia*, 16 (1958), 266–80; 18 (1960), 163–85, with Fig. 1, p. 164. Noyers-sur-Serein: ibid., 18 (1960), 354–6; 22 (1964), 331–2, with Fig. 51, p. 331. Württemberg: O. Paret, *Die Römer in Württemberg*, iii (1932)

28. On the invasions generally, see L. Musset, *Les Invasions: les Vagues Germaniques* (1965); R. Remondon, *La Crise de l'Empire Romain* (1970). For Gaul, see H. Koethe, *32 Bericht der Römisch-Germanisch Kommission*, (1950), 199–224

29. cf. A. Longnon, *Les noms de lieux de la France* (1920–9), nos. 522–47; A. Dauzat, *La toponymie française* (1946), 18

30. E.A. Thompson, *Past and Present*, 2 (1952), 11–23

31. cf. Dio, lxxii, 2, 2; lxxi, 11, 2; *Scriptores Historiae Augustae, Proculus*, 12, 1–2, 5

32. See the works referred to in Note 28, and also A.H.M. Jones, *Econ.H.R.*, 5 (1953), 293–318 (= *The Roman Economy*, ed. P.A. Brunt (1974), 187–227)

33. It may well be, as Jones has argued (*The Later Roman Empire* (1964), 737–57), that the financial burdens on decurions have been exaggerated; what matters, however, is that the decurions themselves were increasingly reluctant to shoulder them

34. Jones, *Econ. H.R.*, 5 (1953), 294–7 (= *The Roman Economy* (1974), 191–6)

35. For a discussion in general terms, see (for example) E.T. Salmon, *A History of the Roman World, 30 B.C. to A.D. 138* (1944), 275–6

36. Jones, op. cit. (Note 32), 297f.

37. ibid., 296; cf. Remondon, op. cit. (Note 28), 87–9

38. For a discussion, with full bibliography and references, cf. J.F. Gilliam, *American Journal of Philology*, 82 (1961), 225–51

39. See above, p. 36, with Notes 9 and 10

40. Britain, perhaps, should be considered separately, in view of the resurgence which followed (cf. the doubts expressed by R. Goodburn, *Britannia*, 1 (1970), 320). Nevertheless, destruction and decay there certainly was (see the summaries in Rivet, *The Roman Villa in Britain* (1969), 200–1, and S. Applebaum, *The Agrarian History of England and Wales*, ed. H.P.R. Finberg (1972), 228–9)

41. Possible candidates are Eccles, in Kent, which seems actually to have expanded at this period (*Arch. Cant.*, 84 (1969), 93–106), Sorde-l'Abbaye (Landes), which had no signs of decay or destruction at any stage (*Gallia*, 19 (1961), 393–6), and oddly enough Mayen (*Bonner Jahrbücher*, 133 (1928), 51–152)

42. *Gallia*, 16 (1958), 279–80

43. *Gallia*, 26 (1968), 366

44. cf. E.M. Wightman, *Roman Trier and the Treveri* (1970), 162–3

45. *The Roman Villa in Britain* (1969), 201

46. On the history of the period, see Jones, *Later Roman Empire* (1964), 37–111: E. Stein, *Histoire du Bas-Empire*, i (1959)

47. *The Ancient Economy* (1973), 87

48. J. Dhondt, *L'Antiquité Classique*, 16 (1947), 261–86; G. Faider-Feytmans, *Actes des Journées de Poitiers, 1–3 mai, 1952* (1953), 103–9

49. Palaminy: *Gallia*, 26 (1968), 528. Plouhinec: ibid., 29 (1971), 241–2

50. ibid., 27 (1969), 352–4

51. ibid., 19 (1961), 426–8

52. Banon: ibid., 16 (1958), 392–9. Noyers-sur-Serein: ibid., 18 (1960), 354–6

53. *La Physiophile*, 32 (1956), 17–30; 34 (1958), 4–30

54. op. cit. (Note 44), 163–4

55. L. Joulin, *Les établissements gallo-romaines de la plaine de Martres-Tolosanes* (1901)

56. op. cit. (Note 14), 836–7

57. *Pallas*, 3 (1955), 89–115

58. cf. R.G. Goodchild, *Antiq. Journ.*, 23 (1943), 148–53

59. *J.R.S.*, 57 (1967), 198

60. Witcombe: *T.B.G.A.S.*, 73 (1954), 5–69. Frocester Court: ibid., 77 (1959), 23–30, and reports since then in *J.R.S.* and *Britannia*

61. Rivet, *Roman Villa in Britain* (1969), 208–9

62. ibid., 202

63. See Note 40

64. Rivet, op. cit., 202; for a more cautious view, see M. Fulford, *Britannia*, 4 (1973), 163–4

65. North Leigh: *V.C.H. Oxfordshire*, i (1939), 316–8. Bignor: *V.C.H. Sussex*, iii (1935), 20–3

66. M. Biro, *Acta Archaeologica Academiae Scientiarum Hungaricae*, 26 (1974), 52–4; cf. A. Mócsy, *Pannonia and Upper Moesia* (1974), 299–308

67. E.M. Wightman, op. cit. (Note 44), 164–70

68. op. cit. (Note 14), 864

69. *Mosella*, 20, 318–48; one thinks, particularly, of the area around Ausonius' birthplace of Bordeaux (see below, p. 72)

Chapter 4

1. On the problem of definitions, see above, p. 13, and on the confusion between villas and towns, J. Harmand, *Les origines des recherches françaises sur l'habitat rural gallo-romain* (1961), Chapter IV

2. On Italy and the Mediterranean provinces generally, see M. Cary, *The Geographic Background of Greek and Roman History* (1949)

3. See, for example, *P.B.S.R.*, 33 (1965), 55f.

4. R.C. Carrington, *J.R.S.*, 21 (1931), 110–30; but see now J.H. d'Arms, *Romans on the Bay of Naples* (1970), esp. pp. 171–232, and K.D. White, *Roman Farming* (1970), 415–45

5. Veii: *P.B.S.R.*, 36 (1968). Capena: ibid., 30 (1962), 116–207; 31 (1963), 100–58

6. ibid., 36 (1968), 145f.

7. ibid., 152f.; see also 31 (1963), 146

8. Carrington, op. cit. (Note 4), 111–15

9. G.A. Mansuelli, *La villa romana di Russi* (1962)

10. The classification here followed is essentially that of Rostovtzeff, *Social and Economic History of the Roman Empire* (2nd ed., 1957), 552f.

11. The nine Campanian sites are nos. 3, 13, 16, 27, 29, 30, 31, 33 and 35 (of which nos. 27, 31 and 33 are illustrated on Fig. 16, p. 120 of Carrington's article); for the ager Veientanus sites, see *P.B.S.R.*, 36 (1968), 153–7

12. *P.B.S.R.*, 33 (1965), 55–69, comparing Figs 3, p. 60 and 7, p. 69

13. op. cit. (Note 10), 552

14. The Pompeian sites are nos. 26 and 34 in Carrington's article; for those in Africa, see below, p. 64

15. *De Architectura*, vi, 6

16. xliv, 1, 4

17. cf. Livy, xxx, 26, 6 (203 BC); Strabo, iii, 2, 6; Dio, lx, 24, 5

18. On colonization here and elsewhere, see A.J.N. Wilson, *Emigration from Italy in the Republican Age of Rome* (1966); for Spain, see particularly 22–7, 38–40

19. For a general introduction to Roman Spain, see J.J. van Nostrand in *An Economic Survey of Ancient Rome*, ed. Tenney Frank, iii (1937); C.H.V. Sutherland, *The Romans in Spain, 217 B.C.–A.D. 117* (1939); R. Thouvenot, *Essai sur la province romaine de Bétique* (1940). The second volume of R. Menendez Pidal, *Historia de España* (1935) contains a number of plans and other useful material; see also Cary, op. cit. (Note 2), 231–43

20. Fraga: *Ampurias*, 5 (1943), 5f. La Cocosa: J. de C. Serra Ráfols, *La villa romana de La Cocosa* (1952); cf. *Archivo Espanol de Arqueología*, 26 (1953), 207f.

21. *Principe de Viana*, 10 (1949), 353f.; 11 (1950), 9f.

22. Cuevas de Soria: R. Menendez Pidal, op. cit. (Note 19), 329, Fig. 206. Ramalete: *Principe de Viana*, 10 (1949), 9f.; *Archivo Espanol de Arqueología*, 26 (1953), 207f.; cf. also the big courtyard villa at Santervas del Burgo (Soria): *Noticiario Arqueologico Hispanico*, 3 (1954), 169–94

23. *Ampurias*, 21 (1959), 323–9, with plan, opp. p. 324; on the size of holdings generally, see Thouvenot, op. cit. (Note 19), 247–8

24. On Roman Africa generally, see R.M. Haywood in *An Economic Survey of Ancient Rome*, ed. Tenney Frank, iv (1937); T.R.S. Broughton, *The Romanization of Africa Pro-*

consularis (1929); G.C. Picard, *La civilisation de l'Afrique romaine* (1959)

25. cf. Varro, *Res Rusticae*, i, 1, 10; Columella, *De Re Rustica*, i, 1, 13; xi, 4, 2; Pliny, *Naturalis Historia*, xviii, 5, 7, etc.; on Mago himself, see K.D. White, op. cit. (Note 4), 17–18

26. White, op. cit.

27. cf. A.J.N. Wilson, op. cit. (Note 18), 42–54

28. *Naturalis Historia*, xviii, 6, 35

29. cf. *Atlas archéologique de la Tunisie* (1893); *Atlas archéologique de l'Algérie* (1911), and the more recent surveys referred to in Note 31 below

30. On all of this, see R.M. Haywood, op. cit. (Note 24), 15–25, 39–51

31. cf. R.G. Goodchild, *P.B.S.R.*, 19 (1951), 43–77; David Oates, ibid., 21 (1953), 81–117

32. See, for example, Oates's sites nos. 10 and 14 (Figs 8, p. 100 and 11, p. 108)

33. ibid., Fig. 7, p. 98

34. T. Prêcheur-Canonge, *La vie rurale en Afrique romaine d'après les mosaïques* (1961), 27f., with Planches iii, iii bis and iv

35. M. Ponsich, *Bull. arch. marocaine*, 5 (1964), 235–52, with Fig. 3, p. 242 (Jorf el Hamra); A. Luquet, ibid., Fig. 2, p. 299 (Bab Tisra)

36. Sabratha: L. Alcock, *P.B.S.R.*, 18 (1950), (92–100). Tagiura: P. Romanelli, *Enciclopedia Classica*, Sezione iii, Vol. x, Tomo vii (1970), 252f. Tipasa: *Fasti Archaeologici*, 12 (1957), no. 5638. Hippo Regius: ibid., 10 (1955), no. 4615

37. op. cit. (Note 31), 92f.

38. cf. J. Boardman, *The Greeks Overseas* (1964), 223–30

39. For a general introduction to Roman Gaul, see A. Grenier in *An Economic Survey of Ancient Rome*, ed. Tenney Frank, iii (1937); O. Brogan, *Roman Gaul* (1953); J.J. Hatt, *Histoire de la Gaule romaine* (2nd ed., 1967)

40. For a more lengthy treatment of villas in Gaul, see the standard work of A. Grenier, *Manuel d'archéologie gallo-romaine*, ii (1934)

41. *Gallia*, 24 (1966), 460–2

42. ibid., 27 (1969), 430–2, with Fig. 14, p. 431

43. G. Combarnous, *Actes du 86ᵉ Congrès National des Sociétés Savantes* (Montpellier, 1961), 117–28, with Fig. 1, p. 118

44. *Gallia*, 22 (1964), 588–90, with Fig. 30, p. 589

45. P. Barrière, *Bull. soc. hist. et arch. Périgord*, 73 (1946), 95–101

46. St-Emilion: *Gallia*, 29 (1971), 345–8. Pompogne: *Rev. de l'Agenais*, 77 (1951), 55–7

47. *Gallia*, 11 (1953), 41–67, with Fig. 2, opp. p. 48

48. Chiragan: L. Joulin, *Les établissements gallo-romaines de la plaine de Martres-Tolosanes*

(1901). Montmaurin: G. Fouet, *La villa gallo-romaine de Montmaurin (Hte-Garonne)* (1969). Arnesp: H.-P. Eydoux, *Résurrection de la Gaule* (1961), 333–60; cf. *Gallia*, 9 (1951), 133–4; 17 (1959), 430–3; 22 (1964), 449–50

49. *Bull soc. sciences, lettres, arts de Pau*, 25 (1963), 55–63; more recent plan in *Gallia*, 27 (1969), Fig. 45, opp. p. 376

50. On continuity in general, see below, pp. 168f.

51. *Gallia*, 12 (1954), 186

52. *Bull. soc. hist. et arch. Limousin*, 74 (1932–3), 5–22; *Gallia*, 10 (1952), 1–30, with Fig. 2, p. 4

53. *Gallia*, 12 (1954), 189

54. *Rev. Arch.*, 16 (1940), 46–61, with Fig. 1, p. 48

55. *Gallia*, 27 (1969), 267–8, with Fig. 12, p. 267

56. See note 44

57. *Bulletin Monumental*, 23 (1857), 178f.

58. Carnac: Grenier, op. cit. (Note 40), Fig. 330, p. 872. Concarneau: *Gallia*, 25 (1967), 231–5, with Fig. 10, p. 231. Plouneventer: *Annales de Bretagne*, 70 (1963), 25–36; 71 (1964), 153–60; cf. plan in *Gallia*, 25 (1967), Fig. 1, p. 227

59. Sizun: *Gallia*, 13 (1955), 156–7, with Fig. 4, p. 156

60. ibid., 27 (1969), 254–6; 29 (1971), 246–7

61. *Rev. Arch.*, (1964), 172–6, with Fig. 1, p. 174

62. cf. J. Soyer, *La Beauce ancienne* (1943), and the review in *Rev. Arch.*, (1951), 105–6; on the area generally, see now D. Jalmain, *Archéologie aérienne en Ile-de-France* (1970)

63. Verneuil: *Revue du Nord*, 38 (1956), 289–306, with Fig. 1, p. 292. St-Maximin: *Gallia*, 25 (1967), 197; 27 (1969), 234; 29 (1971), 228

64. cf. ibid., 21 (1963), 370–2

65. Châteaubleau: Jalmain, op. cit. (Note 62), 67–9, with air photograph, Fig. 30, p. 68

66. *Gallia*, 16 (1958), 266–80; 18 (1960), 163–85, with Fig. 1, p. 164

67. J.B.D. Cochet, *La Seine-Inférieure historique et archéologique* (1864); L. Deglatigny, *Inventaire archéologique de la Seine-Inférieure* (1931)

68. Cochet, op. cit. (last note), 301–2

69. ibid., 83–6

70. See his surveys in *Archéologie aérienne de la Somme* (1964) and *Détection aérienne de vestiges protohistoriques, gallo-romains et médiévaux* (1970)

71. Malapart: *Détection aérienne*, Fig. 415. Grivesnes: *Archéologie aérienne*, Fig. 220. Warfusée: *Archéologie aérienne*, Fig. 221; *Détection aérienne*, Figs 473–5. See also the discussion of these and other sites in *Revue du Nord*, 47 (1965), 541–76

72. H. Stern, *Receuil général des mosaïques de la Gaule*, i. 3 (1963), 145–6, with Planches xcii–xciv

73. Andilly-en-Bassigny: *Les Cahiers Haut-Marnais*, 74 (1963), 108–26; 92 (1968), 1–17; cf. plan in *Gallia*, 25 (1967), Fig. 29, p. 288. Noyers-sur-Serein: *Gallia*, 22 (1964), 331–2, with Fig. 51, p. 331

74. Fontenay-près-Vézelay: *Gallia*, 22 (1964), 329–31, with Fig. 49, p. 330; 24 (1966), 405–6; 26 (1968), 508–9. Fontaines-sur-Marne: *Les Cahiers Haut-Marnais*, 77 (1964), 49–74

75. Grange: F. Stähelin, *Die Schweiz in römischer Zeit* (3rd ed., 1948), 374–5, with Abb. 82, p. 375. Zofingen: ibid., 374, with Abb. 78, p. 371

76. Attricourt: H. Stern, op. cit. (Note 72), 88–91, with Planche XLV. Mantoche: ibid., 91–3, with Planches XLIX and L

77. A.L.F. Rivet, *The Roman Villa in Britain* (1969), 177

78. op. cit. (Note 40), 859–67

79. Frécourt and Courcelles-Urville: *Ann. soc. hist. et arch. Lorraine*, 18 (1906), 413–49, with Figs XIII–XIV (Courcelles-Urville) and XV–XVI (Frécourt). Lorquin: ibid., 20 (1908), 153. Marly-aux-Bois: A. Grenier, *Habitations gauloises et villas latines dans la cité des Médiomatrices* (1906), 67

80. St-Ulrich: *Ann. soc. hist. et arch. Lorraine*, 10 (1898), 171–94; *Les Cahiers Lorrains* (1952), 46–8; cf. the plan in Grenier, op. cit. (Note 40), 830. Rouhling: *Ann. soc. hist. et arch. Lorraine*, 16 (1904), 259–92. Téting: Grenier, *Habitations gauloises* (see last note), 159f., with Fig. 11

81. See Note 78

82. E. Linckenheld, *Une villa romaine avec tombes de l'époque barbare à Gondrexange* (Moselle) (1932)

83. R. de Maeyer, *De Romeinsche Villa's in Belgie: een Archaeologische Studie* (1937); id., *De Overblijfselen der Romeinsche Villa's in Belgie* (1940). For a more critical comment, see G. de Boe, *Archaeologia Belgica*, 132 (1971)

84. Sauvenière: *Ann. soc. arch. Namur*, 24 (1900), 11–20. Chastres-lès-Walcourt: ibid., 121–8

85. Hosté: *Ann. soc. arch. Bruxelles*, 19 (1905), 303f.; cf. the plan in Grenier, op. cit. (Note 40), Fig. 295, p.823. Anthée: *Ann. soc. arch. Namur*, 14 (1877), 165–94; 15 (1881), 1–40; cf. Grenier, op. cit., 845. Haccourt: *Archaeologia Belgica*, 132 (1971), 15–32; cf. also 168 (1974) and 171 (1975)

86. On this and other representations of the harvesting machine, see M. Renard, *Technique et agriculture en pays trévire et rémois* (1959)

87. E.M. Wightman, *Roman Trier and the Treveri* (1970), especially 139–72

88. ibid., 13–16

89. Bollendorf: ibid., 139–43, with Fig. 13, p. 140. Sotzweiler: *Germania*, 39 (1961), 474–8, with Abb. 1, p. 476

90. Konz: *Germania*, 39 (1961), 204–6, with Abb. 1, p. 205; cf. Wightman, op. cit., 165–8. Pfalzel: *Germania*, 19 (1935), 40–53; cf. Wightman, Fig. 20, p. 168

91. *Mosella*, 20, 318–48

92. See Note 80

93. Nennig: Wightman, op. cit., 145–8, with Fig. 16, p. 146. Odrang: ibid., 143–5

94. Grenier, op. cit. (Note 40), 819–20, 822

95. Stahl: ibid., 798, with Fig. 275. Weitersbach: *Trierer Zeitschrift*, 24–6 (1956–8), 511–26

96. *Bonner Jahrbücher*, 133 (1928), 51–152; cf. Grenier, op. cit. (Note 40), 784–95

97. Tacitus, *Annals*, i, 11, 7

98. Köln-Müngersdorf: F. Fremersdorf, *Der römische Gutshof Köln-Müngersdorf* (1933); cf. Grenier, op. cit., 814–9. Merklingen: O. Paret, *Die Römer in Württemberg*, iii (1932), Abb. 74, p. 117. Burgweinting: F. Wagner, *Die Römer in Bayern* (1924), 56–8, with Abb. 17

99. op. cit. (Note 40), 865–7

100. op cit. (Note 98), 27

101. H. von Petrikovits, *Germania*, 34 (1956), 99–125, with Abb. 1, p. 101

102. id., *Das römische Rheinland* (1960), 64–7

103. *Mainzer Zeitschrift*, 18–19 (1921–4), 79–107, with Abb. 10, p. 98

104. J. Harmand, *Rev. Arch.*, (1954), 103–4; cf. the reply by J.J. Hatt, ibid., (1955), 229–32

105. *Gallia*, 22 (1964), 373–4

106. *Helvetia Archaeologica*, 2 (1970), 38–40

107. Zofingen: see Note 75. Kulm: F. Stähelin, *Die Schweiz in römischer Zeit* (3rd ed., 1948), 374, with Abb. 78, p. 371

108. G. Alföldy, *Noricum* (1974), 106–42, 205–12

109. Löffelbach: ibid., 120–1, with Fig. 14, p. 121. Thalerhof: ibid., 173, with Fig. 30, p. 172

110. ibid., 121, with Fig. 15, p. 122

111. For the establishment of the northern frontier generally, see R. Syme, *Cambridge Ancient History*, x (1952), 351–73; cf. also Fergus Millar, *The Roman Empire and its Neighbours* (1967), 221–38

112. J.J. Wilkes, *Dalmatia* (1969), xxi–xxvii

113. ibid., 394–406

114. ibid., Fig. 22, p. 397

115. ibid., 399; cf. Pliny, *Naturalis Historia*, iii, 31

116. ibid., Figs 23, p. 401 and 24, p. 404

117. cf. Millar, op. cit. (Note 111), 229

118. On the geographical features, see Cary, op. cit. (Note 2), 281–9

119. On the villas, see E.B. Thomas, *Römische Villen in Pannonien* (1964); and on the province generally, A. Mócsy, *Pannonia and Upper Moesia* (1974)

120. Thomas, 344–9, with Abb. 167, p. 346

121. ibid., 216–24, with Abb. 112, p. 217

122. ibid., 232–7, with Abb. 118, p. 233

123. ibid., 73–107, with Abb. 40, p. 75

124. ibid., 60–8, with Abb. 29, p. 61

125. Parndorf: ibid., 177–92, with Abb. 99, p. 178. Mediana: Mócsy, op. cit. (Note 119), 302

126. cf. C. Daicoviciu, *La Transylvanie dans l'Antiquité* (1945), 215f.

127. cf., for example, the sites at Cinciș, near Hunedoara (*Fasti Archeologici*, 18 (1963), no. 11019) and Hobita, in the same region (ibid., 12 (1957) no. 7077)

128. cf. Daicoviciu, op. cit. (Note 126), 234

129. Armira: R.F. Hoddinott, *Bulgaria in Antiquity* (1975), 217–20, with Fig. 51, p. 217. Chatalka: ibid., 209–12, with Figs. 47, p. 210 and 48, p. 211

130. Bela Palanka: Mócsy, op. cit. (Note 119), 300, with Fig. 49, p. 301. Kolarovgrad: Millar, op. cit. (Note 111), 230

131. *De Bello Gallico*, v, 14, 1; for the Cantiaci, and for the other main peoples of Britain, see Rivet's survey in *Town and Country in Roman Britain* (2nd ed., 1964), Chapter 6

132. Eccles: interim reports in *Arch. Cant., J.R.S.* and *Britannia* since 1962; most recent published plan, *Arch. Cant.*, 85 (1970), Fig. 2, opp. p. 56. Lullingstone: G.W. Meates, *Lullingstone Roman Villa* (1955)

133. Cobham Park: *Arch. Cant.*, 76 (1961), 88–109

134. Little Chart: ibid., 71 (1957), 130–46, with Fig. 2, p. 132. Otford: ibid., 39 (1927), 153–8; cf. Applebaum, *The Agrarian History of England and Wales*, ed. H.P.R. Finberg, 1. ii (1972), 72

135. *Arch. Cant.*, 22 (1896), 49–84, with plan, opp. p. 49

136. Rivet, *Town and Country*, 145

137. Maidstone: *Arch. Cant.*, 10 (1876), 163–72, with plan, opp. p. 164. East Malling: ibid., 71 (1957), 228–9. Wingham: ibid., 14 (1882), 134–9; cf. plan in *J.R.S.*, 58 (1968), Fig. 21, p. 205

138. Folkestone: S.E. Winbolt, *Roman Folkestone* (1925); cf. *Rural Settlement in Roman Britain*, ed. C. Thomas (1966), 123

139. Barry Cunliffe, *The Regni* (1973); cf. Rivet, *Town and Country*, 158–9

140. ibid., 95; his discussion of the villas mentioned in this section is on pp. 74–107

141. Fishbourne: B. Cunliffe, *Excavations at Fishbourne, 1961–1969* (1971). Angmering: *Sussex Arch. Coll.*, 79 (1938), 3–44; 86 (1947), 1–21. Southwick: ibid., 73 (1932), 13–32. Pulborough: Cunliffe, op. cit. (Note 139), 78. Eastbourne: *Sussex Arch. Coll.*, 90 (1952), 1–12

142. West Blatchington: *Sussex Arch. Coll.*, 89 (1950), 1–56, with Fig. 19, opp. p. 56. Rapsley: ibid., 65 (1968), 1–70. Bignor: *V.C.H. Sussex*, iii (1935), 20–3, with plan, p. 21; cf. *J.R.S.*, 53 (1963), 155–6

143. op. cit. (Note 139), 79

144. See Note 142, and cf. Applebaum, op. cit. (Note 134), 212–14

145. Farnham: *Surrey Arch. Coll.*, 54 (1953–4), 47–57, with Fig. 2, opp. p. 50. Rapsley: see Note 142

146. Rivet, *Town and Country*, 139–40

147. *Berks. Arch. Journ.*, 60 (1962), 62–91

148. *Arch. Journ.*, 54 (1897), 349–54, with plan, opp. p. 342

149. Eling: *V.C.H. Berkshire*, i (1906), 210. Cranhill: ibid., 211

150. Rivet, *Town and Country*, 145–8

151. *Britannia*, 4 (1973), 115–27, with Fig. 2, p. 117

152. Park Street: *Arch. Journ.*, 102 (1945), 21–110. Lockleys: *Antiq. Journ.*, 18 (1938), 339–76. Gadebridge Park: D.S. Neal, *The Excavation of the Roman Villa in Gadebridge Park, Hemel Hempstead, 1963–8* (1974). Boxmoor: *Britannia*, 1 (1970), 156–62, with Fig. 3, opp. p. 162. Latimer: Keith Branigan, *Latimer* (1971)

153. Dicket Mead: *Britannia*, 1 (1970), 289; 2 (1971), 270, with Fig. 10, p. 269

154. Rivet, *Town and Country*, 146, with references

155. ibid., 146–7; cf. *Ordnance Survey Map of Roman Britain* (3rd ed., 1956), Fig. 3, p. 22

156. Apethorpe: *V.C.H. Northamptonshire*, i (1902), 191–2. Whittlebury: ibid., 199. Great Weldon: ibid., 193. Brixworth: *Britannia*, 3 (1972), 322, with Fig. 7, p. 323. Cosgrove: ibid., 1 (1970), 288

157. op cit. (Note 134), 61–9

158. Rivet, *Town and Country*, 156–7, 162–3

159. Gayton Thorpe: *Norfolk Archaeology*, 23 (1928), 166–209. Lidgate: *Britannia*, 3 (1972), 330–1

160. *J.R.S.*, 50 (1960), 228

161. *Proc. Suffolk Inst. of Arch.*, 22 (1936), 339–41; cf. Rivet, *Town and Country*, 157

162. Rivet, ibid., 140–1

163. cf. R.G. Collingwood, *Roman Britain and the English Settlements* (2nd ed., 1937), 224; Applebaum, op. cit. (Note 134), 30

164. Clanville: *V.C.H. Hampshire*, i (1900), 295–7. Newport: ibid., 317; *Antiq. Journ.*, 9 (1929), 141–51

165. Sparsholt: *Britannia*, 4 (1973), 318, with Fig. 15, p. 319. Stroud: *Arch. Journ.*, 55 (1908), 57–60; 56 (1909), 33–52. Rockbourne: *Britannia*, 3 (1972), 348, with Fig. 18, opp. p. 348. Brading: *V.C.H. Hampshire*, i (1900), 313–16, with Fig. 21, p. 313

166. West Meon: *Arch. Journ.*, 64 (1907), 1–14. North Warnborough: *Proc. Hampshire Field Club*, 10 (1931), 225–36

167. op. cit. (Note 163), 236–7

168. Wellow: *V.C.H. Somerset*, i (1906), 312. Pitney: ibid., 326–8. Atworth: *Wilts Arch. Mag.*, 49 (1940–2), 46–95. Box: ibid., 33 (1904), 236–69; cf. *V.C.H. Wiltshire*, i (1957), 44

169. Whatley: *V.C.H. Somerset*, i (1906), 317. Keynsham; *Archaeologia*, 75 (1926), 109–38. Newton St Loe: *V.C.H. Somerset*, i (1906), 302; cf. *J.R.S.*, 26 (1936), Fig. 4, p. 43

170. Camerton: W.J. Wedlake, *Excavations at Camerton* (1958), Mendips: J.W. Gough, *The Mines of Mendip* (1930); cf. *V.C.H. Somerset*, i (1906), 334f.

171. Rivet, *Town and Country*, 155–6

172. Littleton: *V.C.H. Somerset*, i (1906), 323–4. Yeovil: *Proc. Somerset Arch. and Nat. Hist. Soc.*, 74 (1928), 122–43, with Plate 16, opp. p. 142

173. ibid., 96 (1951), 41–77, with Fig. 4, p. 60

174. Lufton: ibid., 97 (1952), 91–112. Ilchester: *J.R.S.*, 48 (1958), 147; 58 (1968), 199

175. Low Ham: *Proc. Somerset Arch. and Nat. Hist. Soc.*, 92 (1946), 25–8; cf. C.A.R. Radford and H.S.L. Dewar, *The Roman Mosaics from Low Ham and East Coker* (1954). Pitney: see Note 168, and R. Colt Hoare, *The Pitney Pavement* (1832).

176. *Proc. Dorset Nat. Hist. and Arch. Soc.*, 85 (1964), 116–21; 86 (1965), 150–4; for the pavement, see *British Museum Quarterly*, 32 (1967), 15–35

177. Dewlish: *Britannia*, 5 (1974), 453, with Fig. 21, p. 454. Frampton: *Royal Commission for Historical Monuments, Dorset*, i (1952), 150. Tarrant Hinton: *Proc. Dorset Nat. Hist. and Arch. Soc.*, 91 (1969), 189–90; cf. plan, *Britannia*, 3 (1972), Fig. 17, p. 347

178. *Town and Country*, 154; cf. *Antiq. Journ.*, 12 (1932), 71–2

179. Llantwit Major: *Archaeologia Cambrensis*, 102 (1953), 89–163; cf. the recent discussion by G. Webster, in *The Roman Villa in Britain*, ed. A.L.F. Rivet (1969), 238–43, and A.H.A. Hogg, *Britannia*, 5 (1974), 225–50. Ely: *J.R.S.*, 11 (1921), 61. Whitton: interim reports in *J.R.S.*, *Britannia* and *Morgannwg* from 1966 to 1971; cf. plan, *J.R.S.*, 59 (1969), Fig. 26, p. 201

180. Rivet, *Town and Country*, 160, 151–3; M.G. Jarrett and J.C. Mann, *Welsh History Review*, 4 (1968), 170–1

181. Chedworth: *Arch. Journ.*, 44 (1887), 322–36; *T.B.G.A.S.*, 78 (1958), 5–23, 162–5. Woodchester: *T.B.G.A.S.*, 48 (1926), 75–96; 74 (1956), 172–5

182. Spoonley Wood: *Archaeologia*, 52 (1891), 651–68. Tockington Park: *T.B.G.A.S.*, 12 (1888), 159–69; 13 (1889), 196–204. Bisley: *Arch. Journ.*, 2 (1846), 42–5

183. Rodmarton: *Archaeologia*, 18 (1817), 113–16. Frocester Court: *T.B.G.A.S.*, 77 (1959), 23–30; interim reports since then in *J.R.S.* and *Britannia* (see plan, *J.R.S.*, 58 (1968), Fig. 18, p. 199). Witcombe: *T.B.G.A.S.*, 73 (1954), 5–69; cf. plan, *Britannia*, 1 (1970), Fig. 9, p. 294

184. Interim reports in *J.R.S.* and *Britannia* since 1963; see plan, *J.R.S.*, 59 (1969), Fig. 40, p. 226; cf. also *T.B.G.A.S.*, 86 (1967), 74–87

185. D.J. Smith, in *The Roman Villa in Britain*, ed. A.L.F. Rivet (1969), 97–102

186. *T.B.G.A.S.*, 68 (1960), 5–23, 162–5

187. Ditchley: *Oxoniensia*, 1 (1936), 24–69, with Fig. 8, p. 28. Islip: *Britannia*, 5 (1974), 257, with Plate xxv B. Little Milton: ibid., 254. Callow Hill: *Oxoniensia*, 22 (1957), 11–53

188. North Leigh: *V.C.H. Oxfordshire*, i (1939), 316–18, with Fig. 33, p. 317; cf. *J.R.S.*, 34 (1944), 81. Stonesfield: *Oxoniensia*, 6 (1941), 1–8; cf. *V.C.H. Oxon.*, i (1939), 315–16

189. Rivet, *Town and Country*, 150–1

190. Acton Scott: *Archaeologia*, 21 (1846), 339–45; cf. *V.C.H. Shropshire*, i (1908), 259. Linley: *V.C.H. Shropshire*, i (1908), 257

191. Rivet, *Town and Country*, 148–9; M. Todd, *The Coritani* (1973)

192. Norfolk Street; *V.C.H. Leicestershire*, i (1907), 196f. Southwell: *Trans. Thoroton Soc.*, 70 (1966), 13–54. Scampton: C. Illingworth, *Topographical Account of the Parish of Scampton* (1808), 6f.

193. Thistleton Dyer: *J.R.S.*, 51 (1961), 175, with Fig. 22, p. 176. Empingham: *Britannia*, 1 (1970), 286; 2 (1971), 258–9; 3 (1972), 316. Winterton: *Antiq. Journ.*, 46 (1966), 72–84. Mansfield Woodhouse: *Trans. Thoroton Soc.*, 53 (1953), 1–14; cf. *V.C.H. Nottinghamshire*, ii (1910), 28–32. Norton Disney: *Antiq. Journ.*, 17 (1937), 138–78, with Plate xlv, opp. p. 158. Medbourne: *Arch. Journ.*, 68 (1911), 218–20; cf. *V.C.H. Leicestershire*, i (1907), 214–15

194. East Denton: *Reports and Papers, Lincs. Architectural and Arch. Soc.*, 9 (1961), 1–25; 10 (1964), 75–104. Barholme: *Britannia*, 5

(1974), 255. Wilsthorpe Mill: ibid., 256
195. Lockington: ibid., 253, with Plate XXII
    A. Cromwell: ibid., with Plate XXIII
196. Todd, op. cit. (Note 191), 92
197. Rivet, *Town and Country*, 157–8
198. Harpham: *Yorks. Arch. Journal*, 38 (1955), 117–18; 39 (1965), 55. Brantingham: *Britannia*, 4 (1973), 84–106, with Fig. 2, p. 86. Rudston: *Yorks. Arch. Journal*, 31 (1934), 366–76; 32 (1936), 214–20; 33 (1938), 81–6, 222–4, 320–38
199. *Britannia*, 1 (1970), 277–9, with Fig. 5, p. 278
200. *Arch. Journ.*, 32 (1875), 135–54

Chapter 5

1. Livy, iii, 26
2. By the terms of the *Lex Claudia* of 218 BC; cf. Livy, xxi, 63
3. See the brief survey above, pp. 25–8; and cf. W.E. Heitland, *Agricola* (1921)
4. A useful guide to all aspects of the subject is that of K.D. White, *Roman Farming* (1970); cf. also his *Agricultural Implements of the Roman World* (1967) and *A Bibliography of Roman Agriculture* (1970). The interpretation of Mediterranean agriculture in terms of modern 'dry farming' techniques will be found in M. Cary, *The Geographic Background of Greek and Roman History* (1949), and more recently in C.E. Stevens's contribution to the *Cambridge Economic History of Europe*, i (2nd ed., 1966), 92–124. For northern Europe, the section by S. Applebaum in *The Agrarian History of England and Wales*, ed. H.P.R. Finberg, 1. ii (1972) is fundamental
5. cf. Stevens, op. cit. (last note), 96f.
6. White, *Roman Farming*, 36–7, with his references
7. ibid., 47f.; cf. Stevens, op. cit., 97
8. A.G. Haudricourt and M.J.-B. Delamarre, *L'Homme et la charrue à travers le monde* (3rd ed., 1955); R. Aitken, *J.R.S.*, 46 (1956), 97–106; cf. White, *Roman Farming*, 174–5. The standard description is in Virgil, *Georgics*, i, 179f.
9. White, *Roman Farming*, 177–8, with references
10. Stevens, op. cit. (Note 4), 98–9
11. White, *Roman Farming*, 225–9
12. ibid., 229–46
13. ibid., Chapter 10
14. ibid., Chapter 3, with Appendixes A–D
15. Though cf. White, ibid., 121–3 for a more charitable view
16. On manuring generally, see White, Chapter 5, and cf. Stevens, op. cit., 96
17. Pliny, *Naturalis Historia*, xviii, 296; Palladius,

vii, 2; for a discussion, with references to earlier work, see M. Renard, *Technique et agriculture en pays trévire et rémois* (1959)
18. cf. Stevens, op. cit., 99; on the subject generally, see R.J. Forbes, *Studies in Ancient Technology*, ii (1955), 88–111
19. cf. White, *Roman Farming*, Chapter 6; cf. Stevens, op. cit., 101–3
20. Stevens, ibid., 105
21. cf. White, *Roman Farming*, 246–61
22. *Georgics*, iv, 125–46
23. Referred to by Stephens, op. cit., 101
24. *De Re Rustica*, ii, 4, 11
25. cf. Applebaum, op. cit. (Note 4), 5–6
26. *Agricola*, 12, 3
27. R.G. Goodchild, *Antiq. Journ.*, 23 (1943), 148–53
28. White, *Agricultural Implements*, 98–103; cf. Applebaum, op. cit. (Note 4), 76f.
29. cf. White, *Roman Farming*, 113–14 (and on rotation generally, 121–3); S. Applebaum in *Rural Settlement in Roman Britain*, ed. C. Thomas (1966), 99 (cf. his paper in *Proc. Prehist. Soc.*, 20 (1954), 103–14); Stevens, op. cit. (Note 4), 107; C. Parain, ibid., 136–42
30. cf. Applebaum, op. cit. (Note 4), 76–8
31. cf. J.G.D. Clark, *Antiquity*, 18 (1944), 1–15
32. See above, p. 107
33. Pliny, *Naturalis Historia*, xviii, 48; Servius, ad Virgil, *Georgics*, i, 174; cf. Stevens, op. cit. (Note 4), 107–8; C. Parain, ibid., 128
34. W.H. Manning, *J.R.S.*, 54 (1964), 62
35. ibid., 56; cf. Varro, *Res Rusticae*, i, 19, 2
36. ibid., 65
37. ibid., 62–3; cf. C.F.C. Hawkes, *Antiquity*, 9 (1935), 339–41; S. Applebaum, *Agric. Hist. Review*, 6 (1958), 66–86
38. Manning, op. cit., 62–5
39. Sir Cyril Fox, *The Archaeology of the Cambridge Region* (1923), 224; cf. Applebaum, op. cit. (Note 4), 56–72
40. cf. Note 38, and for the different periods of advance in Britain and Gaul, see Chapter 4
41. cf. the article by G. Mickwitz, *E.H.R.*, 52 (1937), 577–89; the question is discussed more fully below, pp. 147–8

Chapter 6

1. Livy, iii, 26, with the note by R.M. Ogilvie, *A Commentary on Livy, Books 1–5* (1965), 441
2. Livy, i, 43, with Ogilvie's note, op. cit., 166–8
3. For convenient summaries see *Cambridge Ancient History*, ix (1932), 1–19, or H.H. Scullard, *From the Gracchi to Nero* (1959), 19–22; for the archaeological evidence, see

G.D.B. Jones, *P.B.S.R.*, 30 (1962), 146

4. *Naturalis Historia*, xviii, 6, 35

5. *De Gubernatione Dei*, v, 38–44

6. *Epistulae*, iii, 19; iv, 14; ix, 37, etc.

7. What follows is based on A.H.M. Jones's indispensable article 'The Roman Colonate', *Past and Present*, 13 (1958), 1–13 (= *The Roman Economy*, ed. P.A. Brunt (1974), 293–307). There is much of interest also in R. Clausing, *The Roman Colonate. The Theories of its Origin* (1925), from which earlier bibliography can be obtained

8. op. cit. (last note), 293

9. *Cod. Theod.*, v, 17, 1; cf. Jones, op. cit., 294

10. *Cod. Just.*, xi, 68, 3; cf. Jones, ibid.

11. *Cod. Just.*, xi, 52, 1; cf. Jones, 297

12. On the caste system in general, see A.H.M. Jones, *Eirene*, viii (1970), 79–96 (reprinted in *The Roman Economy*, 396–418)

13. The most important are *C.I.L.* viii, 25902 (AD 116–17), 14428 (AD 181) and 10570 (AD 180–3); for an introduction to the extensive bibliography, see J.J. van Nostrand, *The Imperial Domains of Africa Proconsularis* (1925–6); T.R.S. Broughton. *The Romanization of Africa Proconsularis* (1929), Chapter 6; R.M. Haywood, *Roman Africa*, in *An Economic Survey of Ancient Rome*, ed. Tenney Frank, iv (1938), 83–102; G.C. Picard, *La civilisation de l'Afrique romaine* (1959), 61f.

14. *C.I.L.* viii, 10570, 3, 28–9

15. On the subject of seigneurialization in general, see *E.H.R.*, 84 (1969), 449–73; the standard work on patronage in the later Empire is F. de Zulueta in *Oxford Studies in Social and Legal History*, ed. P. Vinogradoff, i (1909)

16. *Cod. Theod.*, v, 19, 1; *Cod. Just.*, xi, 50, 2; xi, 48, 18; i, 3, 16, etc.; on all of this see Jones, *The Roman Economy*, 300

17. Quoted by C.E. Stevens in *Rural Settlement in Roman Britain*, ed. C. Thomas (1966), 108

18. The three approaches here suggested are essentially those set out by S. Applebaum in *The Agrarian History of England and Wales*, ed. H.P.R. Finberg, I. ii (1972), 40

19. L. Joulin, *Les établissements gallo-romaines de la plaine de Martres-Tolosanes* (1901)

20. *La villa gallo-romaine de Montmaurin (Hte-Garonne)* (1969), Chapter 11

21. R. de Maeyer, *De Overblijfselen der Romeinsche Villa's in Belgie* (1940), 111f.

22. R. Boyer, *Études rurales*, 3 (1961), 91–100, with Fig. 1, p. 93

23. R. Baubérot, *Bull. soc. arch. et hist. Limousin*, 83 (1950), 130–46; 92 (1965), 53–78

24. G. Jeanton, *Le Mâconnais gallo-romain*, iii (1926), 27–31

25. For the 23 'villas', see *Gallia*, 11 (1953), 165–6; for the Tête-de-Fer site see the interim reports in *Gallia*, 16 (1958), 320–2; 18 (1960), 354–6; 22 (1964), 331–2, with Fig. 51, p. 331

26. De Maeyer, op. cit. (Note 21), 56–9; see also the group of villas around Tholey in the Saarland, discussed by E.M. Wightman, *Roman Trier and the Treveri* (1970), 154

27. cf. S. Applebaum, *The Agrarian History of England and Wales* (1972), 212–14, with Fig. 41, p. 213

28. ibid., 41, with Fig. 2, p. 42; 170, with Fig. 34, p. 169; see also *Proc. Hampshire Field Club*, 18 (1953), 126–7

29. *Town and Country in Roman Britain* (2nd ed., 1964), 159

30. Among the more promising examples, we may quote those at Rivenhall in Essex (*V.C.H. Essex*, iii (1963), 171–4; *Britannia*, 4 (1973), 115–27), at Hockwold in Norfolk (*Proc. Cambridge Antiq. Soc.*, 60 (1967), 39–80), and at Lockington in Leicestershire (M. Todd, *The Coritani* (1973), 98–9)

31. C.F.C. Hawkes, *Arch. Journ.*, 104 (1947), 27–81

32. Mrs S.J. Hallam in *The Fenlands in Roman Times*, ed. C.W. Phillips (1970), 22–113. For discussions of villa–village associations in general, see C.E. Stevens, *Rural Settlement in Roman Britain* (1966), 122, with Fig. 1, p. 126; S. Applebaum, *The Agrarian History of England and Wales* (1972), 43–4

33. E. del Marmol, *Ann. soc. arch. Namur*, 15 (1881), 220–4

34. La Mouthe: *Rev. Arch.*, 16 (1940), 108. Rouffiac: *Gallia*, 22 (1964), 480–1; 24 (1966), 459–60

35. *Manuel d'archéologie gallo-romaine*, ii (1934), 733–4

36. *Bull. soc. scientif. et artist. Clamecy*, 73 (1949), 55–67; 74 (1950), 63–75; *Mém. soc. Éduenne*, (1844), 319–36

37. Lower Seine: in general see L. Musset, *Rev. Arch.*, 36 (1950), 84–95, and for a typical example L. de Vesly, *Les Fana, ou petits temples gallo-romains de la région normande* (1909), 92–113, with Planche 5. Mayen: *Bonner Jahrbücher*, 163 (1963), 317–41

38. For general discussions, see A. Grenier, op. cit. (Note 35), 752–63; T. Welter, *Bull. soc. préhist. française*, 5 (1908), 41–52; A. Desforges, ibid., 391–5

39. K. Wichmann, *Ann. soc. hist. et arch. Lorraine*, 15 (1903), 218–62, with Tafel 1; T. Welter, ibid., 37 (1924), 196–201

40. A. Nicolai, *Bull. arch. Comité*, (1946–9), 277, 705–23, with Planche 17

41. L. Joulin, op. cit. (Note 19), 162–4, with Fig. 21, p. 162 (Bordier); 13–14, 164–9, with Fig. 22, p. 165 (Sana); 169–71, with Fig. 24, p. 170 (Coulieu); 179–81, with Fig. 27, p. 179 (Tuc-de-Mourlan); 181–2 (Boussens); 14–16, 171–8, with Fig. 26, p. 173 (St-Cizy); J. Boube, *Pallas*, 3 (1955), 89–115, with Fig. 1, p. 99 (Martres-Tolosane)

42. For the theory, see *Digest*, xxxiv, 5, 1; for a vivid illustration in practice, cf. *C.I.L.*, xi, 1147 (the so-called Table of Veleia)

43. For an introductory discussion, see S. Applebaum, *Latomus*, 23 (1964), 774–87; J. Percival, ibid., 25 (1966), 134–8

44. *Gallia*, 7 (1949), 28–30

45. cf. the references given in Note 41, and see also Grenier's summary of the area's overall history, op. cit., 832–7, 850–8, 888–97

46. G. Fouet, op. cit. (Note 20), 289–313; cf. also *Gallia*, 7 (1949), 23–54.

47. *Proc. Hampshire Field Club*, 18 (1953), 126–7; *The Agrarian History of England and Wales* (1972), 41–3, with Fig. 2, p. 42

48. *T.B.G.A.S.*, 69 (1950), 5–58

49. Applebaum, *The Agrarian History of England and Wales* (1972), 168–70; for an alternative explanation, cf. C.E. Stevens, *Rural Settlement in Roman Britain* (1966), 119

50. *Arch. Journ.*, 65 (1908), 57–60; 66 (1909), 33–52; cf. Applebaum, op. cit., 174–7

51. *Archaeologia*, 71 (1921), 141–98

52. C.A.R. Radford, *Oxoniensia*, 1 (1936), 24–69; see in particular pp. 52–3

53. See the references given in Note 13

54. *The Agrarian History of England and Wales* (1972), 28–33

55. Pfalzel: *Germania*, 19 (1935), 40–53. Konz: ibid., 39 (1961), 204–6; cf. E.M. Wightman, op. cit. (Note 26), 165–9

56. E.B. Thomas, *Römische Villen in Pannonien* (1964), 60–8, with Abb. 29–30, pp. 61–2 (Fenékpuszta); 177–92, with Abb. 99, p. 178 and 100, p. 180 (Parndorf)

57. C.E. Stevens, *Rev. Arch.*, 9 (1937), 26–37; for a more general survey of these sites, cf. A. Grenier, op. cit. (Note 35), 742–52

58. R.C. Carrington, *J.R.S.*, 21 (1931), 110–30; for a more recent and much wider survey, cf. J.H. d'Arms, *Romans on the Bay of Naples* (1970), 171–232

59. S. Applebaum, *The Agrarian History of England and Wales* (1972), 19–26

60. *The Roman Villa in Britain* (1969), 210–14

61. e.g. by S. Applebaum, *The Agrarian History of England and Wales* (1972), Chapter viii, especially p. 132

62. For Dalmatia in general, see above, pp. 88–9

There is similar evidence from Pannonia: cf., for example, M. Biro, *Acta Archaeologica Academiae Scientiarum Hungaricae*, 26 (1974), 51; A. Mócsy, *Pannonia and Upper Moesia* (1974), 173

63. For a preliminary discussion, see Applebaum, *The Agrarian History of England and Wales* (1972), 122–41

64. See the discussion above, pp. 36–8

65. Ödheim: O. Paret, *Die Römer in Württemberg*, iii (1932), 36, 124, etc., with Abb. 11, p. 36. Blankenheim: most conveniently, A. Grenier, op. cit. (Note 35), 819–20, with Fig. 294, p. 821. Parndorf: see the references given in Note 56

66. *T.B.G.A.S.*, 69 (1950), 5–58

67. *The Agrarian History of England and Wales* (1972), 132

68. Grémecey: *Gallia*, 24 (1966), 286–8, with Fig. 21, p. 287. Saaraltdorf: T. Welter, *Ann. soc. hist. et arch. Lorraine*, 20 (1908), 152f., with plan, p. 155. Bollendorf: P. Steiner, *Trierer Jahresbericht*, 12 (1923), 1–59; plan in Wightman, op. cit. (Note 26), Fig. 13, p. 140. Legionary sites: cf. H. von Petrikovits, *Das römische Rheinland* (1960), 64–7, with Abb. 21, p. 64. Württemberg: see Note 65

69. *Germania*, 5 (1928), 121–2

70. *Arch. Journ.*, 120 (1963), 13

71. Denton: *Reports and Papers, Lincs. Architectural and Arch. Soc.*, 10 (1964), 75–104. Exning: *J.R.S.*, 50 (1960), 228

72. *V.C.H. Hampshire*, i (1900), 295–7

73. *V.C.H. Nottinghamshire*, ii (1910), 28–32; *Trans. Thoroton Soc.*, 53 (1953), 1–14

74. cf. Applebaum, *The Agrarian History of England and Wales* (1972), 45–8, 227, 231

75. ibid., 227

76. West Blatchington: *Sussex Arch. Coll.*, 89 (1950), 1–56. Tidbury Rings: *Britannia*, 5 (1974), 259, with Plate xxv A

77. For a general introduction, and for earlier bibliography, see H.C. Bowen, *Ancient Fields* (1961); for the extensions, cf. *A Matter of Time: an Archaeological Survey of the River Gravels of England* (R.C.H.M., 1960)

78. cf. S. Piggott in *Roman and Native in North Britain*, ed. I.A. Richmond (1958), 11f.

79. The evidence is conveniently assembled by Applebaum, *The Agrarian History of England and Wales* (1972), 94f.

80. See, for example, C.E. Stevens, *Rural Settlement in Roman Britain* (1966), 113f., 124; cf. his article in *Rev. Arch.*, 9 (1937), 26–37

81. See above, p. 114

82. *The Roman Villa in Britain* (1969), 182f.

83. See especially *De Bello Gallico*, vi, 19, 1–2;

21, 1; 22, 2–3. The passages are discussed by A. Grenier in *An Economic Survey of Ancient Rome*, ed. Tenney Frank (1937), iii, 406–10

84. *De Bello Gallico*, vi, 13; the existence of estate names in -*acum* formed from individual personal names is also a strong indication of the institution of private property, as was realized by H. d'Arbois de Jubainville, *Recherches sur l'origine de la propriété foncière et les noms de lieux habités en France* (1890). The existence of a landlord–tenant arrangement in Gaul at the time of the conquest could well explain the extensive quarters for farm workers in the early phases of such sites as Chiragan or Montmaurin: the facilities would suit depressed clansmen as well as, if not better than, slaves, whose existence in such numbers at this date would in any case need to be argued

85. *De Bello Gallico*, v, 12–13; for the possible exception of the Belgic areas, cf. ibid., v, 14, 1

86. C.E. Stevens, *Rural Settlement in Roman Britain* (1966), 108–28

87. Dio, lxxviii, 9, 5; *The Roman Villa in Britain* (1969), 184–5

88. *Cod. Just.*, viii, 53, 1; op. cit. (Note 86), 109

89. *Cod. Theod.*, xi, 7, 2; discussed by Stevens in *J.R.S.*, 37 (1947), 132–4

90. *E.H.R.*, 84 (1969), 468–72

91. For a detailed study of the Welsh Laws in relation to agriculture and settlement, see G.R.J. Jones, *The Agrarian History of England and Wales* (1972), 299–308, 320–49; for a more general introduction to both Welsh and Irish evidence, see his article in *Welsh History Review*, 1 (1960), 111–32, together with Stevens, op. cit. (Note 86), 110–13

92. op. cit. (last note), 320–39

93. op. cit. (Note 86), 113–18

94. See above, p. 128

95. *The Agrarian History of England and Wales* (1972), 53

96. ibid., 51–3, with Fig. 3, p. 52

97. ibid., 47, 133; for Tidbury Rings, see Note 76

98. ibid., 45–6; cf. *J.R.S.*, 52 (1962), 172–3, with Fig. 19, p. 171. Stroud: *Arch. Journ.*, 65 (1908), 57–60; 66 (1909), 33–52. Thistleton Dyer: *J.R.S.*, 51 (1961), 175, with Fig. 22, p. 176

99. op. cit. (Note 86), 119

100. G.R.J. Jones, op. cit. (Note 91), 321

101. ibid., 324

102. op. cit. (Note 86), 123–5, with Figs 1 and 2, pp. 126–7

103. *Britannia*, 2 (1971), 109–16

104. *The Roman Villa in Britain* (1969), 209–14

Chapter 7

1. *The Roman Villa in Britain* (1969), 181; cf. his *Town and Country in Roman Britain* (2nd ed., 1964), 105

2. See above, p. 15

3. See the discussion above, pp. 133–4

4. For this, the standard view of the situation at this period, see above, p. 119 with the references there given

5. cf. Varro's comment on such houses (*Res Rusticae*, iii, 2, 6): *nam quod extra urbem est aedificium, nihilo magis ideo est villa* ('for the fact that a building is outside the city does not make it any more a villa'). For him such sites are not villas at all, merely an extension to the suburbs

6. One thinks, for example, of the rich houses established in Kent and Sussex in the latter part of the first century AD, for which see Professor Cunliffe's remarks, *The Regni* (1973), 95, 105. For their counterparts in other provinces, see above, pp. 39–40

7. Cato, *De Agri Cultura*, i, 7; Varro, *Res Rusticae*, iii, 2, 16f.; Columella, *De Re Rustica*, iii, 3, 8–10; Pliny, *Epistulae*, iii, 19

8. *De Agri Cultura*, ii, 7

9. *Epistulae*, iii, 19

10. *Epistulae*, vii, 11

11. cf., for example, G. Mickwitz, *E.H.R.*, 52 (1937), 585–6; R. Duncan-Jones, *The Economy of the Roman Empire* (1974), 39–59; M.I. Finley, *The Ancient Economy* (1973), 117

12. Duncan-Jones, op. cit. (last note), 43–4

13. op. cit. (Note 11), 577–89; cf., more recently, G.E.M. de Ste-Croix in *Studies in the History of Accounting*, ed. A.C. Littleton and B.S. Yamey (1956), 14–74

14. op. cit. (Note 11), 117; for a more charitable view, see now M.W. Frederiksen, *J.R.S.*, 65 (1975), 168–9

15. Duncan-Jones, op. cit. (Note 11), 33, with his n. 3

16. Park Street: *Arch. Journ.*, 102 (1945), 21–110. Ditchley: *Oxoniensia*, 1 (1936), 24–69

17. *Town and Country. The Archaeology of Verulamium and the Roman Chilterns* (1973), 44–6

18. A.H.M. Jones, *The Later Roman Empire, 284–602* (1964), 738, 772–3, with n. 61 of his Chapter xix

19. See above, p. 138

20. Caesar, *De Bello Gallico*, iv, 31; Strabo, iv, 4, 3; cf. Applebaum, *The Agrarian History of England and Wales* (1972), 110

21. op. cit. (Note 18), 767

22. *Arch. Journ.*, 104 (1947), 27–81; the section dealing with Woodcuts is pp. 42–8

23. For 'autumn killing', see now E.S. Higgs and J.P. White, *Antiquity*, 37 (1963), 282–9. Figheldean Down: S. Applebaum, *Proc. Prehist. Soc.*, 20 (1954), 103–14.

24. K.D. White, *Agricultural Implements of the Roman World* (1967), 98–103; cf. Applebaum, *The Agrarian History of England and Wales* (1972), 76–7

25. op. cit. (last note), 82

26. *Roman Britain and the English Settlements* (2nd ed., 1937), 208

27. See the discussion by Rivet, *The Roman Villa in Britain* (1969), 189–98

28. C.F.C. Hawkes, op. cit. (Note 22), 44

29. J.G.D. Clark, *Antiq. Journ.*, 29 (1949), 145–63; cf. Applebaum, *The Agrarian History of England and Wales* (1972), 207

30. ibid., 109

31. op. cit. (Note 27), 196–7

32. *De Mortibus Persecutorum*, vii, 3

33. *The Roman Economy* (1974), 83 (= *Antiquity*, 33 (1959), 39)

34. *The Later Roman Empire* (1964), 812f.

35. *The Agrarian History of England and Wales* (1972), 245–6

36. *The Later Roman Empire* (1964), 822

37. *The Ancient Economy* (1973), 107

38. For a detailed analysis of marketing patterns in Roman Britain, see I. Hodder and M. Hassall, *Man*, 6 (1971), 391–407, especially p. 405, where it is argued that a basic unit in settlement was 'the most efficient maximum distance which might be travelled to market in one day'

39. *J.R.S.*, 21 (1931), 101–3; *Oxoniensia*, 19 (1954), 15–37. The discovery of the temple itself has perhaps made the 'market' hypothesis less necessary, though whether it removes it altogether is clearly debatable

40. *Phoenix*, 24 (1970), 333–41, especially 333–4; cf. Oelmann, *Bonner Jahrbücher*, 128 (1923), 82–91

41. *L'Antiquité Classique*, 7 (1938), 295–316

42. MacMullen, op. cit. (Note 40), 335, with his n. 11

43. ibid., 339–41

44. See above, p. 96

45. See above, pp. 76, 80, 96

46. Chedworth: *T.B.G.A.S.*, 78 (1960), 5–23, 162–5. St-Priest-sous-Aixe: *Bull. Arch. Comité* (1946–9), 759–61; *Bull. soc. arch. et hist. Limousin*, 84 (1952–4), 35–42

47. *Roman Trier and the Treveri* (1970), 139–72

48. *Manuel d'archéologie gallo-romaine*, ii (1934), 864–5

49. op. cit. (Note 17), 44–6, 63–4, 135–6, etc.

50. D.J. Smith in *The Roman Villa in Britain*, ed.

A.L.F. Rivet (1969), 95–113

51. For flue tiles, see A.W.G. Lowther's note in *Surrey Arch. Coll.*, 50 (1947), 94–8. For pewter, see W.J. Wedlake, *Excavations at Camerton* (1958), 82–93, with Plate XIX

52. op. cit. (Note 18), 841

53. ibid., 842; on the question of transport generally, see Alison Burford, *Econ. H.R.*, 13 (1960), 1–18

54. *The Ancient Economy*, 127

55. See above, p. 152

56. Most notably by Collingwood, op. cit. (Note 26), 203–7, but frequently since

57. op. cit. (Note 18), 737–57

58. *The Roman Villa in Britain* (1969), 207

59. *The Agrarian History of England and Wales* (1972), 248, following G.C. Dunning, *Archaeological Newsletter*, 8 (1949), 15

60. See in general H. Sumner, *Excavations in New Forest Pottery Sites* (1927), and more recently M. Fulford, *Britannia*, 4 (1973), 160–78

61. What owners seem to have done in many cases is to make do with secondhand products: see, for example, Lowther's work on flue tiles referred to above (Note 51)

62. Above, pp. 47–8

63. *Gallia*, 28 (1970), 313

64. *Ann. soc. hist. et arch. Lorraine*, 16 (1904), 259–92

65. The evidence is set out by Rivet, *The Roman Villa in Britain* (1969), 208–9

66. *De Agri Cultura*, ii, 7; on the doctrine of self-sufficiency in general, see Duncan-Jones, *The Economy of the Roman Empire* (1974), 37, and M.I. Finley, *The Ancient Economy* (1973), 109

67. Though there is inscriptional evidence in certain cases: see, for example, E.M. Wightman, op. cit. (Note 47), 194–5; R. Clausing, *The Roman Colonate. The Theories of its Origin* (1925), 289–91

68. *T.B.G.A.S.*, 78 (1960), 5–23, 162–5

69. *The Agrarian History of England and Wales* (1972), 188

70. *Ann. soc. arch. Namur*, 14 (1877), 165–94; 15 (1881), 1–40; the site at Morville is reported ibid., 15 (1881), 220–4

71. ibid., 24 (1900), 121–8

72. *Rev. Gévaudan, Causses, Cévennes*, 7 (1961), 5–38; subsequent brief reports in *Gallia*, especially 24 (1966), 482–3 and 27 (1969), 413–14

73. op. cit. (Note 47), 201–2

74. *Town and Country in Roman Britain* (2nd ed., 1964), 140; for the sites around Durobrivae, see the *Ordnance Survey Map of Roman Britain*

(3rd ed., 1956), Fig. 3, p. 22, and also above, p. 98

75. See above, pp. 72, 79
76. Auterive: *Gallia*, 22 (1964), 435–7. Fayence: ibid., 18 (1960), 317–18
77. Hambledon: *Archaeologia*, 71 (1921), 141–98. Spoonley Wood: ibid., 52 (1890), 651–68. Thistleton Dyer: *J.R.S.*, 51 (1961), 175
78. *Gallia*, 22 (1964), 588–90; cf. above, p. 70
79. *Rev. arch. Est*, 1 (1950), 180–4
80. As, for example, does Applebaum, *The Agrarian History of England and Wales* (1972), 16, n. 1
81. For the details, see Duncan-Jones, op. cit. (Note 11), 111, 209–15
82. For an admirable statement of what can and cannot be done in this area, see Rivet, *The Roman Villa in Britain* (1969), 174
83. See, for example, Applebaum, *The Agrarian History of England and Wales* (1972), Chapter IX
84. cf. Wightman, op. cit. (Note 47), 153–6

Chapter 8

1. On the invasions generally, see L. Musset, *Les Invasions: les Vagues Germaniques* (1965); R. Latouche, *Les grandes invasions et la crise de l'Occident au Ve siècle* (1946). Of interest also, as illustrating the reactions of contemporary writers, is P. Courcelle, *Histoire littéraire des grandes invasions germaniques* (3rd ed., 1964)
2. Libanius, *Orationes*, xii, 44
3. cf., for example, A. Grenier, *Manuel d'archéologie gallo-romaine*, ii (1934), 899f.; J.J. Hatt, *Histoire de la Gaule romaine* (2nd ed., 1967), 294–5
4. On Bagaudae and similar movements, see E.A. Thompson, *Past and Present*, 2 (1952), 11–23
5. *Epistulae*, 123, 15
6. *Commonitorium*, ii, 181–4
7. *Germania*, 26
8. A.H.M. Jones, *The Later Roman Empire, 284–602* (1964), 194–6; the point was made originally by J.B. Bury, *The Invasion of Europe by the Barbarians* (1928), 42–3
9. See above, pp. 17f.
10. *The Roman Villa in Britain*, ed. A.L.F. Rivet (1969), 226–7; cf. the statement by K. Branigan, *Town and Country. The Archaeology of Verulamium and the Roman Chilterns* (1973), 136, that the villas of the Chilterns were 'largely unaffected by the 367 invasion', and the more cautious comments of S.S. Frere,

Britannia (1967), 356–7 and S. Applebaum, *The Agrarian History of England and Wales*, ed. H.P.R. Finberg, I. ii (1972), 235–6

11. op. cit. (last note), 231–4
12. Llantwit: *Archaeologia Cambrensis*, 102 (1953), 89–163; cf. Webster's reassessment, op. cit., 238–43. Lullingstone: G.W. Meates, *Lullingstone Roman Villa* (1955), 159
13. Whittington Court: *T.B.G.A.S.*, 71 (1953), 43. Great Wymondley: *V.C.H. Hertfordshire*, iv (1914), 170
14. cf. Branigan, op. cit. (Note 10), 135–8
15. *Rev. arch. Est*, 1 (1950), 180–4; cf. *Gallia*, 6 (1948), 239–41
16. *Ann. soc. arch. Namur*, 14 (1877), 165–94; 15 (1881), 1–40
17. *Gallia*, 9 (1951), 131–3; cf. G. Fouet, *La villa gallo-romaine de Montmaurin (Hte-Garonne)* (1969), 92–3
18. Beaucaire: *Gallia*, 28 (1970), 415–16. Colleville: ibid., 26 (1968), 369–70; 28 (1970), 276
19. ibid., 30 (1972), 505; for the burials, cf. 24 (1966), 445; 26 (1968), 552; 28 (1970), 433
20. Latimer: K. Branigan, *Latimer* (1971), 89–99. The evidence for Britain generally is conveniently summarized by Applebaum, op. cit. (Note 10), 253–4
21. op. cit. (Note 10), 234–6
22. cf. C.H.V. Sutherland, *Coinage and Currency in Roman Britain* (1937), 93f.; J.P.C. Kent, in *Anglo-Saxon Coins*, ed. R.H.M. Dolley (1961), 2; J.N.L. Myres, in *Dark-Age Britain*, ed. D. Harden (1956), 16f.; *Arch. Journ.*, 106 (1949), 69–71; S.S. Frere, *Medieval Archaeology*, 6–7 (1962–3), 351–2; J. Morris, in *Britain and Rome*, ed. M.G. Jarrett and B. Dobson (1965), 176, n. 15
23. cf. his *Arthur's Britain: History and Archaeology, A.D. 367–634* (1971)
24. e.g. Sorde-l'Abbaye (Landes): *Gallia*, 19 (1961), 393–6. Lalonquette (Basses-Pyrénées): *Bull. soc. sciences, lettres, arts de Pau*, 25 (1963), 55–63
25. cf. R. Lantier, *Secondes journées de synthèse historique* (1953), 23f.; S. Gagnière, *Cahiers Rhodaniens*, 7 (1960); J. Rigon, *Provence Historique*, 10 (1960), etc.
26. See above, p. 29
27. *Epistulae*, ii, 2
28. *Epistulae*, viii, 4; *Carmina*, 22
29. Fortunatus, *Carmina*, i, 18, 19, 20
30. ibid., iii, 12; cf. x, 9
31. *Bull. et mém. soc. arch. Bordeaux*, 46 (1929), 1–23
32. Preignac: ibid., 55 (1938–40), 119–41; cf. C. Higounet, *Bordeaux pendant le haut moyen age* (1963), 208f. Aydat: C.E. Stevens, *Sido-*

nius Apollinaris and his Age (1933), 185–96

33. It is a pity we do not know more about the presumed villa at Beremend-Idamajor in Pannonia (E.B. Thomas, *Römische Villen in Pannonien* (1964), 271–3), which has produced an inscription of the late fourth or early fifth century commemorating the senator Valerius Dalmatius, perhaps the villa's owner. He could be a sort of Pannonian Sidonius

34. See above, pp. 31–3

35. cf. M. Toussaint, *Répertoire archéologique du département de Seine-et-Marne* (1953), ad locc.

36. Frontenac: *Gallia*, 15 (1957), 247–50. Loupiac: ibid., 12 (1954), 208–9; 15 (1957), 250–2, with Fig. 13, p. 251. Plassac: ibid., 23 (1965), 416–20; 25 (1967), 335; 27 (1969), 350–2; 29 (1971), 338; 31 (1973), 456, with Fig. 8, p. 455

37. Grépiac: *Gallia*, 12 (1954), 214. Moissac: ibid., 9 (1951), 136–7

38. See above, p. 31

39. M. Toussaint, *Répertoire archéologique du département de la Seine* (1953), 24–6 (Chevilly), 26–8 (l'Hay)

40. The detailed results are in an unpublished D.Phil. thesis, *Roman Agricultural Organisation in Western Europe* (1967), 107–49 (available in the Bodleian Library, Oxford)

41. A. Albenque, *Les Rutènes* (1948), 114f.; cf. his *Inventaire de l'archéologie gallo-romaine du département de l'Aveyron* (1947)

42. For fortification, see R. Paribeni, *Mitteilungen des deutschen archäologischen Instituts, Römische Abteilung*, 55 (1940), 131–48; for nucleation, see A. Grenier, op. cit. (Note 3), 843

43. Sidonius, *Carmina*, 22

44. Fortunatus, *Carmina*, iii, 12, 1–4

45. For *castellum*, see *C.I.L.*, viii, 8426, 26274 etc.; and for the Gebel farms, D. Oates, *P.B.S.R.*, 21 (1953), 81–117

46. *Cahiers d'arch. et d'hist. Alsace*, 130 (1949), 253–6; cf. *Gallia*, 16 (1958), 341

47. *Germania*, 19 (1935), 40–53

48. *Roman Trier and the Treveri* (1970), 169

49. Sümeg: Thomas, op. cit. (Note 33), 111–16, with Abb. 51, p. 112. Keszthely-Fenékpuszta: ibid., 60–8, with Abb. 29, p. 61. On fortified sites in the Danube provinces generally, see A. Mócsy, *Pannonia and Upper Moesia* (1974), 303–8

50. *Genava*, 1 (1953), 74–5; 2 (1954), 210–16, with Fig. 143, p. 214

51. Isle-d'Abeau: *Rhodania*, 20–2 (1938–46), 60–6. Isle-Aumont: H.-P. Eydoux, *Résurrection de la Gaule* (1961), 279–309; cf. *Gallia*, 8 (1950), 87–9

52. cf. H. Dubled, *Le Moyen Age*, 59 (1953), 1–9

53. e.g. *Historia Francorum*, ii, 1; ix, 37; x, 31, etc.; the point was made originally by E. Beaudoin, *Les grands domaines dans l'empire romain* (1899), 15–16

54. For the practice generally, see F. de Zulueta, in *Oxford Studies in Social and Legal History*, ed. P. Vinogradoff, i (1909)

55. Frontinus, *De Controversiis Agrorum*, 53

56. cf., for example, the Roman building under the church at Lyminge, near Folkestone (V.C.H. Kent, iii (1932), 121; *Arch. Cant.*, 69 (1955), 38–9), discussed by H.P.R. Finberg, *The Agrarian History of England and Wales*, i. ii (1972), 391–2. There is now, of course, a striking example at Rivenhall, in Essex (cf. *Britannia*, 4 (1973), 115–27). On the association generally of churches and Roman material, see Applebaum, op. cit. (Note 10), 260

57. Ornézan: *Gallia*, 22 (1964), 454. Penol: ibid., 16 (1958), 381–2. St-Romain-de-Jalionas: ibid., 26 (1968), 588–9; 29 (1971), 428–9. Sion: ibid., 24 (1966), 528. St-Léon-sous-Vézère: ibid., 21 (1963), 525. Néoules: ibid., 18 (1960), 315. Mazères-sur-Salat: ibid., 28 (1970), 406–7. Bernex: *Helvetia Archaeologica*, 1 (1970–1), 12–15; 13 (1973), 12–17. Böckweiler: *Germania*, 39 (1961), 478–9, with Abb. 1, p. 479. Konz: ibid., 204–6, with Abb. 1, p. 205

58. Montcaret: *Congrès arch. France*, 192 (1939), 182–95; cf. plan, *Gallia*, 9 (1951), Fig. 1, p. 115. Martres-Tolosane: *Pallas*, 3 (1955), 89–115, with Fig. 1, p. 99

59. *Gallia*, 22 (1964), 595

60. ibid., 20 (1962), 580

61. The surveys are published in *Archéologie aérienne de la Somme* (1964) and *Détection aérienne de vestiges protohistoriques, gallo-romains et médiévaux* (1970); cf. the general discussion in *Revue du Nord*, 47 (1965), 541–76

62. id., *Détection aérienne*, 207–14

63. The area is covered by Sheet XXIII. 15 (Corbeil–Essonnes) of the 1:50,000 map of France

64. Sheet 52 (Thuin) of the 1:50,000 map of Belgium

65. cf. J. Warichez, *Bull. Comm. Roy. d'Histoire*, 78 (1909), 245–67

66. As has been done, for example, in southern Etruria, where a survey of sites in the region of Veii has led to the suggestion that 'the system of land tenure . . . at the end of the eighth century was still one of villas and large, open estates on the later Roman model', and that 'the transition from the classical to the

medieval pattern took place between the beginning of the ninth and the latter part of the tenth centuries.' (J.B. Ward-Perkins, *Geographical Journal*, 128 (1962), 401–2; for the survey itself, see *P.B.S.R.*, 36 (1968))

67. On seigneurialization generally, cf. *E.H.R.*, 84 (1969), 449–73

Chapter 9

1. S. Applebaum in *The Agrarian History of England and Wales*, ed. H.P.R. Finberg, I. ii (1972), 256, 259 lists Llantwit Major (Glamorgan), Banwell (Somerset), Denton and Worlaby (Lincs.), Southwell Minster (Notts.) and Great Tew (Oxon.). We might add Well House (Berks.: *V.C.H. Berkshire*, i (1906), 209) and Wigginton (Oxon.: *V.C.H. Oxfordshire*, i (1939), 309), but surely not many more

2. E. Linckenheld, *Une villa romaine avec tombes de l'époque barbare à Gondrexange* (Moselle) (1932), 3f., said that the use of villa buildings for cemeteries was rare: examples of it now run into hundreds. As late as 1944 it was thought appropriate to appeal for proper excavation and reporting of post-Roman levels on Roman sites: cf. M. Chaume, *Annales de Bourgogne*, 16 (1944), 60–2

3. Though cf. E. Salin, *La civilisation mérovingienne* (1952), ii, 15f.

4. *Études Rurales*, 3 (1961), 91–100, with Fig. 2, pp. 96–7

5. *Rev. arch. Est*, 7 (1956), 369–76

6. ibid., 1 (1950), 180–4; cf. *Cahiers Lorrains*, (1949), 52–3

7. *Revue de l'Agenais*, 77 (1951), 55–7

8. See above, p. 169

9. cf. the suggestion, later withdrawn, that the burials at Berthelming were 'une geste de vainqueur' (M. Lutz, *Rev. arch. Est*, 1 (1950), 184

10. E. Eblé, *Gallia*, 6 (1948), 365–83, with plan, Fig. 3, opp. p. 368

11. ibid., 374–5, with Fig. 6, p. 374

12. Sulpicius Severus, *Vita S. Martini*, 13, 9

13. For a general description of the site, with references, see H.-P. Eydoux, *Résurrection de la Gaule* (1961), 333–60; the religious sector is reported in *Gallia*, 17 (1959), 430–3, with Fig. 28, p. 431

14. *Congrès arch. France*, 192 (1939), 182–95; for plan, see *Gallia*, 9 (1951), Fig. 1, p. 115

15. Unfortunately, a passing mention only: there is no coin list, and it may simply be that there were a few post-Roman items scattered about the site. The summary article of H.-P.

Eydoux, *Lumières sur la Gaule* (1960), 131–55, gives little further detail

16. On the whole question of burials in and near churches in the Merovingian period, see Salin, op. cit. (Note 3), ii, 12f., with his notes

17. *Pallas*, 3 (1955), 89–115, with Fig. 1, p. 99

18. *Gallia*, 18 (1960), 374

19. ibid., 23 (1965), 421–2, with Fig. 18, p. 422

20. ibid., 9 (1951), 136–7

21. ibid., 26 (1968), 435–7; 28 (1970), 348–50

22. ibid., 26 (1968), 551; 28 (1970), 431–2; 30 (1972), 504

23. ibid., 21 (1963), 261–75

24. *Cahiers ligures de préhist. et d'arch.*, 12 (1963), 103–30

25. *Provincia*, 10 (1930), 104–6; cf. *Gallia*, 18 (1960), 315

26. *Gallia*, 12 (1954), 222–3; 13 (1955), 213

27. Flayosc: *Gallia*, 25 (1967), 419. La Roquebrusanne: ibid., 12 (1954), 438. Prusly-sur-Ource: ibid., 28 (1970), 369–71. St-Symphorien: ibid., 23 (1965), 337. Bouxières-aux-Dames: ibid., 17 (1959), 360. Trinquetaille: ibid., 22 (1964), 575–6

28. H. Hinz, *Die Ausgrabungen auf der Kirchberg in Morken, Kreis Bergheim* (1969), with Falttafel 1

29. R. Agache, *Archéologie aérienne de la Somme* (1964); *Détection aérienne de vestiges protohistoriques, gallo-romains et médiévaux* (1970)

30. *Ann. acad. Mâcon*, 40 (1950–1), 15–23, with Planche 1

31. *Gallia*, 17 (1959), 455–7; cf. H.-P. Eydoux, *Lumières sur la Gaule* (1960), 191–215, with Fig. 37, p. 203

32. E.B. Thomas, *Römische Villen in Pannonien* (1964), 299–326, with Abb. 158, p. 303

33. Sümeg: ibid., 111–16, with Abb. 51, p. 112 and 54, p. 115. Donnerskirchen: ibid., 130–7, with Abb. 67, p. 131 and 70, p. 134

34. Eydoux, op. cit. (Note 31), 183–6, with Fig. 34, p. 185

35. H. Eiden, *Neue Ausgrabungen in Deutschland* (1958), 361, with Abb. 12

36. Konz: *Germania*, 39 (1961), 204–6, with Abb. 1, p. 205. Odrang: E.M. Wightman, *Roman Trier and the Treveri* (1970), 143–5, with Fig. 15, p. 144. Téting: A. Grenier, *Habitations gauloises et villas latines dans la cité des Médiomatrices* (1906), 159f., with Planche 11. Cadeilhan-St-Clar: *Gallia*, 11 (1953), 41–67, with Fig. 2, opp. p. 48. Chateaurenard: ibid., 21 (1963), 405–7, with Fig. 34, p. 406. La Chapelle-Vaupelteigne: ibid., 26 (1968), 509, with Fig. 50, p. 510

37. Cuevas de Soria: R. Menendez Pidal, *Historia de Espana* (1935), ii, 329, with Fig. 206.

Lullingstone: G.W. Meates, *Lullingstone Roman Villa* (1955). Parndorf: E.B. Thomas, op. cit. (Note 32), 177–92, with Abb. 100, p. 180. Csúcshegy: ibid., 224–6, with Abb. 115, p. 225

38. L. Joulin, *Les établissements gallo-romaines de la plaine de Martres-Tolosanes* (1901), 165, with Fig. 22

39. See Note 31. For the reference to *Elusio*, see Paulinus of Nola, *Epistulae*, i, 11

40. *Gallia*, 19 (1961), 317–22, with Fig. 8, p. 318

41. *Habitations gauloises* (see Note 36), 185f.

42. cf. H. Reinhardt, *Der St-Gallen Klosterplan* (1952); the plan is reproduced also in J. Boussard, *The Civilisation of Charlemagne* (1968), 158

43. W. Seston, *Mélanges d'arch. et d'hist., École fr. de Rome*, 51 (1934), 79–113

44. *Confessions*, viii, 5, 6; *De Mor. Eccl. Cath.*, i, 33

45. *Epistulae*, 83

46. *Institutiones* (ed. R.A.B. Mynors, 1937), 73; for the location, see P. Courcelle, *Mélanges d'arch. et d'hist., École fr. de Rome*, 55 (1938), 259–307

47. Paulinus of Nola, *Epistulae*, xxxi, 1; xxxii, 7; see also F. Mouret, *Cahiers d'arch. et d'hist. (Nîmes)*, (1932), 244–56

48. See Note 20

49. St-Ulrich: Grenier, *Habitations gauloises*, 145–59. Eschau: *Cahiers d'arch. et d'hist. Alsace*, (1928–9), 190–211. Loupiac: *Gallia*, 12 (1954), 208–9. Kergollet: ibid., 23 (1965), 336. Sorde-l'Abbaye: ibid., 21 (1963), 532–5, with Fig. 45, p. 532

50. *Vitae Patrum*, 15, 1: *Reperit enim . . . parietes antiquos, quos eruderans a ruinis habitationes aptavit dignas; reperitque ibi oratorium, in quo ferebatur celebre nostrum orasse Martinum. Quod diligenti cura compositum, erecto altari, loculumque in eo ad recipiendas sanctorum reliquias praeparatum, ad benedicendum invitat episcopos*

51. *Revue Mabillon*, 44 (1954), 45–94, with Planche II; cf. *Gallia*, 12 (1954), 380–9

52. cf., for example, A. Dopsch, *The Economic and Social Foundations of European Civilization* (1937), 70–88

53. op. cit. (Note 3), ii, 12f.

54. op. cit. (Note 2), 3f.

55. See above, pp. 47–8

Select Bibliography

Note: Bibliography for individual sites is given as they occur in the text; for this reason the only excavation reports to appear in the following list are those which contain material or discussion of a more general interest.

AGACHE, R., VASSELLE, F. and WILL, E. 'Les villas gallo-romaines de la Somme: aperçu préliminaire', *Revue du Nord*, 47 (1965), 541–76

AGACHE, R. *Archéologie aérienne de la Somme* (Amiens, 1964)

AGACHE, R. *Détection aérienne de vestiges protohistoriques, gallo-romains et médiévaux* (Amiens, 1970)

AITKEN, R. 'Virgil's Plough', *Journal of Roman Studies*, 46 (1956), 97–106

ALFÖLDY, G. *Noricum* (The Provinces of the Roman Empire) (London, 1974)

APPLEBAUM, S. 'Agriculture in Roman Britain', *Agricultural History Review*, 6 (1958), 66–86

APPLEBAUM, S. 'Peasant economy and types of agriculture', in C. Thomas (ed.), *Rural Settlement in Roman Britain* (C.B.A. Research Report, No. 7) (London, 1966), 99–107

APPLEBAUM, S. 'Roman Britain', in H.P.R. Finberg (ed.), *The Agrarian History of England and Wales*, I. ii (Cambridge, 1972), 1–277

D'ARMS, J.H. *Romans on the Bay of Naples* (Harvard, 1970)

BEAUDOIN, E. *Les grands domaines dans l'Empire romain* (Paris, 1899)

BIRO, M. 'Roman Villas in Pannonia', *Acta Archaeologica Academiae Scientiarum Hungaricae*, 26 (1974), 23–57

DE BOE, G. 'De Stand van het Onderzoek der Romeinse Villa's in Belgie', *Archaeologia Belgica*, 132 (1971), 5–14

BOWEN, H.C. *Ancient Fields* (London, 1961)

BRANIGAN, K. *Town and Country. The Archaeology of Verulamium and the Roman Chilterns* (Bourne End, Bucks., 1973)

BROGAN, O. *Roman Gaul* (London, 1953)

BROUGHTON, T.R.S. *The Romanization of Africa Proconsularis* (Baltimore, 1929)

BURFORD, A. 'Heavy Transport in Classical Antiquity', *Economic History Review*, 13 (1960), 1–18

CARRINGTON, R.C. 'Studies in the Campanian Villae Rusticae', *Journal of Roman Studies*, 21 (1931), 110–30

CARY, M. *The Geographic Background of Greek and Roman History* (Oxford, 1949)

CLAUSING, R. *The Roman Colonate. The Theories of its Origin* (New York, 1925)

COLLINGWOOD, R.G. and MYRES, J.N.L. *Roman Britain and the English Settlements* (2nd ed., Oxford, 1937)

COURCELLE, P. *Histoire littéraire des grandes invasions germaniques* (3rd ed., Paris, 1964)

CUMONT, F. *Comment la Belgique fut romanisée* (Bruxelles–Paris, 1914)

CUNLIFFE, B. *The Regni* (Peoples of Roman Britain) (London, 1973)

DAICOVICIU, C. *La Transylvanie dans l'antiquité* (Bucarest, 1945)

DAUZAT, A. *La toponymie française* (Paris, 1946)

DHONDT, J. 'Essai sur l'origine de la frontière linguistique', *L'Antiquité Classique*, 16 (1947), 261–86

DUNCAN-JONES, R. *The Economy of the Roman Empire* (Cambridge, 1974)

FINBERG, H.P.R. *The Agrarian History of England and Wales*, I. ii (Cambridge, 1972)

FINLEY, M.I. *The Ancient Economy* (London, 1973)

FOUET, G. *La villa gallo-romaine de Montmaurin (Hte-Garonne)* (Gallia, Supplement 20) (Paris, 1969)

FOX, Sir C. *The Archaeology of the Cambridge Region*

(Cambridge, 1923)

FREMERSDORF, F. *Der römische Gutshof Köln-Müngersdorf* (Römisch-germanische Forschungen, 6) (Berlin, 1933)

GILLIAM, J.F. 'The plague under Marcus Aurelius', *American Journal of Philology*, 82 (1961), 225–51

GOODCHILD, R.G. 'T-shaped corn-drying ovens in Roman Britain', *Antiquaries Journal*, 23 (1943), 148–53

GRENIER, A. *Habitations gauloises et villas latines dans la cité des Médiomatrices* (Paris, 1906)

GRENIER, A. *Manuel d'archéologie gallo-romaine*, II (Paris, 1934)

GRENIER, A. 'La Gaule romaine', in Tenney Frank (ed.), *An Economic Survey of Ancient Rome*, III (Baltimore, 1937)

HALLAM, S.J. 'Settlement round the Wash', in C.W. Phillips (ed.), *The Fenlands in Roman Times* (London, 1970)

HARMAND, J. 'Sur la valeur archéologique du mot villa', *Revue archéologique*, 38 (1951), 155–8

HARMAND, J. *Les origines des recherches françaises sur l'habitat rural gallo-romain* (Collection Latomus, 51) (Bruxelles–Berchem, 1961)

HATT, J.J. *Histoire de la Gaule romaine* (2nd ed., Paris, 1966)

HAUDRICOURT, A.G. and DELAMARRE, M. J-B. *L'homme et la charrue à travers le monde* (3rd ed., Paris, 1955)

HAVERFIELD, F. *The Romanization of Roman Britain* (4th ed., Oxford, 1923)

HAWKES, C.F.C. 'The Roman Villa and the Heavy Plough', *Antiquity*, 9 (1935), 339–41

HAWKES, C.F.C. 'Britons, Romans and Saxons round Salisbury and in Cranborne Chase', *Archaeological Journal*, 104 (1947), 27–81

HAYWOOD, R.M. 'Roman Africa', in Tenney Frank (ed.), *An Economic Survey of Ancient Rome*, IV (Baltimore, 1938)

HEITLAND, W.E. *Agricola* (Cambridge, 1921)

HIGGS, E.S. and WHITE, J.P. 'Autumn Killing', *Antiquity*, 37 (1963), 282–9

HODDER, I. and HASSALL, M. 'The non-random spacing of Romano-British walled towns', *Man*, 6 (1971), 391–407

HODDINOTT, R.F. *Bulgaria in Antiquity* (London and Tonbridge, 1975)

JALMAIN, D. *Archéologie aérienne en Ile-de-France* (Paris, 1970)

JONES, A.H.M. *The Later Roman Empire, 284–602* (Oxford, 1964)

JONES, A.H.M. *The Roman Economy* (ed. P.A. Brunt, Oxford, 1974)

JONES, G.D.B. 'Capena and the Ager Capenas', *Papers of the British School at Rome*, 30 (1962), 116–207; 31 (1963), 100–158

JONES, G.R.J. 'The tribal system in Wales: a re-assessment in the light of settlement studies', *Welsh History Review*, 1 (1961), 111–132

JONES, G.R.J. 'Post-Roman Wales', in H.P.R. Finberg (ed.), *The Agrarian History of England and Wales*, I. ii (Cambridge, 1972), 279–382

JOULIN, L. *Les établissements gallo-romains de la plaine de Martres-Tolosanes* (Paris, 1901)

KAHANE, A., MURRAY THREIPLAND, L. and WARD-PERKINS, J.B. 'The Ager Veientanus, North and East of Veii', *Papers of the British School at Rome*, 36 (1968)

KOETHE, H. 'Zur Geschichte Galliens im dritten Viertel des 3 Jahrhunderts', *32 Bericht der Römisch-Germanisch Kommission* (1950), 199–224

LATOUCHE, R. *Les grandes invasions et la crise de l'Occident au Ve siècle* (Paris, 1946)

LONGNON, A. *Les noms de lieu de la France* (Paris, 1920–9)

MacMULLEN, R. 'Market-days in the Roman Empire', *Phoenix*, 24 (1970), 333–41

DE MAEYER, R. *De Romeinsche Villa's in Belgie* (Antwerpen, 1937)

DE MAEYER, R. *De Overblijfselen der Romeinsche Villa's in Belgie* (Antwerpen, 1940)

MANNING, W.H. 'The Villa in Roman Britain', *Antiquity*, 36 (1962), 56–8

MANNING, W.H. 'The plough in Roman Britain', *Journal of Roman Studies*, 54 (1964), 54–65

A Matter of Time: an Archaeological Survey of the River Gravels of England (R.C.H.M., London, 1960)

MENENDEZ PIDAL, R. *Historia de Espana*, II (3rd ed., Madrid, 1962)

MICKWITZ, G. 'Economic Rationalism in Graeco-Roman Agriculture', *English Historical Review*, 52 (1937), 577–89

MILLAR, F.G.B. *The Roman Empire and its Neighbours* (London, 1967)

MÓCSY, A. *Pannonia and Upper Moesia* (The Provinces of the Roman Empire) (London, 1974)

MUSSET, L. *Les Invasions: les Vagues Germaniques* (Paris, 1965) (English translation by E. and C. James, *The Germanic Invasions*, London, 1975)

VAN NOSTRAND, J.J. 'The Imperial Domains of Africa Proconsularis', *University of California Publications in History*, 14 (1925–6), 1–88

VAN NOSTRAND, J.J. 'Roman Spain', in Tenney Frank (ed.), *An Economic Survey of Ancient Rome*, III (Baltimore, 1937)

PARET, O. *Die Römer in Württemberg*, III (Stuttgart, 1932)

PARIBENI, R. 'Le dimore dei potentiores nel basso impero', *Mitteilungen des Deutschen Archaeologischen Instituts, Römische Abteilung*, 55 (1940), 131–48

PERCIVAL, J. 'Seigneurial Aspects of Late Roman Estate Management', *English Historical Review*,

84 (1969), 449–73

PETRIKOVITS, H. VON *Das römische Rheinland: archäologische Forschungen seit 1945* (Köln, 1960)

PICARD, G.C. *La civilisation de l'Afrique romaine* (Paris, 1959)

PRÊCHEUR-CANONGE, T. *La vie rurale en Afrique romaine d'après les mosaiques* (Paris–Tunis, 1961)

REMONDON, R. *La crise de l'Empire romain* (Paris, 1970)

RENARD, M. *Technique et agriculture en pays trévire et rémois* (Collection Latomus, 38) (Bruxelles, 1959)

RICHMOND, I.A. *Roman Britain* (2nd ed., Harmondsworth, 1963)

RIVET, A.L.F. *Town and Country in Roman Britain* (2nd ed., London, 1964)

RIVET, A.L.F. (ed.) *The Roman Villa in Britain* (London, 1969)

ROSTOVTZEFF, M. *The Social and Economic History of the Roman Empire* (2nd ed., London, 1957)

DE STE-CROIX, G.E.M. 'Greek and Roman Accounting', in A.C. Littleton and B.S. Yamey, *Studies in the History of Accounting* (London, 1956), 14–74

SALIN, E. *La civilisation mérovingienne* (Paris, 1949–52)

SHERWIN-WHITE, A.N. *The Roman Citizenship* (2nd ed., Oxford, 1973)

SMITH, D.J. 'The Mosaic Pavements', in A.L.F. Rivet (ed.), *The Roman Villa in Britain* (London, 1969), 71–125

STÄHELIN, F. *Die Schweiz in römischer Zeit* (3rd ed., Basel, 1948)

STEIN, E. *Histoire du Bas-Empire*, 1 (Paris, 1959)

STEVENS, C.E. 'A possible conflict of laws in Roman Britain', *Journal of Roman Studies*, 37 (1947), 132–4

STEVENS, C.E. 'Agricultural and Rural Life in the Later Roman Empire', in *Cambridge Economic History of Europe*, 1 (2nd ed., Cambridge, 1966), 92–124

STEVENS, C.E. 'The Social and Economic Aspects of Rural Settlement', in C. Thomas (ed.), *Rural Settlement in Roman Britain* (C.B.A. Research Report, No. 7) (London, 1966), 108–28

SUTHERLAND, C.H.V. *The Romans in Spain, 217 B.C.–A.D. 117* (London, 1939)

THOMAS, E.B. *Römische Villen in Pannonien* (Budapest, 1964)

THOMPSON, E.A. 'Peasant Revolts in Late Roman Gaul and Spain', *Past and Present*, 2 (1952), 11–23

THOUVENOT, R. *Essai sur la province romaine de Bétique* (Paris, 1940)

TODD, M. *The Coritani* (Peoples of Roman Britain) (London, 1973)

WAGNER, E. *Fundstätten und Funde in grossherzogtum Baden* (Tübingen, 1908–11)

WAGNER, F. *Die Römer in Bayern* (München, 1924)

WARD-PERKINS, J.B. 'Etruscan towns, Roman roads and Medieval villages: the historical geography of southern Etruria', *Geographical Journal*, 128 (1962), 389–405

WEBSTER, G. 'The Future of Villa Studies', in A.L.F. Rivet (ed.), *The Roman Villa in Britain* (London, 1969), 217–49

WHITE, K.D. *Agricultural Implements of the Roman World* (Cambridge, 1967)

WHITE, K.D. *Roman Farming* (London, 1970)

WHITE, K.D. *A Bibliography of Roman Agriculture* (Reading, 1970)

WIGHTMAN, E.M. *Roman Trier and the Treveri* (London, 1970)

WILKES, J.J. *Dalmatia* (The Provinces of the Roman Empire) (London, 1969)

WILSON, A.J.N. *Emigration from Italy in the Republican Age of Rome* (Manchester, 1966)

ZULUETA, F. DE 'De Patrociniis Vicorum', in P. Vinogradoff (ed.), *Oxford Studies in Social and Legal History*, 1 (Oxford, 1909)

Index of individual villa sites

General Index